Writing Chinese Laws

The legal institutions of the short-lived Qin dynasty (221–207 BCE) have been vilified by history as harsh and draconian. Yet ironically, many Qin institutional features, such as written statutory law, were readily adopted by subsequent dynasties as the primary means for maintaining administrative and social control.

This book utilizes both traditional texts and archeologically excavated materials to explore how these influential Qin legal institutions developed. First, it investigates the socio-political conditions which led to the production of law in written form. It then goes on to consider how the intended function of written law influenced the linguistic composition of legal statutes, as well as their physical construction. Using a function and form approach, it specifically analyses the Shuihudi legal corpus. However, unlike many previous studies of Chinese legal manuscripts, which have focused on codicological issues of transcription and translation, this book considers the linguistic aspects of these manuscripts and thus their importance for understanding the development of early Chinese legal thought.

Writing Chinese Laws will be useful to students and scholars of Chinese Studies, as well as Asian law and history more generally.

Ernest Caldwell is Assistant Professor in the School of Law at SOAS, University of London, UK. He specializes in legal history, environmental law, and public law in China, Taiwan, and Southeast Asia.

Routledge Studies in Asian Law

Asian Law in Disasters
Toward a Human-Centered Recovery
Edited by Yuka KANEKO, Katsumi MATSUOKA and Toshihisa TOYODA

Judicial Review of Elections in Asia
Edited by Po Jen Yap

Rethinking South China Sea Disputes
The Untold Dimensions and Great Expectations
Katherine Hui-Yi Tseng

Civil Unrest and Governance in Hong Kong
Law and Order from Historical and Cultural Perspectives
Edited by Michael H.K. Ng and John D. Wong

Writing Chinese Laws
The Form and Function of Legal Statutes Found in the Qin Shuihudi Corpus
Ernest Caldwell

For more information about this series, please visit: www.routledge.com/asian studies/series/RSIAL

Writing Chinese Laws

The Form and Function of Legal Statutes Found in the Qin Shuihudi Corpus

Ernest Caldwell

Routledge
Taylor & Francis Group
LONDON AND NEW YORK

First published 2018 by Routledge

2 Park Square, Milton Park, Abingdon, Oxon OX14 4RN
605 Third Avenue, New York, NY 10017

Routledge is an imprint of the Taylor & Francis Group, an informa business

First issued in paperback 2021

British Library Cataloguing-in-Publication Data
A catalogue record for this book is available from the British Library

Library of Congress Cataloging-in-Publication Data
Names: Caldwell, Ernest, author.
Title: Writing Chinese laws : the form and function of legal statutes found in the Qin Shuihudi corpus / Ernest Caldwell.
Description: Abingdon, Oxon [UK] ; New York : Routledge, 2018. | Series: Routledge studies in Asian law | Includes bibliographical references and index.
Identifiers: LCCN 2018003737 | ISBN 9780815396925 (hardback) | ISBN 9781351180689 (ebook)
Subjects: LCSH: Law–China–History. | Law–China–Language. | China–History–Qin dynasty, 221-207 B.C. | Shuihudi Site (China)
Classification: LCC KNN122 .C355 2018 | DDC 340.5/31–dc23
LC record available at https://lccn.loc.gov/2018003737

ISBN: 978-0-8153-9692-5 (hbk)
ISBN: 978-0-367-44522-5 (pbk)

Typeset in Times New Roman
by Wearset Ltd, Boldon, Tyne and Wear

For Leigh, Casimir, and Claude

Contents

Tables

Acknowledgments

This book developed out of my PhD dissertation completed at the University of Chicago in 2014. I wish to thank my advisors Edward L. Shaughnessy and Donald J. Harper for their assistance throughout my doctoral studies. Both provided a great deal of support throughout the writing process. In particular, Professor Shaughnessy read several drafts of individual chapters and provided copious notes and questions that allowed me to refine both the scope of the project and its findings. I also received a great deal of support from my fellow University of Chicago classmates during seminars and study sessions. My knowledge of paleography and manuscript studies was further reinforced by several visiting scholars at Chicago, especially Professors Qiu Xigui, Chen Jian, Chen Songchang, and Chen Wei.

Several others have helped along the way and though I am sure that I will leave out some names (with apologies), Tamara Chin, Michael Gagarin, Caroline Humfress, Michael Loewe, Geoffrey MacCormack, Michael Nylan, Yuri Pines, Matthias Richter, Laura Skosey, Karen Turner, Robin Yates, as well as my colleagues and students at SOAS.

Finally, I wish to thank my family. My partner, Leigh Jenco, read over several drafts of both the dissertation and the final book manuscript. And our two sons Casimir and Claude provided me with the impetus to finish the project. Casimir's birth forced me to buckle down and complete the dissertation whilst still a PhD student, and Claude's birth forced me to complete this book. Without the love and support of all three, I would have never been able to finish.

**I wish to thank Cambridge University Press and the *Law and History Review* for allowing me to republish Chapter 2 which is a slightly altered version of the article "Social Change and Written Law in Early China," *Law and History Review* 32, no. 1 (2012): 1–30.

1 Introduction

Introduction: law, writing and social change in Qin

The legal institutions of the short-lived Qin 秦 dynasty (221–207 BCE) have been vilified by history as harsh and draconian. Yet ironically, many Qin institutional features, such as written statutory law, were readily adopted by subsequent dynasties as the primary means for maintaining administrative and social control. How did the influential Qin legal institutions based on written law develop? This book will utilize both traditional received texts and archeologically excavated legal materials in an attempt to ascertain first, what socio-political conditions provided the rationale for the production of law in written form in the kingdom of Qin; and second to consider how the intended function of written law influenced the linguistic composition of legal statutes, as well as their physical construction.

From amidst the endemic warfare of the aptly named Warring States Period (戰國, 481–221 BCE) one kingdom, the Qin, rose to successfully consolidate its authority over the other kingdoms through military conquest. In so doing, it established the first imperial dynasty of China administered by a centralized, impersonal bureaucratic government. The success of this consolidation depended upon the effective implementation of government policies, whose origins predate the unification of 221 BCE, that were to replace the increasingly defunct systems of aristocratic political order based primarily on the reciprocal obligations defined through lineage affiliation. Over time, such lineage affiliations weakened, and resulted in the rise of powerful ministerial families capable of directly challenging the authority of the ruler and sometimes leading to rulers being deposed or even assassinated. The new order envisioned by the Qin would be headed by a central government represented in and connected to the periphery through an impersonal bureaucracy of officials with legally defined jurisdictions. The establishment of various socio-political institutions of the Qin, such as universal standards for all regions (e.g., axle widths, weights, written script), were also vital to the effort of creating a level of institutional homogeneity and administrative predictability within geographic boundaries formerly governed by disparate institutions. This grand-scale restructuring over such a large territory required a high level of social and administrative control. This was secured through a legal framework in which bureaucratic and social existence came to be defined and judged according to written legal statutes.

Yet how did writing come to be used for the purpose of composing and transmitting law? And how were laws composed so as to maximize their efficacy in attaining the desired goals of the legislative drafters? This book seeks to answer these two questions by applying a *function* and *form* approach to the study of excavated legal manuscripts from Qin. To understand the function ascribed to law by the Qin, I draw upon theories from Law and Society literature to illustrate the ways in which social and political changes influence legal changes, and also how legal reforms can in turn be directed to elicit targeted social or political change. The received philosophical literature and traditional Chinese histories recording the socio-political milieu of Qin provide evidence with which we can reconstruct certain elements of these socio-legal processes. The addition of "new" sources of Qin law in the form of archeologically excavated legal manuscripts over the past 70 years allows us to further refine such reconstructions. With a clearer understanding of the role of law in Qin culture, I then turn my attention to the form of written laws by applying legal-linguistic methods to a codicological and compositional analysis of a corpus of legal documents from the tomb of a county-level Qin official discovered by archeologists in 1975. Such an approach allows me to demonstrate how the envisioned function of legal statutes directly influenced the linguistic composition and physical production of such legal texts. In this way, this book elucidates the role of writing in the conceptualization and composition of written law in Qin.

Methodology: socio-legal changes and legal linguistics

I analyze the function and form of written law in Qin through the perspective lenses of two fields of legal research: socio-legal studies and legal linguistics. For the purposes of this book, I typically take a fairly narrow, positivist definition of law: I am primarily concerned with legislation handed down by the ruler or on the ruler's behalf, which prescribes or proscribes behavior and is backed by threat of force or some other measure of coercion.[1] Yet to confine myself to such a simplistic definition, while certainly heuristically convenient, would tell us little about the factors influencing legal development and would likely devolve to an examination of the First Emperor's (Qin Shi Huang Di 秦始皇帝) megalomania or despotism.[2] To truly understand how legal innovations arise from within a society, one must fully comprehend the relationship between law and society, or, more specifically, the dynamics of social and legal change. In this section, I briefly examine the theories of socio-legal change as developed in the field of socio-legal studies, and then, in the next chapter, I will apply these theories to an analysis of several passages from the *Zuo zhuan* 左傳. In doing so, I will demonstrate how the early Chinese understanding of the dynamics of socio-legal change influenced the implementation of written laws.

Theorizing socio-legal change

As Lawrence Friedman noted, social theories of law "look at law as a dependent variable, as an effect, a product, as a system molded by social forces, rather than as an isolated insulated subsystem."[3] Therefore, law should be understood as a social construct embedded into and developed within a specific social setting. As such, effective law is not simply the whim of the ruler completely divorced from social reality, but should instead be understood as a calculated measure meant to respond to, and subsequently to direct, social and political circumstances. This responsive nature can of course be constructed based upon a ruler's desires, yet even still it requires a measure of legitimacy to be enforced. This legitimacy need not be endorsed by all of society, but merely those people who actually matter (holding some form of political, economic, social, or military power), such as a ruling elite, a bureaucracy dependent upon state resources for support.[4]

Furthermore, while a measure of legitimacy is certainly necessary, equally important for promulgating efficacious legal reforms is a firm understanding of the dynamics of socio-legal change. A socio-legal perspective considers law to be a social construct; therefore, legal reforms are conceptualized by scholars as *responsive* to specific social or political issues giving rise to disorder. This "disorder" need not be understood as imminently detrimental to society or the state, but rather a single change or series of changes to the socio-political landscape which either gradually or quickly erode the efficacy of previous laws or institutions to maintain order.[5] Legal reform or innovation thus becomes an attempt to reestablish control over the "new" social circumstances. Therefore, to fully comprehend the development of certain legal innovations (i.e., what function a legal innovation or reform serves), one must understand which social or political changes serve as a catalyst for legal reform. Furthermore, we should also ask how new legal forms or institutions were understood to reestablish control over specific social problems.[6]

With that in mind, we can then ask what societal factors prompt the shift from legal practices based upon oral or customary law to the development of new legal institutions predicated upon bodies of written law.[7] Certainly the presence within a given society of a functional writing system, whether indigenously developed or cross-culturally borrowed, is a prerequisite for the creation of written law. Yet several scholars, notably legal anthropologists and socio-legal theorists, have argued that the mere presence of writing does not necessarily result in the immediate, or inevitable, development of certain socio-political institutions dependent upon the technological capacities writing offers.[8] These same scholars warn that assigning such a mono-causal role to writing reduces the multifaceted complexity of a social phenomenon such as the development of written law to a teleological inevitability. Instead, many believe that writing provides what Jack Goody has called "potentialities" for types of developments and alternative configurations of social organization.[9] That is to say, the technological capacities of writing provide the potential for specific institutional developments, such as the use of written law; yet for such potential to be actualized, there must first exist within the society an acknowledgment of a social need with a concomitant consciousness that that need can best be satisfied through the implementation of a form of writing.

Legal linguistic analysis of statutes

Understanding the intended function of written law in Qin will be the first step taken in this book. The next step, however, will be a comprehensive codicological and linguistic analysis of extant Qin legal statutes. To do this, I employ various theories and methods derived from the fields of literary theory and legal linguistics (also called forensic linguistics). Below, I briefly outline the guiding principles of my analysis of Qin statutes; however, these methods are contextualized in greater detail in Chapters 3 and 4.

Following the work of Edward Finegan, I argue that the form of a text—meaning its physical as well as linguistic form—is dependent upon two factors.[10] The first factor is the intended *function* of the text. Positive law functions as a normative statement of right and wrong applicable to a specified group of people. When placed in written form, the intention is that the efficacy of these norms transcends the proximity of space and time to the legislator. To accomplish this, the written law must be composed in such a way as to elicit a textual interpretation that accurately conveys the desired meaning encoded by the legislator.[11] Overcoming the problem of interpretive ambiguity is crucial to producing a legal text that can be consistently interpreted and applied by different people in different geographic locations. For this reason, drafters in various legal traditions have devised numerous compositional strategies designed to eliminate, to the greatest extent possible, any linguistic ambiguity in legal writing.[12] Because legal language is not necessarily a technolect, a great deal of emphasis is placed on reducing terminological indeterminancy.[13] That is, legal language is commonly derived from ordinary language which has been embedded with specialized legal meaning in specific legal contexts.[14] This creates the legislative need for increased attention to compositional methods that can ensure that those individuals reading a legal statute, for example, completely and unambiguously comprehend the *legal* meaning of the words used. Specific textual layouts,[15] clearly articulated sentence structures,[16] as well as formulaic language[17] can also be employed to facilitate directed readings of legal texts.

The second important factor is the intended audience of the text. Chartier has noted that the way in which material is presented in written form depends greatly upon to whom the text is addressed.[18] If one wishes to convey a specific meaning, then one must be conscious of the literacy of the intended audience. The language used by playwrights to convey political satire, to use one of Chartier's extended examples, differs greatly if they are commissioned by a royal family as opposed to being commissioned by the owner of a playhouse that caters to "common tastes." We see similar features in modern law-making. For example, the Napoleonic French legal codes were originally written with the intention that they could be read and understood by the general public. Law was meant to be accessible to all citizens and, as such, they were composed in non-technical language.[19] Contra this, the German tradition of codification assumes that the reading, use, and interpretation of laws will be done by a highly trained legal profession.[20] This has resulted in legislative forms which are extremely long, complex, and highly technical. When examining Qin legal statutes, I will be conscious of compositional features which illustrate a drafter's consciousness of the intended audience.

The socio-legal and the legal linguistic approaches will guide my analysis of the development of Qin statutory law and legal language throughout this book. I now turn my attention to the primary sources of Qin law: namely, the excavated legal statutes from Shuihudi, as well as the administrative tablets from Liye.

"New" sources of Qin law

Until the 1970s, scholars researching Qin history, society, or law relied heavily upon philosophical texts ascribed to the so-called "Legalist" school of thought, *fa jia* 法家, as well as post-Qin historical records written with overtly anti-Qin bias. This reliance upon received materials, however, was dramatically changed in 1975. During that year, workers excavating a drainage ditch in the Xiaogan district of Yunmeng Hubei 孝感地區, 云夢縣, 湖北 uncovered a Qin period tomb. Archeologists soon arrived and from December 1, 1975 to February 9, 1976, they surveyed and discovered a total of 12 tombs.[21]

Of particular interest was the tomb designated M11, *mu*11, 墓11. Within the center coffin chamber of this tomb, archeologists discovered numerous pieces of Qin style lacquer ware, bronze ware, and pottery indicative of a lower-ranking member of the elite.[22] They also discovered two sets of writing implements, including two brushes with protective bamboo covering sleeves.[23]

Table 1.1 List of manuscripts found in Shuihudi Tomb 11

Title	*English title*	*# of slips*[1]
編年記	*Recorded Annals*	53
南郡守騰文書	*Letter from Governor Teng of Nan Commandery*	16
秦律十八種	*Eighteen Varieties of Qin Statutes*	201
效律	*Statute on Checking*	60
秦律雜抄	*Miscellaneous Transcriptions of Qin Statutes*	42
法律答問	*Questions and Answers on Laws and Statutes*	210
封診式	*Models for Seals and Findings*	99
爲吏之道	*The Path to Becoming a Good Official*	51
日書: 甲	*Almanac A*	166
日書: 乙	*Almanac B*	261

Note

1 The number of slips for each manuscript is based upon the findings in Shuihudi Qin mu zhujian zhengli xiaozu, ed., *Shuihudi Qin mu zhujian* (Beijing: Wenwu chuban she, 1990).

Archeologists were more surprised with what they discovered once the lid of the inner coffin was removed. Inside, they found the intact corpse of the tomb occupant, who was subsequently determined to be a male between the ages of 40 and 45. More importantly, however, the corpse was surrounded by over 1000 bamboo slips. Upon closer examination, many of the slips were found to have writing on them. In total, archeologists discovered roughly 1300 bamboo slips comprising ten separate texts.

The legal statutes and statutory excerpts found on the 303 bamboo slips comprising the *Xiao lü*, the *Qin lü shiba zhong*, and the *Qin lü zachao* will be the focus of this book.[24] An extensive codicological and linguistic analysis of these three texts is found in Chapters 3 and 4, but I will briefly provide a very general overview of the principle features and contents of the manuscripts.

The *Xiao lü* is a single legal statute consisting of 30 individual articles written on a total of 60 bamboo slips.[25] The manuscript's title, *xiao* 效 "to check" or "to audit" is written on the back of Slip 1. This title is missing the graph *lü* or "statute" after the graph *xiao*; however, the opening line of the front of Slip 1 clearly self-references the text as the *xiao lü*. The editors of the Shuihudi corpus believe that this manuscript represents a complete Qin legal statute.[26] Because of the length of the manuscript, the complexity of its individual articles, and the completeness of the text, it provides a wonderful opportunity to conduct a detailed study of the codicological and linguistic features of Qin legal statutes. The *Xiao lü* consists of a series of articles covering administrative auditing of county-level offices and the government accounts and provisions these offices oversee. The articles cover situations ranging from ensuring all county military weapons are properly marked, catalogued, and stored to maintaining proper registration accounts of individual households within the county. The majority of articles are composed in a casuistic format whereby single or multiple protasis elements containing a prescribed or proscribed action are first listed. This is followed by a single or multiple apodosis statements containing various levels of corresponding penal or administrative sanctions.

Unlike the *Xiao lü* manuscript, the *Qin lü shiba zhong* and *Qin lü zachao* manuscripts are not single legal statutes, but instead represent composite texts consisting of individual or multiple excerpts of articles drawn from a variety of legal statutes. The *Qin lü shiba zhong* is an eclectic document comprising 110 excerpts drawn from 18 different Qin legal statutes. The manuscript was discovered on the right side of the tomb occupant. It is one of the longest extant legal manuscripts from early China. The document does not have a visible title; therefore, the editors named the manuscript, *Qin lü shiba zhong*, based on its textual contents. Although the overall text lacks a title, each statutory excerpt ends with direct reference to the title of the original "complete" statute from which it was excerpted. For example:

Qin lü shiba zhong—Slip 66
布袤八尺幅廣二尺五寸布惡其廣袤不如式者不行　　金布[66]

> Cloth measures eight *chi* in length and two *chi* and five *cun* in width. When cloth is inferior or its width and length do not accord with the standard-model, do not circulate. [Statute on] Currency (66)

The content of the excerpts range from articles concerning the control of artisans to rationing of convict laborers engaged in public construction work. Similarly, the *Qin lü zachao* is a compilation text consisting of 26 statutory excerpts written on 42 bamboo slips. The manuscript was located between the legs of the tomb occupant. The contents also cover a wide range of topics including the maintenance of royal parks, the registration of adult males for conscripted service, as well as statutory articles concerning the appointment of officials. These two texts will be featured throughout this book; however, their eclectic nature is problematic for conducting a comprehensive linguistic analysis of "complete" statutes. That is, they are quite useful for studying the linguistic compositional features of individual phrases or articles, but these texts have limited use for studying the internal coherence of complex legal statutes. For this reason, I use the contents of these two texts throughout the book to demonstrate certain features related to the production of legal manuscripts, but they function primarily as comparands for similar observations made about the *Xiao lü* manuscript.

Before turning to an overview of the book chapters, I wish to briefly consider the life of the individual interred, and his possible relationship to the tomb texts examined above. Following the arguments of many scholars in China and the West, I consider the Shuihudi legal texts to represent *functional* documents that were likely used during the lifetime of the tomb occupant as part of his official post.

One text found in M11 is extremely important for what it tells us about the life and career of the tomb occupant. The *Biannian ji* is a short text consisting of 53 bamboo slips and roughly 560 individual graphs.[27] The text is divided into upper and lower registers chronologically recording specific events, primarily notations of military excursions, related to the political history of the Qin kingdom. It also contains a series of entries written in another hand which relate to the life and career of the tomb occupant, Xi 喜.[28] The contents of the additional entries allow us to trace the career of Xi and postulate a potential relationship between the tomb occupant and the tomb texts prior to Xi's death. Establishing the potential for such a relationship is important as it will influence how we view these manuscripts as representative of actual Qin style government documents an official would normally engage. Regarding Xi's life and career, the *Biannian ji* notes:

> 卌卌五年 … 十二月甲午鷄鳴時喜產 [45A][29]
>
> Forty-fifth year (262 BCE) … In the twelfth month on *jiawu* day in the hour of the cock crowing, Xi was born. (45A)
>
> 今元年 … 喜傅 [8B]
>
> In the current first year (246 BCE) … Xi was registered. (8B)

三年 … 八月喜揄史 [10B]

Third year (244 BCE) … in the eighth month, Xi served as a scribe in Yu.[30] (10B)

四年 … 十一月喜X安陸X史 [11B]

Fourth year (243 BCE) … in the eleventh month Xi [illegible] Anlu [illegible] scribe. (11B)

六年四月為安陸令史 [13B]

Sixth year (241 BCE), in the fourth month [Xi] served as the chief scribe of Anlu. (13B)

七年正月甲寅鄢令史 [14B]

Seventh year (240 BCE), in the first month on *jiayin* day [Xi served as] the chief scribe of Yan. (14B)

十二年四月癸丑喜治獄鄢 [19B]

Twelfth year (235 BCE), in the fourth month on *guichou* day, Xi began adjudicating legal cases in Yan. (19B)

From the *Annals*, we know that Xi was born in the twelfth month of the forty-fifth year of King Zhaoxiang (262 BCE). At 17 *sui* 歲, Xi was officially registered as an adult, *fu* 傅 with the local government. This registration would have placed him in a category obliging Xi to perform conscripted military service, as well as corvée labor service on an annual basis.[31] Two years after his registration, the *Annals* text indicates that Xi obtained an initial appointment as a scribe in Yu County. Only a year later, Xi was transferred to Anlu County where he also served as a scribe. Xi remained in Anlu for approximately three years, and it is possible that he received a promotion to the position of chief scribe, *ling shi* 令史 in 241 BCE. Xi was transferred once again in 240 BCE to serve as the chief scribe of Yan County. Xi remained in Yan for at least six years before "following the army" in 234 BCE.[32]

A curious entry for the year 235 BCE records that during the fourth month on *guichou* day, Xi adjudicated legal cases in Yan. This implies that Xi was tasked to perform certain legal duties in Yan County; however, the date is fairly specific and it is difficult to assess whether this was a temporary instatement or a long term position. I would argue that a likely reading of the passage *shier nian yue guichou* Xi *zhi yu yan* 十二年四月癸丑喜治獄鄢 is that "In the twelfth year on the fourth month on the day *guichou*, Xi *began* adjudicating legal cases in Yan." The precision of the dating possibly indicates the beginning of the appointment. One sees a similar occurrence of temporal precision with Xi's appointment to be the *ling shi* of Yan. The fact that no other entry during this time period signals a change in location or position leads me to postulate that in the twelfth year Xi actually began presiding over the adjudication of legal disputes in Yan County and likely continued to do so until his departure with the military a year later in 234 BCE.

Given the career of Xi as noted in the *Biannian ji*, the genres of document interred with him are perhaps understandable. As a scribe, Xi would have undergone specialized training to perform the tasks required of administrative scribal officials under Qin rule. In European contexts, there are scholarly arguments that a great number of early medieval scribes were illiterate and performed their tasks merely as "artists" recreating the textual image of one page upon another. For early China, however, it seems that greater care was taken to ensure that scribes were not only capable of reproducing the image of the text, but were functionally literate to the extent that they could understand the meaning of the texts they were copying or even composing.[33] Excavated administrative documents from Liye 里耶 (discussed below) further demonstrate the ubiquitous employment of scribes to compose, copy, and transmit written materials. As a scribe, and later chief scribe, Xi was likely charged with numerous administrative tasks that would have required a base knowledge of the Qin written script and the grammar of the Qin language. The content of one statutory excerpt found in the *Qin lü shiba zhong* manuscript provides that local-level administrative offices are required to copy and maintain accurate editions of statutory provisions affecting their respective offices.[34] The *Annals* also record that Xi was trained as a scribe and served in that function in two different counties until he was appointed to handle legal cases in 235 BCE. Drawing on all this evidence, several scholars have noted that it seems likely the legal documents interred with Xi represent documents he used during his life.[35] That is, these manuscripts were functional texts used by Xi in the execution of his duties as a Qin scribal official, and were not merely tomb texts produced solely for the purpose of interment.

With that in mind, I would argue that the Shuihudi legal texts allow us to examine the physical and textual form of Qin legal statutes (and other legal genres) in the same format that a local-level official—meant to copy, read, interpret, and consistently apply them—would have engaged such texts.

Other sources of Qin legal statutes

Although the Shuihudi legal statutes serve as the primary source material for this study, they are by no means the only legal statutes dated to the Qin that have been uncovered in recent years. In 1989, archeologists discovered several fragments of Qin legal statutes buried with the occupant of Tomb 6 in Longgang 龍崗, Yunmeng County, Hubei 湖北. The editors of the Longgang bamboo slips believe the tomb occupant was a lower Qin official named, Bi Si 辟死. This name is mentioned on a wooden tablet found in the tomb. The tablet records what appears to be part of a trial record, wherein Bi Si was originally found guilty and sentenced to serve as a wall builder, or *chengdan* 城旦, possibly in the Forbidden Gardens. His case was reviewed and the decision was overturned.

The Assistant Prefect and a scribe mandated that Bi Si's sentence be expunged and ordered him to be released. After this, the editors of the manuscript postulate that Bi Si served in an official capacity as the warden of the gardens. This career scenario is used to explain why the contents of the Longgang statutory material focus on issues related to the maintenance of the Forbidden Gardens, such as forestry and animal husbandry. Unfortunately, these bamboo slips were not well preserved and only small fragments, typically upper portions of slips, remain today. It is for this reason that I make limited use of these materials throughout this book.

One final corpus of Qin legal materials should be mentioned here, the Yuelu corpus. In 2007, the Yuelu Academy 嶽麓書院 in Henan 河南 purchased a large collection of Qin bamboo slip manuscripts off the Hong Kong antiquities market.[36] Among the 2100 bamboo slips contained in the purchase, nearly 1600 slips contain textual material related to Qin law. These legal materials were divided into roughly three primary categories: legal statutes, legal ordinances, and "exemplary criminal cases."[37] Although the Yuelu corpus of legal statutes and ordinances potentially makes a wonderful comparand for my analysis of the Shuihudi corpus, I will make limited use of them in this book for two reasons. First, this study is intended to be a corpus-based analysis focusing on a single set of texts from the Shuihudi tomb for which we have an archeological provenance, as well as possible evidence of who might have copied and used these texts. The Yuelu materials were looted from a tomb and later surfaced on the antiquities market.[38] As such, we do not know their geographic origins; nor do we know anything (rank, official post, etc.) about the person who possessed them. This poses problems not only for authenticating the materials, but it also precludes us from making explicit interpretive statements about the possible *use* of the manuscripts and their relationship to their "owner."[39] Second, by constraining my study to a single corpus of legal texts, Shuihudi, it is my intention that the methods of analysis and finds of this study will serve as a guide for other scholars working on the legal manuscripts of Yuelu, or other legal manuscripts from the Qin and Han periods. Indeed, for the subsequent dynasty, the Han, there are many more excavated materials currently available for study.[40] As such, I will make only minor use of the Yuelu materials, and focus more intently on Shuihudi and other legal and administrative documentation for which we have archaeological provenance.

Administrative documents from Liye

Excavated manuscript copies of legal statutes and statute excerpts are certainly important for the study of written law in Qin legal culture; however, additional excavation sites have yielded numerous materials for the study of Qin culture, specifically its administrative culture. In April of 2002, the Hunan Provincial Institute of Archaeology carried out salvage excavations on the grounds of the future site of a hydroelectric plant along the You River 酉水 near Liye Village 里耶村, in Longgang County, Hunan Province.[41] This area along the You River had long been known as the site of an ancient city, as parts of the old city walls were still visible. After the initial surveys, archaeologists uncovered all four sides of the old city wall which enclosed a rectangular area measuring north–south 235 meters and east–west 150 meters. Within these walls, several ancient wells were discovered and it was Well number 1 (井1) which was first chosen to be fully excavated. On July 3, 2002 workers excavating the well uncovered a bamboo slip with writing upon it in distinctive Chu calligraphy. Shortly thereafter, they discovered something that will likely become one of the greatest archaeological discoveries of the twenty-first century, a cache of over 37,000 wooden tablets dating from the twenty-fifth year of King Zheng of Qin 秦正王 to the second year of the Qin Emperor Er Shi 二世 (roughly 222–208 BCE). Initial reports of the 37,000 Qin documents immediately caused a stir in the academic community, which compared the discovery to that of the Dunhuang cache in the nineteenth century. It should be noted, however, that the initial report of 37,000 wooden tablets did not specify the total number of tablets containing written text (though many scholars assumed all the tablets contained writing) and it is now known that of the 37,000 a little less than half have writing on them. Regardless, the 15,000 written documents still constitute one of the largest single site caches of written documents discovered in China to date.

The majority of manuscripts excavated from Well 1 are written upon long rectangular wooden tablets. These average 23 cm long, with a few longer tablets. The widths of the tablets are far from standardized and range from 1.3 cm to over 5 cm. Wang Huanlin 王焕林 believes that this width variation is due to the practice of using one tablet for one affair. Thus, if an issue needed to be recorded, but the required number of graphs was low, a thinner piece of wood could be used.[42] There are some problems with this hypothesis as many of the Liye manuscripts published to date contain large amounts of blank space, making it difficult to assume that this particular tablet was chosen after considering the space requirements for the text to be written.

The medium used is primarily wood from Chinese fir trees (*shan mu* 杉木; *Cunninghamia lanceolata*) or Chinese pine trees (*song mu* 松木; *Pinus armandii*). The wood is hard with very fine grains that run from top to bottom of the document. Previously excavated Qin manuscripts from Shuihudi contain instructions for the Minister of Works, *sikong* 司空 to select certain trees with wood that are conducive for writing with ink and to "square them," *fangzhi* 方之. It further states that if trees are unavailable, then reeds can be woven together to form a writing surface.[43]

Most of the Liye manuscripts found in Well 1 are classified as administrative documents pertaining to the mundane affairs of a single county called Qianling 遷陵 located in Dongting Commandery 洞庭郡. Additional documents were discovered in trash pits in the surrounding area. Many of these documents are badly damaged and show evidence of substantial fire damage. These particular documents are household registration ledgers that record the names of individual families, the families' "head" or father, the number of family members, the names, gender, age, and ranks of each family member, and even servants are listed.[44] These particular documents demonstrate the use of writing to provide the extensive reach of the Qin government into the lives of the general populace.

Although only part of the Liye materials has been published to date, these materials have already made a tremendous impact upon our knowledge of the historical development of early imperial administration.[45] The manuscripts, consisting of administrative documents in the form of communications on various county-level affairs, allow us to reevaluate how the Qin government actually functioned by giving us the ability to compare the normative aspects of statutory law with the more "realistic" issue of the practical application.[46] For the purposes of this book, I use the Liye documents as a comparand for observations made about the Shuihudi materials, particularly in the areas of punctuation usage and the citation of legal statutes or ordinances within administrative contexts. These documents provide a large cache of daily administrative documents and allow us to see how ubiquitous certain codicological and linguistic features were. This comparative analysis will tell us whether such features could be considered part of a greater scribal practice or merely the idiosyncratic habits of a single scribe, Mr. Xi.

The above-mentioned legal manuscripts, specifically the Shuihudi corpus along with supplementary citations of other collections, constitute the primary sources for this book. The fact that they are archeologically excavated allows us to examine them as contemporary examples of local-level documents used by lower officials who were legally obligated to follow their dictates as precisely as possible or risk sanction.

Chapter summary

This book utilizes a function and form approach to examine two specific features of written law in Qin legal culture. First, I wish to answer the question of how the Qin conceptualized the function of law, specifically written legal statutes. To do this, I ask what the Qin government expected written law to accomplish and attempt to uncover the underlying reasons for the Qin belief that written law could actually accomplish such goals. Second, having addressed the issue of function I will turn my attention to the physical and linguistic form of Qin legal statutes. Drawing on the work of legal linguists, I argue that the intended function and intended audience of a text directly influence a text's physical and linguistic composition.

This approach informs the structure of my book. Chapter 2 traces the development of early Chinese theories of written law as evidenced in the text, *Zuo zhuan*. To do this, I ask which dynamic societal factors produced a conscious need for legal change in early China and why the introduction of written law was considered to be an integral part of that legal change. In answering these questions, I bring to light three new facets of early Chinese views on the value and role of written law. First, that the early Chinese use of written laws arose in direct response to a growing need for an alternative method of social control, precipitated by the deteriorating socio-political conditions of the late "Spring and

Autumn" and "Warring States" Periods.[47] Second, unlike previous scholarship, I argue that the reliance on written law was not envisioned as merely having vertical legal effect on the socio-legal relations between the traditional aristocracy and the general populace, but was also thought to be capable of mediating the escalating inter-clan conflict among the aristocracy which threatened the internal stability of individual kingdoms. Third, I demonstrate a growing consciousness within several early Chinese kingdoms of the ability of written media to increase the efficacy of law.

Chapter 3 employs a law and society approach to examine the possibility that the development of written law in the kingdom of Qin (and potentially elsewhere) was a direct response to the growing need for an alternative method of social control precipitated by the deteriorating socio-political conditions of the late Spring and Autumn and Warring States Periods. The first half of the chapter examines the political turmoil wrought by the ministerial elite within Qin and the social and legal reforms that developed in response as depicted in philosophical texts and traditional Chinese histories. Central to these reforms was the limitation of the political power of the aristocracy through the establishment of a centralized bureaucracy staffed with impersonal officials, the maintenance of social and political order by the universal promulgation of clear, understandable laws through which bureaucratic and social existence could be defined and adjudged, and, finally, as a response to Qin's later territorial expansion, the production of universal social institutions based on a Qin paradigm. The second half of the chapter utilizes a variety of excavated Qin manuscripts ranging from military tallies to household registers to demonstrate how writing, particularly written law, was employed to produce and maintain strict centralized control over the bureaucracy and the general populace.

Chapters 4 and 5 employ legal linguistic methods to consider the influence of the intended function of written law on the physical and linguistic manifestation of legal statutes. Chapter 4 begins an extensive examination of the *Xiao lü* manuscript of the Shuihudi corpus and illustrates how the Qin employed specific codicological features designed to facilitate transmission of legal texts and, at least in theory, ensure textual fidelity and interpretative consistency over a large and geographically dispersed audience. To do this, I consider the impact of using bamboo slips as the primary medium platform for legal statutes, the use of Qin clerical script to produce a text that could be read and understood by any individual trained to work in a Qin government office, and finally the use of punctuation markers to provide a visual guide to ensure accurate and consistent readings of individual provisions within legal statutes.

Chapter 5 also employs methods from the field of legal linguistics to analyze the compositional structure of Qin legal statutes. In so doing, I consider what compositional features within the *Xiao lü* manuscript demonstrate a conscious effort to craft a text in such a way as to eliminate as much interpretative ambiguity as possible. If the Qin rulers truly intended (however naïvely) for their legal statutes to be merely applied and not interpreted by local official, then how does one compose such a text? To answer this, I begin with an analysis of methods of legal definition to show how the Qin attempted to unambiguously embed legal meaning to individual terms placed within a legal context. I then examine the compositional organization features of several individual articles of varying levels of complexity within the *Xiao lü* manuscript. And finally, I consider the use of internal textual-mapping, or cross-referencing, as a compositional strategy designed to produce a conceptually coherent composite text formed of multiple articles, as well as external textual-mapping as a strategy to embed the *Xiao lü* manuscript into the existing corpus of Qin legal statutes.

Chapter 6 concludes the book by synthesizing the findings of the previous chapters in order to contextualize the written statute within Qin legal culture. Through this synthesis, and the previous chapters, I hope to contribute to our understanding of how socio-political conditions of the Warring States Period, as well as the needs of the pre- and post-unification Qin government precipitated the adoption and continued use of a legal system predicated upon written legal statutes. By delving further into questions of statutory composition, I also advance our knowledge of the ways in which writing was employed to compose documents which would elicit consistent and predictable responses when read by different people in different locations. In methods of interpretation, writing was again employed to seek out clarification of statutory provisions. Thus, it was the technology of writing that provided the potential for such administrative homogeneity and judicial predictability by allowing for the clear, understandable encoding of legal principles into a written form, which could then be accurately transmitted over great distances and predictably implemented. The book ends by considering how the methods of this project can be applied to other legal texts of the Qin and later periods to expand our understanding of the development of Chinese legal language and the use of written law.

Notes

1 The archetypes of legal positivist theories of law are drawn from John Austin and H.L.A Hart. See Roger Cotterrell, *The Sociology of Law*, 2nd ed. (Oxford: Oxford University Press, 1992), 12.

2 Indeed, many studies of early Chinese law overemphasize the ruler's harsh use of law to coerce society. In so doing, they often fail to reconstruct a full picture of how law was truly conceptualized by early Chinese philosophers and statesmen. For examples of this rather narrow approach, see Zhengyuan Fu, *China's Legalists : The Earliest Totalitarians and Their Art of Ruling*, New Studies in Asian Culture. (Armonk, NY: M.E. Sharpe, 1996); Yongping Liu, *Origins of Chinese Law: Penal and Administrative Law in Its Early Development* (Oxford: Oxford University Press, 1998); T'ung-tsu Chü, *Law and Society in Traditional China* (Paris: Mouton, 1961).

3 Lawrence M. Friedman, *Law and Society: An Introduction* (Englewood Cliffs, NJ: Prentice-Hall, 1977), 95.

4 Ibid., 77–78; Cotterrell, *The Sociology of Law*, 152–153.

5 Some scholars have argued for a greater disjunction between law and society. Most notably Alan Watson has shown that laws that are completely out of touch with social reality can be retained for generations. However, Watson admits that such laws lose their legitimacy and enforceability early on and that if *all* laws or the majority of those laws ceased to correspond to society, then there would be need for a greater

change. See in general Alan Watson, *The Evolution of Law* (Baltimore, MD and London: Johns Hopkins University Press, 1985); Alan Watson, "Legal Change: Sources of Law and Legal Culture," *University of Pennsylvania Law Review* 131 (1983): 1121–1157.

6 Drawing on the works of Niklas Luhmann, Roger Cotterrell notes that "law as a communication system is open to cognitive input in the sense that it can, and does, routinely recognise and respond to economic, scientific, political, and other events or phenomena." Cotterrell, *The Sociology of Law*, 67.

7 Throughout this book I will refrain from using the term "codification" when referring to the collections of written law in ancient China prior to third century BCE. Even modern attempts to produce a universal definition typically fail in the face of the diversity of theoretical and interpretative traditions informing codified legal systems throughout the world. The problem is multiplied when attempting to apply such a term anachronistically to the legal traditions of the ancient world. For attempts to construct a multi-tiered conceptual paradigm for studying "codification" in chronologically and geographically diverse legal traditions, see Mark D. Rosen, "What Has Happened to the Common Law? Recent American Codifications, and Their Impact on Judicial Practice and the Law's Subsequent Development," *Wisconsin Law Review* 5 (1994): 1119–1286; Geoffrey MacCormack, "The Transmission of Penal Law (Lü) from the Han to the T'ang: A Contribution to the Study of the Early History of Codification in China," *Revue Internationale Des Droits de L'antiquité* 51 (2004): 47–83. For more critical assessments of the utility of such a term applied to ancient civilizations, see Martha T. Roth, "The Law Collection of King Hammurabi: Toward an Understanding of Codification and Text," in *Codification Des Lois Dans L'Antiquite*, ed. E. Lévy (Paris: De Boccard, 2000), 9–31; Raymond Westbrook, "Codification and Canonization," in *Codification Des Lois Dans L'Antiquite*, ed. E. Lévy (Paris: De Boccard, 2000), 33–47; John K. Davies, "Deconstructing Gortyn: When Is a Code a Code?" in *Greek Law in Its Political Setting: Justification Not Justice*, ed. Lin Foxhall and Andrew Lewis (Oxford: Oxford University Press, 1996), 33–56.

8 Classic examples of these debates can be found in Jack Goody, *The Power of the Written Tradition* (Washington, DC: Smithsonian Institution, 2000); Jack Goody, *The Logic of Writing and the Organization of Society* (Cambridge: Cambridge University Press, 1986); Erik Havelock, *The Muse Learns to Write: Reflections on Orality and Literacy from Antiquity to the Present* (New Haven, CT: Yale University Press, 1986); Walter Ong, *Orality and Literacy*, 2nd ed. (London and New York: Routledge, 2002). Such scholars also show that although writing as a technology provides new possibilities for the transmission of knowledge, the power and presence of the *oral* is retained well after writing takes the stage.

9 Some of Jack Goody's earlier work received much criticism for implicitly ascribing to writing a "mono-causal" role in the development of particular socio-political institutions. For an overview of these critiques and Goody's response, see Goody, *The Power of the Written Tradition*, 2–9.

10 Edward Finegan, "Form and Function in Testament Language," in *Linguistics and the Professions: Proceedings of the Second Annual Delaware Symposium on Language Studies*, ed. Robert Di Pietro (Norwood, NJ: Ablex, 1982), 113–120.

11 Lawrence Solan, *The Language of Statutes: Laws and Their Interpretation* (Chicago, IL: University of Chicago Press, 2010), chap. 2.

12 Peter M. Tiersma, *Legal Language* (Chicago, IL: University of Chicago Press, 1999), chap. 2.

13 Timothy A.O. Endicott, "Legal Indeterminacy," *Oxford Journal of Legal Studies* 16, no. 4 (1996): 667–697.

14 Heikki Mattila, "Legal Vocabulary," in *The Oxford Handbook of Language and Law*, ed. Peter M. Tiersma and Lawrence M. Solan (Oxford: Oxford University Press, 2012), 27–38.

15 Maurizio Gotti, "Text and Genre," in *The Oxford Handbook of Language and Law*, ed. Peter M. Tiersma and Lawrence M. Solan (Oxford: Oxford University Press, 2012), 52–66.

16 Risto Hiltunen, "The Grammar and Structure of Legal Texts," in *The Oxford Handbook of Language and Law*, ed. Peter M. Tiersma and Lawrence M. Solan (Oxford: Oxford University Press, 2012), 39–51; Vijay Bhatia, "Cognitive Structuring in Legislative Provisions," in *Language and the Law*, ed. John Gibbons (Harlow, UK: Longman Group UK, 1994), 136–155; Vijay Bhatia, "Textual-Mapping in British Legislative Writing," *World Englishes: Journal of English as an International and Intranational Language* 6, no. 1 (1987): 1–10.

17 Joanna Kopaczyk, *The Legal Language of Scottish Burghs: Standardization and Lexical Bundles 1380–1560* (Oxford: Oxford University Press, 2013).

18 Roger Chartier, *Forms and Meanings: Texts, Performances, and Audiences from Codex to Computer* (Philadelphia: University of Pennsylvania Press, 1995).

19 Heikki Mattila, *Comparative Legal Linguistics* (Farnham, UK: Ashgate, 2006), 187–198.

20 Ibid., 173–179.

21 For more on the initial discovery, see Ji Xun, "Yunmeng Shuihudi Qin Jian Gaishu," *Wenwu* 5 (1976): 1–6; A.F.P. Hulsewé, "The Ch'in Documents Discovered in Hupei in 1975," *T'oung Pao* 64, no. 4–5 (1978): 175–217; Yunmeng Shuihudi Qin mu bianxie zu, ed., *Yunmeng Shuihudi Qin Mu* (Beijing: Wenwu chuban she, 1981).

22 Yunmeng Shuihudi Qin mu bianxie zu, *Yunmeng Shuihudi Qin Mu*, 10.

23 Ibid., 26–27.

24 In Table 1.1, I provide translations for each manuscript; however, throughout this book I will use the *pinyin* transcription for individual manuscript titles and provide English translations for individual statute titles mentioned within a single manuscript.

25 Hulsewé incorrectly states the *Xiao lü* contains 29 individual articles. This is due to him reading articles 8 and 9 as a single textual unit. Upon examination, however, it is clear that these are two distinct articles and the correct number of articles for the *Xiao lü* should be 30. See A.F.P. Hulsewé, *Remnants of Ch'in Law* (Leiden: E.J. Brill, 1985).

26 Shuihudi Qin mu zhujian zhengli xiaozu, ed., *Shuihudi Qin Mu Zhujian* (Beijing: Wenwu chuban she, 1990), 69.

27 As mentioned, the *Biannian ji* consists of 53 bamboo slips that were originally bound together by 3 leather or silken throngs (since deteriorated). The *Annals* manuscript was originally rolled up and placed under the head of the tomb occupant. It records political events over a period of 90 years, from 306 to 217 BCE. This coincides with the reigns of King Zhaoxiang (昭襄王, r. 306–251 BCE), King Xiaowen (孝文王, r. 250 BCE), King Zhuangxiang (狀襄王, r. 249–247 BCE), and reign of King Zheng/Qin Shihuang di.

28 It is commonly agreed that the manuscript was written by two distinct "hands"; however, there are numerous debates concerning the actual authorship of the additional private entries to the *Recorded Annals*. These debates go beyond the scope of the present study. For more, see Achim Mittag, "The Qin Bamboo Annals of Shuihudi: A Random Note from the Perspective of Chinese Historiography," *Monumenta Serica* 51 (2003): 556–560; Xinfang Liu, "Guanyu Yunmeng Qin Jian Bian Nian Ji de Bushu, Xubian, He Xiaogai Deng Wenti," *Jiang-Han Kaogu* 3 (1991): 79–84.

29 This citation method employs the letters (A) and (B) to demonstrate the *upper* register (A) and the *lower* register (B). The number refers to the slip number as assigned by the Shuihudi editors.

30 The Shuihudi editors argue that the graph *yu* 揄 represents the word *yu* 揄 "to enter into service"; however, other scholars have argued that the graph, in fact, refers to a place name. Ma Feibai argues that *yu* 揄 should be read as designating the geographic location of Xi's appointment, that is the Yu County (modern Yuci 揄次, Shanxi 山西). If we

follow the Shuihudi editors, then the present entry would lack a geographic designator while all the other entries contain such designators. I, therefore, follow the reading of Ma for this entry. See Shuihudi Qin mu zhujian zhengli xiaozu, *Shuihudi Qin Mu Zhujian*, 9, n.47; Ma Feibai, "Yunmeng Qin Jian Dashi Ji Ji Zhuan," *Zhongguo Lishi Wenxian Yanjiu Jikan* 2 (1981): 81–83.

31 Hsing I-tien, "Qin-Han Census and Tax and Corvee Administration: Notes on Newly Discovered Materials," in *Birth of an Empire: The State of Qin Revisited*, ed. Yuri Pines, Lothar von Falkenhausen, Gideon Shelach, and Robin D.S. Yates (Berkeley: Global, Area, and International Archive, University of California Press, 2014), 155–186; Robin D.S. Yates, "Social Status in the Ch'in: Evidence from the Yun-Meng Legal Documents. Part One: Commoners," *Harvard Journal of Asiatic Studies* 47, no. 1 (1987): 197–237.

32 An entry in the lower register of the *Biannian ji* states: "In the thirteenth year (234 BCE), [Xi] followed the army." 十三年從軍 [20B]

33 Robin D.S. Yates, "Soldiers, Scribes, and Women: Literacy among the Lower Orders in Early China," in *Writing and Literacy in Early China: Studies from the Columbia Early China Seminar*, ed. Feng Li and David Prager Branner (Seattle: University of Washington Press, 2011), 339–369.

34 The *Qin lü shiba zhong* excerpt found on Slip 186 states:

> 縣各告都官在其縣者寫其官之用律　　　內史雜
>
> Counties shall each inform those offices in their county to write the statutes used by their offices. Miscellanea of the Nei shi.

35 In saying this, I do not imply that the manuscripts found in Xi's tomb are necessarily representative of his entire "library." It is possible that some measure of selection took place when these specific texts were placed in the tomb. Without further evidence, however, it is impossible to know.

36 For an overview of the Yuelu Qin corpus, see Chen Songchang, "Yuelu Shuyuan Suo Cang Qin Jian Zongshu," *Wenwu*, no. 3 (2009): 75–88.

37 For a translation of the exemplary cases, see Ulrich Lau and Thies Staack, *Legal Practice in the Formative Stages of the Chinese Empire: An Annotated Translation of the Exemplary Qin Criminal Cases from the Yuelu Academy Collection* (Leiden: Brill, 2016).

38 See, generally, Songchang Chen, ed., *Yue Lu Shu Yuan Cang Qin Jian de Zheng Li Yu Yan Jiu* (Shanghai: Zhong xi shuju, 2014).

39 For more on the problems of dealing with Chinese manuscripts that lack an archaeological provenance, see Paul R. Goldin, "Heng Xian and the Problem of Studying Looted Artifacts," *Dao: A Journal of Comparative Philosophy* 12, no. 2 (2013): 153–160.

40 For a general survey of relevant Han legal materials, see Anthony J. Barbieri-Low and Robin D.S. Yates, *Law, State, and Society in Early Imperial China: A Study with Critical Edition and Translation of the Legal Texts from Zhangjiashan Tomb No. 247* (Leiden: Brill, 2015), 39–47.

41 An overview of the site as well as the archeological excavation schedule can be found in Hunan sheng wenwu kaogu yanjiu suo, *Liye Fajue Baogao* (Changsha: Yuelu shushe, 2006).

42 Wang Huanlin, *Liye Qinjian jiaoku* (Beijing: Zhongguo wenlian chubanshe, 2007), 5–6.

43 See *Qin lü shiba zhong*, Slips 131–132.

44 See Zhang Chunlong, "Liye Qin Jian Suojian de Huji He Renkou Guanli," in *Liye Gucheng: Qin Jian Yu Qin Wenhua Yanjiu*, ed. Zhongguo shehui kexue yuan kaogu yanjiu suo, Zhongguo shehui kexue yuan lishi yanjiu suo, and Hunan sheng wenwu kaogu yanjiu suo (Beijing: Kexue chuban she, 2009), 188–195.

45 Several tablets were published in the *Liye fajue baogao*; however, the first formal volume of manuscripts was not published until 2013. See Hunan sheng wenwu kaogu yanjiu suo, ed., *Liye Qin Jian*, vol. 1 (Beijing: Wenwu chuban, 2012); Wei Chen, ed., *Liye Qin Jiandu Jiaoyi*, vol. 1 (Wuhan: Wuhan daxue chuban she, 2012).

46 For an initial English language survey of the Liye corpus and its potential value for the study of Qin legal and administrative culture, see Robin D.S. Yates, "The Qin Slips and Boards from Well No. 1, Liye, Hunan: A Brief Introduction to the Qin Qianling County Archives," *Early China* 35–36 (2012–2013): 291–329.

47 The chronology of early China can be daunting for those not familiar with its intricacies. The Zhou royal family ostensibly governed the central plains region of China from roughly 1046–256 BCE. Their reign is divided into two large periods, the Western Zhou (1046–771 BCE) and the Eastern Zhou (771–221 BCE). The latter is further subdivided into two additional eras, the Spring and Autumn Period (*c.*771–476 BCE) and the Warring States Period (*c.*476–221 BCE).

2 Social change and written law in pre-imperial China

Introduction

What societal factors prompt the shift from legal practices based upon oral or customary law to the development of new legal institutions predicated upon bodies of written law?[1] Certainly the presence within a given society of a functional writing system, whether indigenously developed or cross-culturally borrowed, is a prerequisite for the creation of written law. Yet several scholars, notably anthropologists and sociologists, have argued that the mere presence of writing does not necessarily result in the immediate, or inevitable, development of certain socio-political institutions dependent upon the technological capacities writing offers.[2] These same scholars warn that assigning such a mono-causal role to writing reduces the multifaceted complexity of a social phenomenon such as the development of written law to a teleological inevitability. Instead, many believe that writing provides what Jack Goody has called "potentialities" for types of developments and alternative configurations of social organization.[3] That is to say, the technological capacities of writing provide the potential for specific institutional developments, such as the use of written law; yet for such potential to be actualized, there must first exist within the society an acknowledgment of a social need with a concomitant consciousness that that need can best be satisfied through the implementation of a form of writing.

Ascertaining what societal changes led to the development of written law is a quest that has guided the research of many historians of Western civilization attempting to understand the appearance of written law within a given society, or to explain institutional differences between chronologically and geographically contiguous legal traditions.[4] Scholars of ancient Greek and Roman law, for example, continue to debate the underlying causes of the transition to written law. For some, the institution of written law was an act of conciliation by the ruling aristocratic lineages intended to pacify the growing dissatisfaction of the general populace. Others argue that the transition to written law actually cleverly served to preserve aristocratic legal authority vis-à-vis the populace, while simultaneously mitigating factional aristocratic conflicts.[5]

Similar questions pertaining to the underlying causes and socio-political implications of the transition to written law have concerned scholars of traditional Chinese law.[6] Likewise, the debates appear polarized, with most theories methodologically locked in a struggle to understand the rationale behind this legal transition from the perspective of one of two major schools of thought in early China: Confucianism or Legalism.[7] Confucian interpretations often lament the written law transition, seeing it as detrimental to the moral (and legal) authority of the aristocracy to govern, and warn that as a consequence of writing down laws the populace is afforded greater legal empowerment vis-à-vis the aristocracy.[8] Alternatively, Legalist interpretations focus on written law as a political tool devised by the central government for the purpose of controlling bureaucrats and the populace. Such Legalist interpretations, when applied retrospectively to early Chinese sources, focus too narrowly on the effects of written law along a vertical socio-political axis. That is, scholars of traditional Chinese law, like some scholars of ancient Greece and Rome, are concerned only with the consequences of employing written law on the political and legal relationship between the governed (the populace) and those who govern (the aristocracy). As a result, they look only to potential factors impacting this specific relationship. Such perspectives often fail to consider broader societal factors, such as the influence of theories of writing on theories of law and administration, as well as the changing external and internal dynamics of power among individual kingdoms brought about by the blurring of aristocratic kinship relations.

In this chapter, I ask which dynamic societal factors produced a conscious need for legal change in early China and why the introduction of written law was considered to be an integral part of that legal change. In answering these questions, I bring to light three new facets of early Chinese views on the value and role of written law. First, that the early Chinese use of written laws arose in direct response to a growing need for an alternative method of social control, precipitated by the deteriorating socio-political conditions of the late "Spring and Autumn" and "Warring States" Periods.[9] Second, unlike previous scholarship, I argue that the reliance on written law was not envisioned as merely having vertical legal effect on the socio-legal relations between the traditional aristocracy and the general populace, but was also thought to be capable of mediating the escalating inter-clan conflict among the aristocracy which threatened the internal stability of individual kingdoms. Third, I demonstrate a growing consciousness within several early Chinese kingdoms of the ability of written media to increase the efficacy of law.

To do this, I first examine the changing socio-political conditions of this era as described in the classic historical text, *Zuo zhuan*. Against the backdrop of this societal flux, I analyze five passages within the text that demonstrate a growing consciousness of the value of written law as a tool capable of producing social and political order. I then place the early Chinese development of written law into a global context by comparing it to the development of written law within other premodern legal traditions. From a comparative perspective, a close examination of the relationship between theories of writing and the development of a legal ideology predicated upon written law in the early Chinese case provides new insights for ongoing debates concerning the development of written law in other societies around the world. Likewise, scholars of Chinese legal history can gain a new perspective on Chinese legal developments by considering the developmental trajectories of law in other societies.

The *Zuo zhuan* and social change

If the purpose of one's inquiry is to test how early Chinese reactions to social change manifested in an increased reliance on written law, then the historical contents of the *Zuo zhuan* 左傳 offer several remarkable examples of a society in transition. The *Zuo zhuan*, or *Zuoshi zhuan* 左氏傳, is one of three extant commentaries on the classic text *Chun qiu* 春秋, or *Spring and Autumn Annals*.[10] The latter text is a terse, annalistic chronicle that records the external and internal events affecting the kingdom of Lu from 722–481 BCE.[11] The compilation and editing of the text is ascribed to Confucius and was believed to contain his subtle, embedded moral judgments on the recorded events. As a result, its status was later elevated to that of one of the Confucian classics. The *Zuo zhuan*, on the other hand, is a rather lengthy text covering the years 722–463 BCE. Its compilation is ascribed to Zuo Qiuming, purportedly a disciple of Confucius, and is understood to be an extended commentary meant to elucidate many of the terse and sometimes cryptic entries of the *Chun qiu*. Indeed, a three or four character entry in the *Chun qiu* might correspond to an entry in the *Zuo zhuan* covering several pages, replete with narrative-style historical anecdotes, soliloquys, and dialogues.[12] The authenticity of these soliloquys and dialogues, however, has been questioned for centuries, and dates for these contents range from the fifth century BCE to the first century CE.[13] Many scholars would now agree that the *Zuo zhuan* is likely a collection of historical anecdotes of the Spring and Autumn Period, which were compiled and edited by mid- or late-Warring States Period historiographers.[14] As such, when analyzing the passages from this text, I am not necessarily asserting a genuine chronology to the recorded events, nor am I arguing for the authenticity of the words ascribed to various individuals. I do, however, view these records as representative of a growing and evolving intellectual discourse surrounding the development of written law and nascent theories of codification, which was believed to have begun during the Spring and Autumn Period and was further developed and theorized during the subsequent Warring States Period.[15]

As mentioned above, the *Zuo zhuan* documents the early Eastern Zhou Period, when the sources of authority and legitimacy, traditional power bases, and social hierarchies were in flux. One source of this instability can be traced back to early land enfeoffment policies of the preceding era, known as the Western Zhou Period.

The Western Zhou Period is portrayed in traditional historical texts as the "golden age" of early Chinese civilization. Two rulers of the Zhou people, Wen, and, upon his death, his son Wu, led a "virtuous" series of campaigns to overthrow the debauched Shang dynasty (*c.*1600–1045 BCE). Once completed, Wu established the Zhou dynasty and claimed the title of King of Zhou. Subsequent

Zhou kings led a series of military campaigns to the east, bringing much of the central plains under Zhou royal authority.[16] As a method of control, the Zhou rulers frequently divided the newly incorporated, distant lands into individual principalities and, in exchange for loyalty and military support, installed Zhou family members to serve as royal custodians charged with maintaining social and political order within their jurisdictions. Thus, the extension of central Zhou royal authority over peripheral kingdoms relied heavily upon lineage affiliation and kinship hierarchies. Similar bloodline hierarchies served as the socio-political foundation within individual kingdoms. The gradual dilution of these extended lineage relations—through processes of time and exogamic marriage practices—slowly increased the autonomy of the various kingdoms vis-à-vis the center, while *within* these kingdoms a similar devolution occurred as powerful ministerial families gained increased authority to challenge their rulers.[17] Later, military incursions by non-Zhou peoples forced the weakened Zhou ruler to flee to the east (beginning the Eastern Zhou Period), where he and his successors became ceremonial puppets in the political machinations of powerful individual kingdoms.

An outgrowth of this decentralization of Zhou royal authority was increased regionalism and a collapse of traditional social and political order, evidenced externally by a dramatic increase in warfare between kingdoms vying for political and territorial supremacy, and internally by various, often deadly, political intrigues. This societal flux gave rise to new institutional forms. An example of a new institution designed to re-establish inter-kingdom cohesion was the *ba* 霸, or hegemon system. Whereas previous political unity was maintained through a kinship-based acknowledgment that the Zhou king possessed sole authority to perform certain ritual sacrifices, convene multi-kingdom assemblies, or muster multi-kingdom military forces to attack another "disobedient" kingdom, under the *ba* system the authority (and responsibility) to carry out these functions was ceremonially bestowed by a weakened Zhou king upon the ruler of the most politically and militarily powerful kingdom. Writing played a crucial role in the conferral of this authority, especially during the religio-legal ceremony of the covenant, *meng* 盟. At the covenant, the rulers of various kingdoms would congregate, acknowledge the Zhou king's chosen recipient, and often agree to quasi-contractual statements of allegiance. Afterwards, the written versions of these pledges, as well as sacrificial animals, would be buried together so as to sanctify the conferral.[18] The actual royal institution of Zhou rulers was not directly supplanted, but changing political circumstances (the Zhou now occupied a fraction of their former lands, had lost much of the bloodline-based authority, and could not field a proper army) necessitated the development of an alternative, authoritative institution capable of sustaining inter-kingdom cohesion.[19]

As a consequence of increased political autonomy of the individual kingdoms, there developed more visible regional peculiarities with respect to intra-kingdom institutions. These societal transformations included the development of increasingly regionalized forms of written scripts, administrative practices, arts, and religious practices.[20] The societal sphere of law was also affected. Many of the law-related responses were designed to negotiate changing social conditions, brought about by increased social mobility and weakening internal blood ties within individual kingdoms, either by re-establishing former lines of authority through the manipulation of former institutions, or by establishing new sources of authority through new institutions. Within individual kingdoms, many powerful ministerial families appropriated the religio-legal institution of the covenant to establish quasi-contractual (i.e., non-kinship based) agreements of allegiance within their own lineage, as well as with other families. Written contracts between individual persons, composed upon stone slabs and buried in sacrificial pits, produced a form of internal cohesion that did not rely exclusively on kinship ties.[21] Like the *ba* system, written forms served an important function in the development of a legal institution designed to respond to changing social conditions. The remainder of this chapter examines how this environment of societal change, as depicted within the pages of the *Zuo zhuan*, elicited another intra-kingdom response in which writing, in the form of the increased use of written law collections, played an increasingly more important role.

Social change, legal response, and written law in the *Zuo zhuan*

There are five primary references to written law contained within the *Zuo zhuan*. Below, I analyze these passages from the perspective of social and legal change. In terms of presentation, I opt not to discuss the passages thematically. Instead, I have elected to present and analyze each passage separately and in chronological order as recorded in the *Zuo zhuan*. I do this for two reasons, one logistical and one methodological. As will be seen below, some of the passages are quite lengthy and touch upon multiple themes related to written law. If a thematic arrangement were utilized, segments of translation would be broken up, requiring a great deal of confusing cross-referencing and cross-translating. Methodologically, this practice would destroy the indigenous architectonics of Chinese legal historiography represented in the structural totality of individual passages and by their original arrangement. While the main purpose of this chapter is to examine the development of written law in early China, tangentially I also wish to consider the ways in which the Chinese both understood their own history and contextualized law within that history.

The organizational efficacy of written laws: Zhao Dun's reforms in Jin

The passage quoted below is often overlooked in studies on early Chinese written law, because it does not appear to contain a direct reference to written law.[22] However, when read against the historical backdrop of societal transformation, one can see elements of an underlying theory of written law that can best be viewed as a reaction against increased internal disorder.

In spring of the sixth reign year of Duke Wen of Lu (r. 626–609 BCE), it is recorded in the *Zuo zhuan* that the kingdom of Jin held grand military reviews at Yi and Dong. As a result of these reviews, the Jin military underwent a serious reorganization including the reassignment of several commanders to new posts and the disbandment of two full armies out of Jin's total of five. During the review at Dong, an assistant commander by the name of Zhao Dun was singled out as deserving a higher rank by Yang Chufu, a former subordinate to Zhao Dun's father and a loyalist to the Zhao clan. Yang believed Zhao Dun possessed great ability and argued that, "To employ [those with] ability is beneficial to the kingdom." Thus, Zhao Dun (known afterwards as Xuanzi) was promoted and charged with managing the government of Jin.

It quickly becomes apparent that the Jin government is plagued by a variety of administrative maladies, for Zhao Dun immediately initiates a systematic reform of several government institutions. The *Zuo zhuan* records that:

> 宣子於是乎始為國政.制事典正法罪辟獄刑董逋逃由質要治舊洿本秩禮續常職出滯淹既成以授大傅陽子與大師賈佗使行諸晉國以為常法
>
> Thereupon, Xuanzi began to administer the kingdom. He systematized various posts; rectified laws and offenses; compiled personal suits and punishments; investigated the issue of abscondence; instituted the use of "contracts"; managed outdated and defunct policies; restored the distinctions of rank according to propriety; renewed common offices; brought out men whose path had been stopped, and who were in obscurity. Once completed, [he] presented [the reforms] to Grand Tutor Yangzi and Grand Marshal Jia Tuo, so as to be implemented throughout the kingdom of Jin as constant laws.[23]

Zhao Dun's actions, subsequent to his appointment, provide a crucial window through which we may glimpse early Chinese conceptions of the efficacious use of both law and writing to conceptualize and generate particular social and political transformations.

A very prominent feature of the passage concerns the purposive exploitation of laws and written forms as devices for combating disorder. The kingdom of Jin has long been used as an example of the societal transformations and institutional responses occurring during the early Spring and Autumn Period. Well before Zhao Dun, the often violent ducal succession disputes motivated an institutional change, whereby those sons not appointed to the position of heir-apparent would be sent to other kingdoms.[24] The shifting avenues of power among the ministerial families also led to increased quarreling that often ended in bloodshed or banishment. By the time of Zhao Dun's appointment to administer the government, Jin was experiencing a decline in both its domestic and inter-kingdom power. In 632 BCE, under the sagacious rule of Duke Wen (r. 636–628 BCE), the kingdom of Jin rose politically to claim the title of *ba*, or hegemon over the other kingdoms.[25] Yet, this prominence greatly diminished under the reign of his successor, Duke Xiang (r. 627–621 BCE). Military defeats weakened Jin's external image and necessitated the troop musters at Yi and Dong, as well as the disbandment of two of its armies. Internally, rival court factions, centering on a few powerful ministerial families, vied for control over the Jin ducal family. Their political intrigues and machinations contributed to an increased instability within the government. It was a desire to stabilize the kingdom internally and project a strong image externally that prompted Zhao Dun's reform movement.

From a legal perspective, four of his reform targets, as well as the terminology used to describe the specific actions of reform, demonstrate a belief that the problem of disorder within political and social institutions could be counteracted through a transformation and systematization of those very institutions. Indeed, Zhao Dun's first action is to "systematize" (*zhi* 制) the offices of the government. Such action likely required a transformation of the existing administrative institutions in order to produce a comprehensive network of several interdependent offices and functions.

Zhao Dun then goes on to "rectify the laws and offenses" of Jin. That the laws and offenses were targeted for reform indicates first that the laws of Jin were unsettled, and second that the unsettled nature of the laws of Jin was perceived as contributing in part to a state of disorder. Such a conclusion is supported by the very terminology used to describe Zhao Dun's actions. The word "rectify" (*zheng* 正) is commonly used as a verb within early Chinese philosophical discourses to indicate a practice of organizing things according to a preconceived standard of correctness.[26] The use of the term to describe Zhao Dun's actions then implies that the targets for rectification, the antonymic binary "the laws and offences," were understood to have a proper organization, yet at the same time were perceived by Zhao Dun to be in disarray or incorrectly categorized. The Chinese graph for the word "law" (*fa* 法) is a polysemantic graph that was frequently employed in early China to represent a range of semantically related words, such as, "model," "method," and "practice," all of which possess an implicit indication of the existence of *proper* or *correct* forms, methods, or behaviors.[27] In the present context, this proper behavior signified by the word "laws" is juxtaposed to its antonym "offenses" (*zui* 罪), or that which contravenes the laws. It is clear that Zhao Dun considers the categories of "laws and offenses" to be muddled and confused, and that only through a proper categorization and differentiation of acceptable and unacceptable behavior can a disorderly society be transformed into an orderly one.

The third important reform concerns the compilation (*bi* 辟) of personal and criminal law matters. The use of the term *bi* in this context seems to imply a standardization or compilation of laws related to these two legal spheres. Such a meaning is confirmed by the term's use in later passages of the *Zuo zhuan* where it refers to written collections of penal law promulgated by the ancient rulers Yu, Tang, and Zhou, as well as occurrences of the term in other early Chinese texts.[28] What specific aspects of personal or criminal law were affected is unclear; however, since the previous reforms involved processes of systematizing and categorizing, it is possible that these reforms touched on both substantive and procedural areas of law. The distinctive use of the terms *yu* 獄, "to litigate" or "a suit," and *xing* 刑, "to punish" or "punishment" indicates that the act of compilation (*bi*) would likely entail a degree of differentiation of specific actions as either personal or criminal, and of procedures for dealing with such actions. The final reform concerns the "management" (*zhi* 治) of old and defunct policies. Zhao Dun examines the policies of Jin, categorizes and values them, and then nulls those policies deemed no longer efficacious.

The contribution of writing to Zhao Dun's reform efforts is easily found in the final line of the passage. Once he completed his reforms they were "presented to Grand Tutor Yangzi and Grand Marshal Jia Tuo, so as to be implemented throughout the kingdom of Jin as constant laws." The use of the graph *shou* 授, meaning "to present," indicates that the reforms were first conceptualized, then composed in written form and physically presented to Yangzi and Jia Tuo. Support for this usage can be found on bronze vessel inscriptions dating as early as the Western Zhou Period.[29] The so-called investiture inscriptions of the period typically describe royal audiences in which the Zhou ruler makes a royal proclamation bestowing new duties upon the recipient, awarding gifts for valiant service, or reaffirming the recipient's prior obligations to the ruler.[30] Often a written version of the royal command is presented (the verbal form of *shou*) to the recipient of the mandate.[31] This document is stored by the recipient as a tangible personal referent to his charge, as well as evidential documentation providing proof of the charge or awards. Similarly, Zhao Dun wished for his reforms to become "constant laws" and so presented written versions to two people with the intent that they be referred to in future situations.

The breadth of Zhao Dun's reforms provides further support for the necessity of writing. Zhao Dun conceptualizes the form and content of reforms designed to transform a wide range of administrative fields. His reliance on Yangzi and Jia Tuo to aid in the implementation of these reforms generates the need to convey complex policies with a level of clarity and specificity capable of achieving the desired transformation. The use of writing to satisfy these new administrative requirements evinces an early Chinese awareness that writing provides the technological capacities necessary for composing large, complex systematizing texts capable of transmitting the intent of the author to other individuals in different locations, at different times, and without the presence of the author.[32] This consciousness of writing as an efficacious tool for conceptualizing, composing, and transmitting government directives and laws is present in other early Chinese texts as well. The *Analects of Confucius* (*Lun yu* 論語) contains the passage: "When preparing orders, Pi Shen drafted them. Shi Shu debated and discussed them. The minister of foreign relations, Zi Yu, polished and elaborated them. Zi Chan of Dongli touched up and embellished them."[33] In this passage from the *Analects*, like the present one concerning Zhao Dun, the use of writing to transmit government policy/law is not condemned as something unwarranted or dangerous. In fact, Confucius is offering praise for the procedure used by Pi Shen and others. Nor is there any indication of apprehension associated with the use of the written form and its potential negative effects on aristocratic authority.

Such concerns are clearly voiced, however, in subsequent passages analyzed below.

One final feature of written law in this context concerns the person to whom these reforms are ascribed. Zhao Dun was the aristocratic son of the head of the powerful Zhao ministerial family. He had a military career and was singled out due to his military service as one with "ability." It is also noteworthy that institutional and legal reforms are not attributed to the ruler, but to a person who is invested with the authority to act on the ruler's behalf. The importance of these personal characteristics will be revisited later in this chapter, especially when debates over the inevitability of written law to destroy the aristocracy's power are examined.

Written law as both a product of and catalyst for social change: Shu Xiang's critique of Zichan

It is exceedingly difficult to find a study of early Chinese law that does not ascribe the very origin of publicly promulgated written law to Zichan, minister of the kingdom of Zheng.[34] The *Zuo zhuan* records that in 536 BCE he ordered the casting of a bronze penal text, the *xing shu* 刑書.[35] It states:

> 三 月, 鄭人鑄刑書, 叔向使詒子產書曰, 始吾有虞於子, 今則已矣, 昔先王議事以制, 不為刑辟, 懼民之有爭心也, 猶不可禁禦, 是故閑之以義, 糾之以政, 行之以禮, 守之以信, 奉之以仁, 制為祿位, 以勸其從, 嚴斷刑罰, 以威其淫, 懼其未也, 故誨之以忠, 聳之以行, 教之以務, 使之以和, 臨之以敬, 涖之以 彊, 斷之以剛, 猶求聖哲之上, 明察之官, 忠信之長, 慈惠之師, 民於是乎可任使也, 而不生禍亂, 民知有辟, 則不忌於上, 竝有爭心, 以徵於書, 而徼幸以成之, 弗可為矣, 夏有亂政而作禹刑, 商有亂政, 而作湯刑, 周有亂政, 而作九刑, 三辟之興, 皆叔世也, 今吾子相 鄭國, 作封洫, 立謗政, 制參辟, 鑄刑書,將以靖民, 不亦難乎, 詩曰, 儀式刑文王之德, 日靖四方, 又曰, 儀刑文王, 萬邦作孚, 如是何辟之有, 民知爭端矣, 將棄禮而徵於書, 錐刀之末, 將盡爭之, 亂獄滋豐, 賄賂竝行, 終子之世, 鄭其敗乎, 肸聞之, 國將亡, 必多制, 其此之謂乎. 復書曰, 若吾子之言, 僑不才, 不能及子孫, 吾以救世也, 既不承命, 敢忘大惠士文伯曰, 火見, 鄭其火乎, 火未出而作火, 以鑄刑器, 藏爭辟焉, 火如象之, 不火何為.
>
> In the third month, the people of Zheng cast a penal text. Shu Xiang dispatched to Zichan a text. It stated, "Formerly, I had hope for you, but have now given it up. In the past, former kings consulted on affairs to decide them but did not make penal compilations, for they feared that the people would grow litigious. Still unable to control them, they restrained them with rightness, bound them with [good] governance, and raised them with humanness. They institutionalized emoluments and ranks to encourage their obedience and determined strict punishments so as to overawe their perversity. Fearing that that was not enough, they taught them of loyalty, rewarded good conduct, instructed them in their duties, deployed them with harmony,

> supervised them respectfully, supervised them with might, and adjudged them with firmness. Still they sought sagacious and erudite superiors, intelligent and astute officials, loyal and trustworthy elders, and kind and beneficent masters. It was only under such conditions that the people could be employed without disaster or disorder resulting. When the people are aware of a legal compilation, they will have no wariness of their superiors. All become contentious, appealing to the texts, and achieve their goals through lucky conniving. They cannot be governed. When the Xia had a disorderly government, they composed the *Punishments of Yu*. When the Shang had disorderly administration, they composed the *Punishments of Tang*. When the Zhou had disorderly administration, they composed the *Nine Punishments*. All three of these penal compilations arose in terminal ages. Now as advisor to the kingdom of Zheng you have rectified fields and ditches, established a reviled administration, instituted the tripartite compilation, and cast the penal text [in bronze], in order to calm the populace. Is this not difficult? The *Poetry* states: 'Make King Wen's virtue a guide, a model, a pattern; each day pacify the four quarters.' Again it states: 'Make King Wen a guide and pattern: The ten thousand communities will respond.' Given this, how can one have penal codes? When the people know the points of contention, they cast away propriety and focus instead upon the texts. Even at chisel's tip and knife's edge they will contend. Frenzied litigiousness will flourish, and bribes will circulate everywhere. Will Zheng perhaps perish at the end of your generation? I have heard that 'when a state is about to fall, it has numerous regulations.' Surely it refers to this sort of situation."
>
> Zichan wrote in reply: "It is as you have said. I am untalented and unable to reach for posterity. I have done it to save this generation. Though I am unable to accept your mandate, how should I dare to forget your great kindness?"[36]

This passage contains a wealth of information related to the concept of written law and the dual nature of its relationship to societal change. On the one hand, the institution of written laws is portrayed as a reaction to changing socio-political conditions; on the other hand, it is an active agent producing societal change. This transformative duality will be discussed later in the chapter.

Shu Xiang's rather vehement reaction is commonly taken to reflect the traditional tension between rule-by-man and rule-by-law notions of political legitimacy.[37] The extant historical record contains many narratives indicating a custom of judicial verdicts being given by rulers on the basis of their own judgment.[38] This fact is emphasized by Shu Xiang's polemic of the ruler serving as the model of conduct for the people and the supreme adjudicator of normative behavior. He argues that in the past sagacious rulers considered all the circumstances and made their decisions on a case-by-case basis. By introducing written law, this high degree of judicial flexibility would be curtailed and the people would grow more wary of the interpretative legal authority of the aristocracy. Many scholars argue that Shu Xiang's statements reflect a fear that the introduction of written law carries with it the potential to constrain the aristocratic echelons of society, who for centuries had maintained a monopoly over legal authority.[39] For Shu Xiang, written law upsets the traditional hierarchy and increases social disorder by legally empowering the populace to engage in rampant litigation.

Interestingly, Shu Xiang's remonstrance exposes a belief, or an apprehension, that the literal act of writing down laws and allowing them to be made publicly known can effect transformations of the institutions of law and society. From a bottom-up perspective, the introduction of written law alters the populace's conception of the sources of law, reconfigures their legal relationship to their superiors, and redefines their method of legal engagement and legal argumentation. From a top-down perspective, this transition further transforms the actual legal process by requiring legal judgments of aristocratic "judges" to conform to a written, public standard and forcing them to defend the validity of their judgments to those capable of reading the written laws. In short, Shu Xiang ascribes to the very act of writing laws a transformative capacity to alter the concept of law itself.

Change, however, is not restrictively conceptualized as social transformations unilaterally induced by legal change. In many ways, Shu Xiang's remonstrance implicitly resonates with Zhao Dun's view that written law can be utilized to combat social disorder. Though framed negatively, Shu Xiang's criticism still illustrates the reciprocal nature of a change wherein legal transformation reacts to societal change. Drawing on past practices as authoritative evidence, he states that written law collections arose in times of great social disorder in dynastic rule. When rulers were unable to control the people through example and virtue, they turned to written laws as a "stop-gap" capable of temporarily restoring some measure of social control. From the perspective of traditional Chinese historiography, both Schaberg and Li Wai-yee argue that this passage reflects attempts by early Chinese historiographers to reconcile conflicting views of writing contained within historical records. Those historiographers promote a virtuous rule-by-man ideology through the construction of historical precedents that negatively associate the rise of written law collections with evidence of dynastic decline.[40] However, regardless of the historiographers' intent, the discourse between Shu Xiang and Zichan does display a consciousness that the law changes to accommodate changing social conditions. Zichan makes this clear when he replies to Shu Xiang. Though he admits the futility of long term reliance on written law, Zichan maintains that the promulgation of written law is necessary to cope with the changing social conditions in Zheng; changes that have caused increased disorder within the kingdom.

This passage contains useful information concerning three major themes associated with the development of written law in early China. First, like the problems necessitating reform in the kingdom of Jin by Zhao Dun, the use of written law in the kingdom Zheng arose during a time of social and political crisis. The former systems of social control were no longer deemed efficacious, so the possibility of written law as a means of combating socio-political disorder comes to the forefront. Zichan views the institution of written law as an expedient means of regaining some measure of stability. Second, Shu Xiang's remonstrance illustrates the belief that the institution of written collections of laws would produce a new, visible standard of behavior capable of influencing the actions of not only the general populace, but also the aristocratic lineages traditionally charged with monitoring and judging behavior. Third, this increased efficacy of law to control both the populace and aristocracy was possible because writing was visible and accessible to the general populace. It enabled the actions of those above to be assessed based on a known, public standard. The transformative importance of this shift from oral to written and from private to public forms of law becomes more evident in the following passages.

The transition from private to public writing and the efficacy of the law: the iron cauldrons of Jin

The kingdom of Zheng was by no means the only polity to inscribe portions of their law onto bronze-cast vessels. Nor was Zichan the sole recipient of harsh criticism for condoning such a practice. In 513 BCE, the kingdom of Jin, noted above for providing one of the earliest references to the process of compiling and distributing collections of written law, also utilized the permanence and prominence of cast vessels in the production of public penal laws. And just as Shu Xiang saw the inscribed bronze vessels as portents of the coming demise of the kingdom of Zheng, the casting of Jin's penal vessels receives biting criticism from Confucius as well as the scribe Cai Mo. Despite the harsh commentaries (which voice an opinion quite similar to that of Shu Xiang), this passage contains very interesting perspectives on the relationship between social change, writing, and law in early China.

The *Zuo zhuan* records that in the winter of the twenty-ninth year of Duke Zhao of Lu (r. 541–510 BCE), "Zhao Yang and Xun Yin of Jin led troops to fortify Rubin. Thereafter, they presented one *gu* of iron to the kingdom of Jin, so as to cast penal cauldrons upon which would be inscribed Fan Xuanzi's so-called *Book of Punishments*" (晉趙鞅, 荀寅, 帥師城汝濱, 遂賦晉國一鼓鐵, 以鑄刑鼎, 著范宣子所謂刑書焉).[41]

This extremely brief passage contains some valuable clues concerning the increased use of written law in early China. Foremost, it provides one of the earliest references to the actual source material for written law. From the previous passages, we are unable to ascertain the source of the laws which were transferred to written form by the likes of Zhao Dun or Zichan. Zhao Dun is merely recorded as having "rectified laws and offenses" and "compiled personal suits and punishments," but the textual (or customary) sources informing these disorderly institutions that he engages and corrects are not mentioned. With Zichan, we are likewise in the dark over both the content and provenance of the "penal text" he commissioned.

In the present passage, however, Zhao Yang and Xun Yin, of the Zhao and Zhonghang ministerial clans respectively, contribute a portion of iron with the intent that it be used for the casting of a penal tripod vessel. The legal text to be cast into this vessel is not created *ex nihilo* by either contributor, nor does it come from the Jin ruler. Instead, we are also told explicitly that the content of the cast vessel will be the *Book of Punishments* of Fan Xuanzi.[42] That is, the public writings are based upon another written document previously composed by a single author and on a particular subject. In this case, it is likely penal in nature, due to the use of the term *xing* 刑, "punishment"; however, this does not necessarily imply a total or comprehensive treatment of Jin penology.

Furthermore, this illustrates a consciousness that the capacities of the written form to effect desired changes are in part dependent upon the inscribed medium. A penal text, like the one composed by Fan Xuanzi, will prescribe and proscribe specific behaviors for a particular group of people. Yet, the ability of such a text to produce the intended behavioral conformity depends upon the effective transmission of its contents to those persons for whom such prescriptions or proscriptions were initially created. It is likely that Fan Xuanzi's text originally existed in written form on bamboo slips, and this would potentially limit direct transmission to the smaller communities of learned scholars/aristocrats. It is unclear exactly how the *Book of Punishments* was originally used in Jin; however, the actions taken by Zhao Yang and Xun Yin seems to indicate that its contents, if made public, were believed to be capable of influencing the behavior of a broader, more general audience. To enhance the transformative effects of the text, however, an alternative medium was apparently required and selected. Thus, the process of casting the document into a vessel is indicative of a conscious desire by Zhao Yang and Xun Yin to obtain this enhanced efficacy by supplying a medium capable of broadening its transmission.

This assumption about the public dimension of writing is supported by the appended commentaries offering pessimistic views of both the transition to written law and its results. The objections to written law ascribed to Confucius are remarkably similar to those of Shu Xiang. Prior to Zhao Yang and Xun Yin's actions, the kingdom of Jin was the stage for nearly a century of intense conflicts between powerful ministerial families that resulted in the banishment and/or execution of several family lines.[43] One can then argue that the actions of Zhao Yang and Xun Yin were designed to bring about some form of stability in the kingdom among the aristocracy as well as the populace. Yet, contra all the previous arguments stating that written laws can effectively combat societal disorder, Confucius in his critique claims that the transition to publicly promulgated written forms of law will in fact lead to further disorder (even the destruction of the kingdom) by obfuscating social hierarchies. He argues that the authority for legal interpretation should be entrusted solely to the aristocracy, and assumes that written law will become the sole source of the people's law, thereby undermining the socially distinguishing legal authority of the aristocracy. Confucius is quoted as saying,

> Now they have discarded these standards,[44] and cast penal cauldrons. The populace will dwell only on the cauldrons. How will they revere the noble?

> How will the nobles preserve their patrimony? Without distinction between the noble and the base, how can there be a kingdom?[45]

Though the authenticity of the commentary is debated, it has traditionally been read as the archetypical expression of the Confucian view on law, wherein the efficacy of written law is deemed inferior to a preferred rule-by-man legal institution.[46] Regardless of its philosophical pedigree, the commentary along with the historical anecdote to which it is appended both illustrate, at the very least, an anxiety over the potential capacity of the public dimension of written legal forms to generate alternative social structures, as well as alternative configurations of legal institutions. Additionally, like the casting of penal texts in the kingdom of Zheng, there is an implicit cognizance of a direct relationship between the medium upon which laws are placed and the very efficacy of those laws.

The durability of written law: Deng Xi's Bamboo Book of Punishments

Further evidence linking law to writing on bamboo slips is found in a later reference to events occurring in the kingdom of Zheng. In the ninth year of Duke Ding of Lu (r. 509–495 BCE), the *Zuo zhuan* states:

> 鄭駟歂殺鄧析, 而用其竹刑. 君子謂子然於是不忠, 苟有可以加於國家者, 棄其邪, 可也, 靜女之三章, 取彤管焉, 竿旄何以告之, 取其忠也, 故用其道, 不棄其人, 詩云, 蔽芾甘棠, 勿翦勿伐召伯所茇, 思其人, 猶愛其樹, 況用其道, 而不恤其人乎, 子然無以勸能矣.
>
> Si Chuan of Zheng killed Deng Xi, yet still employed his *Bamboo Book of Punishments*. The superior man says that in so doing Ziran was disloyal. If there is a person who possesses that which could be used to benefit the kingdom, then it is permissible to dismiss his vices. In the third stanza of "Graceful Girl," what one takes is the red tube. In "What shall I report to him?" in "Flagstaffs," what one takes is loyalty.[47] Therefore, when utilizing [a person's] ways, do not discard the person. The *Poetry* states,
>
> Young and tender is this sweet pear tree!
> Do not lop it off or harm it;
> For the Lord of Shao rested under it.[48]
>
> The writer, thinking of the man, loved even his tree; how could we use [a person's] ways, but show no compassion for the person? Ziran did nothing to encourage ability.[49]

From the passage, we can initially infer, based primarily upon the superior man's comment about dismissing his vices, that Deng Xi obviously committed some offense, and because of this was put to death by Si Chuan. Unfortunately, the *Zuo zhuan* does not reveal what offense would warrant an execution.

Like the penal text of Xuanzi (Zhao Dun?), the document implemented by Si Chuan is ascribed to a single author. Therefore, we may assume that the contents of the *Bamboo Book of Punishments* represent a mental product of one individual. And despite his vices, the author of the text, Deng Xi, is also characterized as a person of talent and ability. This characterization of ability is determined by his capacity to produce a written legal text considered beneficial to the kingdom. Thus, unlike the earlier rebukes of Shu Xiang or Confucius, the superior man's criticism of Si Chuan's action is directed not at the implementation of a written penal text, but at his decision to put to death a person capable of benefiting the kingdom. Just like Zhao Dun, in the first passage analyzed above, we find here no condemnation, or even problematization, of the use of written law. Instead, its production and utilization are praised as something positively contributing to the kingdom.

Furthermore, Si Chuan's implementation of Deng Xi's text illustrates the inherent ability of a written legal text to transcend the life of its author. Like Zhao Dun, Deng Xi was able to compose a text on a specific legal subject in such a way that other people would be able to read, understand, interpret, and implement its contents without recourse to the author. This again demonstrates an early Chinese consciousness of the capacity of written forms to enhance the communicative function of laws intended to alter the behaviors of those meant to be affected by the textual contents.

Finally, later commentators for this passage ascribe the motivating element behind the implementation of Deng Xi's penal text to the poor status of Zheng's government and society, which is described as blighted and confused.[50] Thus, as with nearly all the previous passages analyzed thus far, we once again can see social change/disorder inspiring legal change. And that legal change was predicated upon a consciousness of the transformative capacity of written law, wherein a particular written form is perceived to be effective in counteracting disorder. At no place in the present passage is there any condemnation of the use of written law due to its potential negative influence on aristocratic legal authority.

Public display of the law: the xiangwei of Lu

One of the last references to written law contained in the *Zuo zhuan* has clear thematic links to the above passages, in that it emphasizes an early Chinese recognition that introducing a public dimension to a law will increase its efficacy in promoting a desired social transformation. It comes from the third year of Duke Ai of Lu (r. 494–477 BCE). During the summer of that year, a great fire broke out near the duke's palace threatening the ducal repository and treasury, as well as several temples. Various servants and officials were ordered to remove valued documents and keep watch over the treasury contents, while others attempted to put out the flames with tents and curtains soaked in water.

Apparently little could be done to extinguish the conflagration and it eventually consumed the ancestral temples of Huan and Xi. When Ji Huanzi, a minister to Duke Ai, arrived on the scene, he took charge of the duke's chariot and escorted him away from the raging fire to the compound's outer gates. Once there he "ordered those fighting the fire to desist once injured, and leave things to chance. He ordered the *xiangwei* to be stored, stating 'Old statutes cannot be lost.'" (命救火者, 傷人則止, 財可為也, 命藏象魏, 曰, 舊章不可亡也).[51]

Ji Huanzi's concern over preserving the *xiangwei* 象魏 provides important evidence necessary to formulate a more comprehensive understanding of how the early Chinese envisioned the efficacious function of written law.

It has already been shown that at least as early as the sixth century BCE, officials, like Zhao Dun and Zichan, were conscious of the potential use of law as a device capable of transforming socio-political institutions and behavior. Further, within the passages discussed earlier, these same officials demonstrated an understanding of the potential contribution of the visual dimension of writing to the intended function of law, and so exploited the form of bamboo texts or bronze/iron inscriptions for the dual purposes of creating a standardized referent for the laws and making such laws "visibly" transmittable. Yet, if a law is brought into existence with the intention that it will elicit a conditioned behavioral response from those people under its jurisdiction, then actual public knowledge of that law becomes essential.

Before Ji Huanzi's command to rescue the *xiangwei* from the fire, previous references to written law have in fact revealed very little about the public availability or distribution of those laws directed towards the general populace. As mentioned above, those legal texts composed by Zhao Dun and Deng Xi, and those utilized by Si Chuan and Zhao Yang, were most likely written upon bamboo slips. Indeed, the text of Deng Xi is referred to as the *Bamboo Book of Punishments*, indicating the medium upon which it was composed. For these texts, we can construct vague trajectories of transmission, but they are limited to the elite sphere of the official–aristocrat. As critiques of the practice demonstrate, however, it is only when laws are cast in bronze or iron vessels that that they gain the capacity to publicly and directly influence lower-levels of society. Other than that, we lack references to the dynamics of top-down dissemination of legal knowledge through written forms. Even those records of the much criticized production of inscribed laws on bronze or iron vessels suggest remarkably little information about where such vessels would be situated spatially so as to provide public viewing by the populace. The role of the *xiangwei* might shed some light on this issue.

There are varied explanations regarding the physical form of the *xiangwei*. Some scholars interpret it as a post, some an actual raised platform, and still others view it as the framework of a gateway.[52] Regardless of its actual form, we can discern from this *Zuo zhuan* passage some basic features of the *xiangwei*. It was some type of man-made structure, semi-mobile (i.e., capable of being moved away from danger, such as a fire), located near the gates of a palace or town, and used for the public display of official documents. These latter were typically legal documents, in the form of statutes or edicts, either written directly upon the *xiangwei* or on placards hung from it. In the present passage, Ji Huanzi alludes to the legal significance of the *xiangwei* of Lu by stating that "Old statutes cannot be lost." The word "statutes" is represented by the graph *zhang* 章, a term that generally refers to specific passages of writing, but which is used in other early Chinese texts to indicate specific written laws and government policies.[53] Thus, the *xiangwei* represents one medium whereby the rulers of Lu utilized written forms to publicly inform the populace of certain laws, old and new, meant to govern their behavior.

This use of the *xiangwei* to inform the public of changes to the law resurfaces in the *Zhou li* 周禮, a late Warring States Period text constructing an idealized conception of the former Zhou government.[54] In the section detailing the role of an official called the *tai zai* there is a direct reference to the *xiangwei*. One of the official duties of this position was to promulgate new policies throughout the kingdom on the first day of the first month. To ensure that these proclamations were viewed by the populace, they were ordered to be hung from the *xiangwei*.[55]

The *Mozi* 墨子, also a textual product of the Warring States Period, further demonstrates the intentional use of public forms of writing to convey government information to the general populace which, in turn, reflects an implicit expectation by government officials that such written forms would be communicable to a more general audience. One section records: "When making regulations related to defense preparations, set them up stating: 'Regulation X'. Position them in offices, streets, crossroads, stairways, and gateways. Order those passing by to look upon them and follow them."[56]

Interestingly, recently discovered archaeological materials provide additional evidence pointing to the continued practice of publicly posting laws well after the Warring States Period. References to *bianshu* 扁書 found in recently excavated administrative documents, dated to the Western Han dynasty (206 BCE to CE 25), indicate that the conscious use of the legal-didactic function of the *xiangwei*, or *xiangwei*-like forms, as a means to notify officials and the populace of legal changes (i.e., the promulgation of new laws) was eventually institutionalized as a mandated administrative practice. These documents commonly instructed those officials charged with implementing a newly delivered edict or law to:

> 明白大扁書鄉亭市里門外謁舍顯見處令百姓盡知之
>
> Prominently display [the edict/law] on a large *bianshu* in conspicuous locations at townships, stations, markets, outer gates, and hostels causing the hundred names to fully comprehend it.[57]
>
> 明白扁書亭隧顯見處令吏卒盡知之
>
> Prominently display [the edict/law] on *bianshu* at stations and outposts in conspicuous locations, causing officials and troops to fully comprehend it.[58]

Like the *xiangwei* mentioned in the above *Zuo zhuan* passage, these *bianshu* represent public manifestations of new laws and edicts transmitted from the capital to peripheral administrative offices in written form via an extensive official postal service. Once they arrived, orders accompanying these edicts or laws required local officials to display the texts in conspicuous, high traffic areas so as to make their contents known to other officials and the general populace. Thus rulers relied upon the public display of written laws as a method of inculcating new responsibilities into the populace. And, like the cast vessels of Jin and Zheng, the *xiangwei*, and later *bianshu*, became a public referent for legal knowledge.

In saying all of this, I do not mean to imply that such public written forms were the only means used; nor am I claiming the existence of such a high level of literacy that anyone passing the gates would fully comprehend their meaning. At the very least, the existence and use of the *xiangwei*, as a repository of public official and legal information, evinces an underlying ideology that at least some law was not conceived of as an esoteric knowledge jealously guarded by the aristocracy, and that some rulers considered public written law to be efficacious for the purpose of social change.

The development of Chinese written law in global context

A comparative perspective offers analogues to the rationale behind the early Chinese legal transition to written law. Earlier scholars of ancient Greece certainly made arguments similar to those of Shu Xiang and Confucius, that the move to written law in the *poleis* had a "democratizing" effect by legally empowering the populace at the expense of the aristocratic authority;[59] however, archaeological evidence reveals clearly that most of the *poleis* that first instituted written law were aristocratically governed, and remained so well after the institution of written law.[60] With specific reference to ancient Crete, Zinon Papakonstantinou further argues that the formulation and promulgation of written laws should be understood not as an attempt to limit the powers of aristocratic officials over the general populace, but as attempts by specific aristocratic factions to increase political stability by limiting the political influence of opposing aristocratic political factions.[61] Thus, written law was viewed as an expedient tool capable of combating internal political disorder created by aristocratic inter-lineage competition. Likewise, many have argued that the creation of the *Twelve Tables* in ancient Rome represented a concession by the patricians to the plebeians that severely undermined the former patrician legal authority. The nature of this "concession," however, has been called into question. Walter Eder believes that this transition to written law was actually "a measure to ensure aristocratic predominance" in a period of social unrest.[62] Written laws and their subsequent promulgation were viewed as a tool that could homogenize behavior of *both* classes, stabilize social unrest both vertically (competing aristocratic lineages) and horizontally (patrician/plebeian conflicts), and yet still maintain aristocratic predominance.[63] Here, the use of written law was perceived to be an expedient means to consolidate aristocratic power and extinguish social disorder.

With that in mind, contrary to the arguments made by Confucius and Shu Xiang, the aristocratic origin of early Chinese written law does not necessarily seem antithetical to the desired perpetuation of aristocratic authority vis-à-vis the general populace. In fact, the comparative exercise contributes to our understanding of yet another dimension of the early Chinese ideology of written law, the fear that intra-lineage conflict would destroy the kingdom.[64] Though there were objections, many aristocratic ministers placed their faith in the power of written law to combat this disorder. References to Zhao Dun highlight the extent of the internal disorder and the use of written forms (including law) to transform society and bring about stability. Although he was a member of one of several competing ministerial families, his reforms were designed to maintain the unity of the kingdom by systematizing and regulating not only aristocratic offices and behaviors (theoretically limiting inter-aristocratic lineage conflicts), but also the interactions of the general populace. In so doing, there is no indication that the position of the aristocracy was necessarily weakened in relation to the commoners. We can assume, however, that the reforms to the aristocratic offices were meant to curb inter-lineage conflict and provide horizontal stability at the elite level. Likewise, the use of written penal laws in Zheng was (rather weakly) defended by Zichan as an expedient means for bringing about some manner of control. The use of Fan Xuanzi's penal text by Zhao Yang and Xun Yin also comes on the heels of intense lineage conflict that threatened to destroy the kingdom of Jin. Therefore, this increased reliance on written law can be viewed as both a reaction to increased societal disorder, and the manifestation of a consciousness that written law could be employed to effect specific, desired socio-political transformations aimed at combating that disorder without detrimentally affecting traditional aristocratic legal authority.

Laws in other ancient civilizations were also designed to promote a specified social change. They were, therefore, intended to have a communicative function: they conveyed specific images of authority, as well as the desires of the government for the performance of specific behaviors by officials and the general populace. Furthermore, if law was to be utilized for the purpose of altering behaviors, one must effectively, efficiently, and accurately convey the law to those for whom it was conceived. In ancient Babylonia, for example, Hammurabi utilized publicly displayed collections of written law to consolidate his claim over newly annexed and conquered lands and did not consider such an action a threat to his, or his family's, legal authority.[65] Law was viewed as a stabilizing tool for consolidation of power and the use of writing and public display was considered a means to increase the efficacy of laws. For ancient Greece, Michael Gagarin argues that the Greeks conceived of law as being most efficacious if it was understandable and available to the majority of the population. As such, they utilized the public dimension of writing to increase the intended efficacy of law to condition behavior by providing a visible means for communicating official information to large audiences.[66]

The exploitation of the *visual* dimension of written law within these early societies suggests an early Chinese consciousness of the ability of written forms to effectively convey legal information in a manner that would be understood and internalized by its intended audience. This resonates clearly with Zhao Dun, who conceptualized society-altering changes to the laws which were then transmitted to Yangzi and Jia Tuo. The latter were then able to understand the conveyed written legal knowledge and institute the desired transformations. Likewise, Si Chuan was able to read Deng Xi's penal text and institute its contents without recourse to the author. The cast vessels, the *xiangwei*, and the *bianshu* all served to publicly inform the government officials, soldiers, and commoners of the area of their legal responsibilities. Thus, like ancient Babylonians, Greeks, and Romans, the early Chinese understood that specific written forms were capable of enhancing the communicative, and by extension transformative, function of law.

Conclusion

Contemporary scholarship on traditional Chinese law tends to view the development of written law through the lens either of modern notions of universalized "legal codes," or traditional interpretative paradigms that dichotomize Confucianism and Legalism. However, as I have tried to show in this chapter, these lenses unduly constrain our understanding of the socio-political role ascribed to written law by the early Chinese, and obfuscate the societal transformations underlying its increased use. If we turn our attention away from form/content debates and focus instead upon the context in which written law arises and the ideology informing its deployment, we can begin to reconstruct certain elements of an indigenous value system. Within this value system the production of written law was perceived as part of a transformative process capable of producing increased socio-political stability, as well as control over both the aristocracy and the general populace.

The era in which the production of written law became prominent was a time of great societal transformation, and its increased use was a response to a growing sense of disorder resulting from such changes. The continued decline of Zhou royal authority increasingly compromised the proverbial threads maintaining the stability of the region's geo-political fabric. The increased production of collections of *written* positive law, however, was not necessarily a direct response to inter-kingdom contentions for power, but more an intra-kingdom phenomenon meant to combat growing domestic disorder within individual kingdoms. In fact, the same dilution of lineage ties that diminished the traditional Zhou royal authority also affected intra-kingdom socio-political hierarchies, resulting in both increased potential for social mobility and increased conflict between powerful ministerial families vying for more power. Nearly all of the above examples drawn from the *Zuo zhuan* that depict the production of written law are foreshadowed by strong evidence of internal disorder.

The source of this disorder, frequently described as poor governance or hierarchical confusion, can be traced to conflicts between lineages or their various political machinations. Within the same *Zuo zhuan* passages, written law is always conceptualized as the product of a top-down enterprise initiated by a member of the aristocracy. It is used as a social-ordering tool responding to intra-kingdom conflict and the disorder that results. Yet, does the socially stabilizing efficacy of this new legal institution predicated upon written law necessarily come at the expense of the aristocracy's traditional legal power base vis-à-vis the general populace? I would argue that the frequent link between aristocratic, elite authorship and written law calls into question the strength of the objections offered by Shu Xiang and Confucius, as well as the shared ubiquity of their opinion. Both argue that the inevitable consequence of the transition to written law is the further destabilization of some desired social hierarchy, by shifting the source of law away from the aristocratic individual and towards the written text. This, by extension, usurps aristocratic authority to interpret the standards of normative behavior in that the people will no longer be swayed by elite legal rhetoric and command, but instead will insist that aristocrats justify their behavior in reference to law. Yet despite these two critiques (and their dubious provenance), the majority of references contained within the *Zuo zhuan* evince an open willingness on the part of the elite to institute written legal forms, as well as their lack of fear over any potential authority-reducing repercussions.

Finally, each of the passages analyzed provides either explicit or implicit evidence that the early Chinese capitalized on the value of the public dimensions of written law. Zichan's use of bronze vessels, the transition of the Fan Xuanzi's penal text from a bamboo book edition to iron vessels, and the use of the *xiangwei* indicate an early conceptualization of writing, especially public writing, as a technological device capable of increasing law's efficacy to produce and maintain a prescribed socio-political order. The early Chinese, therefore, seem to espouse a positive belief that by writing down laws and making them publicly known, they can provide a visible, written standard of conduct for all levels of society.

Notes

1 Throughout this chapter, I will refrain from using the term "codification" when referring to the collections of written law in ancient China prior to third century BCE. Even modern attempts to produce a universal definition typically fail in the face of the diversity of theoretical and interpretative traditions informing codified legal systems throughout the world. The problem is multiplied when attempting to apply such a term anachronistically to the legal traditions of the ancient world. For attempts to construct a multi-tiered conceptual paradigm for studying "codification" in chronologically and geographically diverse legal traditions, see Mark D. Rosen, "What Has Happened to the Common Law? Recent American Codifications, and Their Impact on Judicial Practice and the Law's Subsequent Development," *Wisconsin Law Review* no. 5 (1994): 1119–1286; Geoffrey MacCormack, "The Transmission of Penal Law (lü) from the Han to the T'ang: A Contribution to the Study of the Early History of Codification in China," *Revue Internationale Des Droits De L'antiquité* 51 (2004): 47–83. For more critical assessments of the utility of such a term applied to ancient civilizations, see Martha T. Roth, "The Law Collection of King Hammurabi: Toward an Understanding of Codification and Text," in *Codification Des Lois Dans L'Antiquite*, ed. E. Lévy (Paris: De Boccard, 2000), 9–31; Raymond Westbrook, "Codification and

Canonization," in *Codification Des Lois Dans L'Antiquite*, ed. E. Lévy (Paris: De Boccard, 2000), 33–47; John K. Davies, "Deconstructing Gortyn: When Is a Code a Code?" in *Greek Law in Its Political Setting: Justification Not Justice*, ed. Lin Foxhall and Andrew Lewis (Oxford: Oxford University Press, 1996), 33–56.

2 Classic examples of these debates can be found in Jack Goody, *The Power of the Written Tradition* (Washington, DC: Smithsonian Institution, 2000); Jack Goody, *The Logic of Writing and the Organization of Society* (Cambridge: Cambridge University Press, 1986); Erik Havelock, *The Muse Learns to Write: Reflections on Orality and Literacy from Antiquity to the Present* (New Haven, CT: Yale University Press, 1986); Walter Ong, *Orality and Literacy*, 2nd ed. (London and New York: Routledge, 2002). Such scholars also show that although writing as a technology provides new possibilities for the transmission of knowledge, the power and presence of the *oral* is retained well after writing takes the stage.

3 Some of Jack Goody's earlier work received much criticism for implicitly ascribing to writing a "mono-causal" role in the development of particular socio-political institutions. For an overview of these critiques and Goody's response, see Goody, *The Power of the Written Tradition*, 2–9.

4 Ancient Mesopotamian civilizations, for example, made use of a complex writing system as early as the Jemdet Nasr period (*c.*3200–3000 BCE), yet the earliest collections of written laws, such as the Laws of Ur-Namma (*c.*2100 BCE), Laws of Eshnunna (*c.*1770 BCE), and the Laws of Hammurabi (*c.*1750 BCE), were promulgated over a millennium after the introduction of writing. See Martha T. Roth, *Law Collections from Mesopotamia and Asia Minor* (Atlanta, GA: Society of Biblical Literature and Scholars Press, 1997).

5 For an excellent analysis of both sides of these arguments for the case of Roman law, see Walter Eder, "The Political Significance of the Codification of Law in Archaic Societies: An Unconventional Hypothesis," in *Social Struggles in Archaic Rome: New Perspectives on the Conflict of the Orders*, ed. Kurt A. Raaflaub (Malden, MA: Blackwell Publishing Ltd, 2005), 239–267. I will return to these debates later.

6 See, for example, T'ung-tsu Chü, *Law and Society in Traditional China* (Paris: Mouton, 1961); MacCormack, "The Transmission of Penal Law (lü) from the Han to the T'ang"; John W. Head and Yanping Wang, *Law Codes in Dynastic China : A Synopsis of Chinese Legal History in the Thirty Centuries from Zhou to Qing* (Durham, NC: Carolina Academic Press, 2005).

7 I acknowledge that terms such as "Confucian" and "Legalist" are anachronistic, categorical labels applied to various Warring States Period philosophers by later scholars. For this dissertation, I merely use the term "Confucian" to describe those early Chinese philosophers who either cited or openly advocated those theories of statecraft predicated upon virtuous rule and ascribed to the historical figure of Confucius. Likewise, the term "Legalist" refers to the theories of statecraft predicated upon bureaucratic centralization, strict laws, and harsh punishments and ascribed to thinkers such as Shang Yang or Han Feizi. In neither case do I imply a direct lineage or self-identifying "school" of thought. See, for example, Scott Cook, "The Use and Abuse of History in Early China from Xunzi to Lüshi Chunqiu," *Asia Major* 18, no. 1 (2006): 48–78; Kidder Smith, "Sima Tan and the Invention of Daoism, 'Legalism,' 'et Cetera,'" *Journal of Asian Studies* 62, no. 1 (2003): 129–156.

8 This interpretation is based upon a particular passage in the *Zuo zhuan* which is dealt with below.

9 The chronology of early China can be daunting for those not familiar with its intricacies. The Zhou royal family ostensibly governed the central plains region of China from roughly 1046–256 BCE. Their reign is divided into two large periods, the Western Zhou (1046–771 BCE) and the Eastern Zhou (771–221 BCE). The latter is further subdivided into two additional eras, the Spring and Autumn Period (*c.*771–476 BCE) and the Warring States Period (*c.*476–221 BCE).

10 There are arguments over the relationship between the three commentaries. Many believe that the *Gongyang zhuan* 公羊傳 and *Guliang zhuan* 穀梁傳 are commentaries for the "New Text" version of the *Chun qiu*, and that the *Zuo zhuan* is a commentary on the "Old Text" version of the *Chun qiu* that survived in the Han imperial archive and was written in old style Chinese characters (*guwen* 古文). For a brief synopsis of these arguments see Anne Cheng, "Ch'un ch'iu, Kung yang, Ku liang and Tso chuan," in *Early Chinese Texts: A Bibliographical Guide*, ed. Michael Loewe (Berkeley, CA: SSEC and Institute of East Asian Studies, 1993), 67–76.

11 The kingdom of Lu was a relatively small polity occupying parts of modern day Shandong Province.

12 Originally these two texts circulated as two independent documents; however, the Jin dynasty commentator on the *Zuo zhuan*, Du Yu (CE 222–284) purportedly combined the two texts into its current, single document format. See Takezoe Kōkō, *Saden kaisen* (Taipei: Tiangong shuju, 1998), 6–7. All citations to the *Zuo zhuan* will be based on Kōkō, *Saden kaisen*. Unless otherwise stated, all translations are those of the author.

13 Cheng, "Ch'un ch'iu, Kung yang, Ku liang and Tso chuan," 70.

14 Many scholars today argue that much of the dialogic contents of the *Zuo zhuan* should be dated to the Warring States Period. They also claim that the text as a whole represents an attempt to come to terms with the developmental trajectory of early Chinese society and, as such, represents a developing style of Chinese historiography. See, for example, David Schaberg, *A Patterned Past: Form and Thought in Early Chinese Historiography* (Cambridge, MA: Harvard University Press, 2001). For arguments that much of the *Zuo zhuan* contents should be accepted as contemporary to the late "Spring and Autumn" and early "Warring States Periods," see Yuri Pines, "Intellectual Change in the Chunqiu Period: The Reliability of the Speeches in the *Zuozhuan* as Sources of Chunqiu Intellectual History," *Early China* 22 (1997): 76–132.

15 This argument is similar to a recent statement by Scott Cook that

> [how] accurate these may reflect statements actually made at the purposed times is, certainly, open to question. They do, however, present an intellectual picture of the times that is historically quite plausible and, for all we know, may well have been based on reliable historical record.
>
> ("The Use and Abuse of History," 47, ft. 3)

16 For an overview of the establishment and later expansion of the Western Zhou, see Edward L. Shaughnessy, "Western Zhou History," in *The Cambridge History of Ancient China: From the Origins of Civilization to 221 B.C.*, ed. Michael Loewe and Edward L. Shaughnessy (Cambridge: Cambridge University Press, 1999), 292–351.

17 The role of weakening kinship affiliation in the decline of Western Zhou central authority has been thoroughly treated in Li Feng, *Landscape and Power in Early China: The Crisis and Fall of the Western Zhou, 1045–771 BC* (Cambridge: Cambridge University Press, 2006).

18 The religio-legal significance of writing within the context of early Chinese covenants has been well documented by W.A.C.H Dobson, "Some Legal Instruments of Ancient China: The *Ming* and the *Meng*," in *Wen-lin: Studies in the Chinese Humanities*, ed. Tse-tsung Chow (Milwaukee: University of Wisconsin Press, 1968); Mark Edward Lewis, *Writing and Authority in Early China* (New York: SUNY, 1999), 18–21.

19 For a detailed analysis of the *ba* system and its implications for Eastern Zhou geo-politics, see Liu Boji, *Chun Qiu huimeng zhengzhi*, 2nd ed. (Taipei: Wen jing shu ju, 1977).

20 Lothar von Falkenhausen, *Chinese Society in the Age of Confucius (1000–250 BC): The Archaeological Evidence* (Los Angeles: Cotsen Institute of Archaeology, University of California, Los Angeles, 2006), esp. chaps. 7 and 8.

21 Archaeological excavations at Houma 侯馬, Shanxi 山西 in 1965, Wenxian 溫縣, and Henan 河南 in 1976, yielded thousands of these covenant "contracts" from the kingdom of Jin that date to the fifth century BCE. Among these texts are several thousand "loyalty" and "pledge" texts, each specifically naming an individual who pledges loyalty to an unnamed covenant lord, *zhu*. See Susan Roosevelt Weld, "The Covenant Texts from Houma and Wenxian," in *New Sources of Early Chinese History: An Introduction to the Reading of Inscriptions and Manuscripts*, ed. Michael Loewe and Edward Shaughnessy (Berkeley: SSEC and the Institute of East Asian Studies, University of California, Berkeley, 1997), esp. 140–148.

22 The majority of scholarly books and articles overlook the importance of this passage and instead refer to the casting of the bronze penal texts in the kingdom of Zheng (see next section below) as the first textual reference to written law in China. The only source I have located which makes direct reference to this passage when discussing written law is Herrlee Glessner Creel, "Legal Institutions and Procedures During the Chou Dynasty," in *Essays on China's Legal Tradition*, ed. Jerome Alan Cohen, R. Randle Edwards, and Chen Chang Fu-mei (Princeton, NJ: Princeton University Press, 1980), 34–37.

23 *Zuo zhuan*, Wen gong 6: *Saden kaisen*, 596–597.

24 Cho-yun Hsu, *Ancient China in Transition: An Analysis of Social Mobility, 722–222 B.C.* (Stanford, CA: Stanford University Press, 1965), 82.

25 Cho-yun Hsu, "The Spring and Autumn Period," in *The Cambridge History of Ancient China: From the Origins of Civilization to 221 B.C.*, ed. Michael Loewe and Edward Shaughnessy (Cambridge: Cambridge University Press, 1999), 558–560.

26 Perhaps the most famous use of the term in early China is found in Confucius' theory of the "rectification of names" (*zhengming* 正名). Confucius argued that disorder arose when standardized/proper hierarchies within society and politics (i.e., names) were not acknowledged or practiced. Socio-political order could only be restored if these hierarchies were rectified according to a prescribed standard. Relatedly, the word *zheng* 正 is also used adjectivally in early China to mean "precise," "standardized," "correct," or "upright."

27 Indeed the meanings ascribed to the graph *fa* 法 in early China are much debated. For an overview of the different meanings, see Perry Ernest Caldwell IV, "Hunting the Xiezhai: Mythology, Methodology, and an Alternative Explication of [灋]" (MA Thesis, University of Kansas, 2006) and Chad Hansen, "Fa (Standards: Laws) and Meaning Changes in Chinese Philosophy," *Philosophy East and West* 44, no. 3 (July 1994): 435–488.

28 For later *Zuo zhuan* usages see section below. The similar use of the term *bi* 辟 as "compilation" referring to collections of written law can be found in *Shi jing* 詩經 (Siku quanshu ed.), 19.44a–b and *Guanzi* 管子 (Siku quanshu ed.), 4.3b and 4.5b.

29 In early China, aristocratic lineages produced elaborate collections of bronze vessels that were typically stored in ancestral temples and filled with sacrificial food and wine offerings during lineage ceremonies. Some of these vessels are quite small, while others weigh more than 100 kg. Furthermore, these bronze vessels often contain inscriptions, ranging from a single graph to several hundred graphs, which record various activities, meetings, battles, and even legal suits. For an overview of the various styles of bronze vessels used during the Western Zhou, see Jessica Rawson, *Ancient Chinese Bronzes from the Arthur M. Sackler Collections*, 2 vols. (Washington, DC and Cambridge, MA: Arthur M. Sackler Foundation; Arthur M. Sackler Museum, Harvard University, 1990). For the significance of bronze vessel inscriptions to Chinese historiography (especially legal historiography), see Laura Skosey, "The Legal System and Legal Tradition of the Western Zhou (ca. 1045–771 B.C.E.)" (PhD dissertation, University of Chicago, 1996).

30 An excellent overview of Western Zhou investiture inscriptions can be found in Virginia C. Kane, "Aspects of Western Chou Appointment Inscriptions: The Charge, the Gifts, and the Response," *Early China* 8 (1982–1983).

31 For more on the role of written documents within Western Zhou investiture ceremonies, particularly the conferral of royal commands, see Edward L. Shaughnessy, "The Writing of a Late Western Zhou Bronze Inscription," *Asiatische Studien/Etudes Asiatiques* 61, no. 3 (2007): 865–868.
32 The potential contributions of writing to various administrative spheres, particularly law and archiving, have been studied by Goody, *The Logic of Writing and the Organization of Society*, 87–171.
33 *Lun yu* (Siku quanshu ed.), 14.5b.
34 See, for example, Henri Maspero, "Le Régime féodal et la proriété foncière dans la Chine antique," in *Mélanges posthumes sur les religions et l'histoire de la Chine*, ed. Henri Maspero (Paris: Presses Universitaires de France and Publications du Musée Guimet, 1950); Geoffrey MacCormack, *The Spirit of Traditional Chinese Law* (Athens: University of Georgia Press, 1995); John W. Head and Yanping Wang, *Law Codes in Dynastic China: A Synopsis of Chinese Legal History in the Thirty Centuries from Zhou to Qing* (Durham, NC: Carolina Academic Press, 2005); T'ung-tsu Chü, *Law and Society in Traditional China* (Paris: Mouton, 1961).
35 The term *xing shu* literally translates as penal (*xing*) text (*shu*).
36 *Zuo zhuan*, Zhao gong 6: *Saden kaisen*, 1440–1444.
37 See Head and Wang, *Law Codes in Dynastic China*, chap. 2. For an examination of these debates as they resurfaced in late imperial and early republican China, see Leigh Jenco, "Rule by Man and Rule by Law in Early Republican China: Contributions to a Theoretical Debate," *Journal of Asian Studies* 69, no. 1: 181–203.
38 Western Zhou bronze inscriptions provide the earliest evidence of "trials" in early China and these typically depict litigants taking their dispute before an official seeking judgment. See Laura Skosey, "The Legal System and Legal Tradition of the Western Zhou," 103–106, 111–115, and 118–121. In addition, there are several references within the *Zuo zhuan*, as well as Warring States texts, depicting personal disagreements being articulated in front of a ruler or high ranking minister. References to law and legal proceedings found in the *Zuo zhuan* and other commentaries to the *Chun qiu* are collected in Yuhao Zhang, " 《*Chun qiu*》 san zhuan falü ziliao jizhu," in *Fa lü wen xian zheng li yu yan jiu*, ed. Boyuan Zhang (Beijing: Beijing daxue chuban she, 2005), 254–308.
39 See, for example, the discussion of Confucian ideals of law in MacCormack, *Spirit of Traditional Chinese Law*, 2–8.
40 Schaberg, *A Patterned Past*, 293–295; Li Wai-yee, *The Readability of the Past in Early Chinese Historiography* (Cambridge, MA: Harvard University Press, 2008), 363–365.
41 *Zuo zhuan*, Zhao 29: *Saden Kaisen*, 1745–1746.
42 One problematic aspect of this passage concerns the person to whom the *xingshu* is ascribed. The *Zuo zhuan* does indeed contain several passages referencing Fan Xuanzi, of the Fan ministerial clan; however, little evidence exists for him ever having composed a legal text. Further complicating matters, the appended criticism of Confucius cites the textual content of the *xingshu* as originating from Zhao Dun. He states: "The punishments of Xuanzi are those from the muster at Yi." It is possible that the Xuanzi to whom Confucius refers is none other than the aforementioned Zhao Dun. See Schaberg, *A Patterned Past*, 430, n. 150.
43 Hsu, *Ancient China in Transition*, 82–83.
44 The standards to which Confucius is referring are distinct models of behavior predicated upon a social hierarchy and entrusted by the former Zhou kings to the founder of the kingdom of Jin, Tang Shu.
45 *Zuo zhuan*, Zhao 29: *Saden kaisen*, 1745.
46 See, for example, Head and Wang, *Law Codes in Dynastic China*, 48–58.
47 The translation of these two poetic references, both found in the *Classic of Poetry*, follows that of David Schaberg. He argues that the purpose of these references is to

show that the person giving a gift is equally valuable as the gift. For example, in the "Graceful Girl," the author is given a red pipe, yet he values the "gift not for itself but for the beauty of the giver." To Schaberg, this implies condemnation of the killing of Deng Xi (the giver of laws), while retaining and valuing his gift (*Bamboo Book of Punishments*). Schaberg, *A Patterned Past*, 299–300.

48 This quote is from the *Shi jing* poem "Gantang" (Mao #16). The translation follows Arthur Waley, *The Book of Songs: The Ancient Chinese Classic of Poetry* (New York: Grove Press, 1996).

49 *Zuo zhuan*, Ding 9: *Saden kaisen*, 1835–1836.

50 In his work *Saden kaisen*, Takezoe Kōkō collects the commentaries of scholars from around CE 200 to the 1800s. For this particular passage, Takezoe merely states that the government was at the time blighted and confused (鄭此時秕政紛紛), see *Saden kaisen*, 1835.

51 *Zuo zhuan*, Ai 3: *Saden kaisen*, 1897–1898.

52 See *Saden kaisen*, 1898.

53 By the end of the Warring States Period the term *zhang* was not used to represent a specific legal document. Its legal meaning was replaced by *lü* (律), the term still used today as the word for a legal statute. For other early Chinese texts which ascribe legal significance to the term *jiu zhang* 舊章, see *Shang shu zhushu* 尚書注疏 (Siku quanshu ed.), 16.4b and *Shi jing zhushu* 詩經注疏 (Siku quanshu ed.), 24.62b.

54 For more information on the authenticity of the *Zhou li* and arguments over its dates, see William Boltz, "Chou li," in *Early Chinese Texts: A Bibliographical Guide*, ed. Michael Loewe (Berkeley, CA: SSEC and Institute of East Asian Studies, 1993), 24–32.

55 *Zhou li jinzhu jinyi* (Taipei: Taiwan Shangwu, 1972), 14–15.

56 *Mozi xiangu* (Beijing: Zhonghua shuju, 1986), 552.

57 2000ES7S: 4A. This alphanumeric citation and the following one are based on Wei Jian ed., *Ejina Hanjian* (Guangxi: Guangxi shifan daxue chuban she, 2005).

58 2000ES9SF4: 3.

59 Many early Greek legal references do imply a desire for laws to be spread throughout all social strata, yet the level of "empowerment" afforded by such action is difficult to assess. See Rosalind Thomas, "Written in Stone? Liberty, Equality, Orality, and the Codification of Law," in *Greek Law in its Political Setting: Justification not Justice*, ed. Lin Foxhall and Andrew Lewis (Oxford: Oxford University Press, 1996), 9–32.

60 Michael Gagarin, *Writing Greek Law* (Cambridge: Cambridge University Press, 2008), 72–76.

61 Zinon Papakonstantinou, "Written Law, Literacy, and Social Conflict in Archaic and Classical Crete," *Ancient History Bulletin* 16, no. 3–4 (2002): 149–150.

62 Eder, "Political Signficance of the Codification of Law," 239.

63 Much like Confucius and Shu Xiang, Eder notes that codification could be viewed as potentially eliminating absolute authority over the law, where the loss of arbitrary jurisdiction (in terms of adjudication) would limit scope of aristocratic capriciousness. However, he argues that the content of the law was still determined by the aristocracy, in that legislation descended from the aristocracy. "'Fixed' law need not necessarily mean 'just law.'" This is strengthened by the fact that very few of the plebeians demanded concessions are represented in codified laws. Eder, "Political Signficance of the Codification of Law," 252–253.

64 The danger was indeed real. There are several recorded instances of dukes of various kingdoms being killed by ministerial families. Furthermore, the kingdom of Jin, known for having high levels of lineage conflict, was eventually partitioned off into three distinct kingdoms, Han 韓, Wei 魏, and Zhao 趙, each ruled by a former Jin ministerial family.

65 Russ VerSteeg, *Early Mesopotamian Law* (Durham, NC: Carolina Academic Press, 2000), 30–33.

66 Gagarin, *Writing Greek Law*, 1.

3 Inscribing control in Qin

Introduction

This chapter examines the extant materials related to the use of writing and law as a form of centralized control over the Qin aristocracy, bureaucracy, and the general populace. As shown in the previous chapter, the *Zuo zhuan* 左傳 debates over the use of written law are best understood within the context of the socio-political turmoil affecting most kingdoms during the latter years of the Spring and Autumn Period. The increased instances of usurpation and political assassinations brought about by the machinations of powerful hereditary ministerial families, as well as the inability of past legal and administrative measures to adequately maintain social order and preserve royal power, necessitated the creation of alternative forms of control. Writing was paired with law as a means to publicly promote a centralized standard of behavior to which ministers and the general populace were held accountable.

In the present chapter, I will examine how the rulers and ministers of the kingdom, and later empire, of Qin came to use various written forms as a means of providing a centralized standard of behavior for all levels of society. More specifically, I ask how excavated epigraphic and manuscript documents can aid us in understanding how the Qin conceptualized the function of written law. To answer this, I will make use of a variety of received and excavated textual sources dating from the mid- to late Warring States period and after the Qin unification (*c.*400–207 BCE). The first section briefly considers the historical representations of Qin political and legal theories as recorded in standard histories and in the philosophical works of those individuals who purportedly influenced the development of Qin imperial thought. These records depict a state of affairs quite similar to that of other Eastern Zhou kingdoms in which the Qin rulers and those advising them attempted to curb ministerial authority and preserve centralized rule. Received texts such as these provide an important window into how such curbs on authority were thought about and theorized. However, in light of the limitations of working with received philosophical materials and the heavily biased materials of the Han historiographical tradition, I go on to offer analysis of excavated manuscripts to provide contemporary evidence of specific Qin perspectives on law, control, and writing. The second section therefore analyzes excavated textual materials dated to the era of Qin's rise and its eventual consolidation (or unification) of the disparate warring kingdoms.

Qin legal innovation as seen in received and historical texts

This section briefly surveys how historical and philosophical sources are used to reconstruct specific elements of Qin theories of law, writing, and control, but it does not offer an exhaustive examination of Qin history or of the entirety of Qin political development. Several studies exist on such topics; however, here I am primarily concerned with illustrating what received and historical texts say about Qin political and legal innovations arising in response to internal disorder brought about by ministerial machinations.[1] Doing so will provide a foundation upon which we can analyze the excavated materials. As such, I will focus my analysis on views of political re-centralization and governmental control systems, particularly during the reigns of Duke Xian (獻公, r. 384–362 BCE), Duke Xiao (孝公, r. 361–338 BCE), and their descendant, King Zheng/Qin Shi Huang Di (秦政王/秦始皇帝 r. 247–210 BCE). It is during the later stages of the Warring States Period that the kingdom of Qin underwent a massive series of social and political transformations.[2] Many of the policies anticipating these reforms are ascribed directly and indirectly to particular scholar-statesmen collectively known in later times as "Legalists," or *fa jia* 法家.[3] Through the policies of Qin rulers and those who influenced them, the Qin transformed its social and political order in an attempt to unify and strengthen the kingdom and, later on, unify the central plains and remnant warring kingdoms. Here I am interested in linking to the historical situation of Qin and the Qin response to some of the ideas mentioned in the previous chapter, which associated the rise of written law with the means to control the hereditary ministerial families.

Disorder and change

As mentioned in Chapter 2, during the late Spring and Autumn Period most kingdoms experienced political devolution in which increased conflicts among hereditary ministerial lineages vying for control over the ducal families threatened the kingdoms' internal stability. As the internal situation of individual kingdoms further deteriorated, usurpations, political assassinations, and court factionalization became increasingly common. During this time, advocates of collections of written law within many kingdoms pointed to the potential stabilizing effects of clearly worded, universally promulgated, and consistently applied written law. They argued that written laws were valuable political tools capable of producing social stability by centralizing legal authority and establishing a fixed, visible legal standard. Such a standard would transform the behavior of the aristocracy and the general populace, both of which would be judged according to the criteria of the centralized standard. Law, writing, and bureaucratic centralization were inextricably linked and conceptualized as a viable method to derive all authority from the person of the ruler. Written law was perceived as capable of eliminating baneful aristocratic political machinations and circumscribing the aristocracy's direct authority over the population. A similar story can be told for the kingdom of Qin.

Although traditional Chinese historiography attempts to portray the westerly kingdom of Qin as an "alien" society or a cultural "other," in terms of its internal politics, especially during the late Spring and Autumn and the Warring States Periods, Qin was in fact culturally quite similar to the eastern kingdoms, and also suffered from many of the same domestic problems.[4] The *Shiji* 史記 provides several examples of internal power struggles headed by ministerial families similar to those that plagued kingdoms such as Jin 晉 and Zheng 鄭 in the text of the *Zuo zhuan*. Such conflict effectively crippled the Qin government for decades. In the *Shiji* chapter that provides an overview of Qin history, the "Annals of Qin," *Qin benji* 秦本紀, the Han dynasty historian, Sima Qian 司馬遷 (d. 86 BCE) records the following political events which occurred in Qin during the Warring States Period (*c.* mid fifth to fourth centuries BCE):[5]

> 躁公二年南鄭反十三年義渠來伐至渭南十四年躁公卒立其弟懷公懷公四年庶長鼂與大臣圍懷公懷公自殺懷公太子曰昭子蚤死大臣乃立太子昭子之子是為靈公[6]
>
> In the second year of Duke Zao (r. 442–429 BCE), Nanzheng revolted. In the thirteenth year, the Yiju came to attack and reached south of the Wei River. In the fourteenth year, Duke Zao died, and his younger brother Duke Huai (r. 428–425 BCE) was established. In the fourth year of Duke Huai, *shuchang* Chao and the grand ministers besieged Duke Huai. Duke Huai killed himself. Duke Huai's eldest son, called Zhaozi, died early; therefore, the grand ministers established the son of elder-son Zhaozi. This was Duke Ling (r. 424–415 BCE).
>
> 惠公十二年子出子生十三年伐蜀取南鄭惠公卒出子立出子二年庶長改迎靈公之子獻公于河西而立之殺出子及其母沈之淵旁秦以往者數易君君臣乖亂故晉復彊奪秦河西地[7]
>
> In the twelfth year of Duke Hui (r. 399–387 BCE), [his] son Chuzi (r. 386–385 BCE) was born. In the thirteenth year, [he] attacked Shu and reclaimed Nanzheng. Duke Hui died, and Chuzi was established. In the second year of Chuzi, *shuchang* Gai escorted the son of Duke Ling, Duke Xian (r. 384–362 BCE), from west of the [Yellow] River and established him. [He] killed Chuzi and his mother, drowning them in the nearby depths. In this earlier period, Qin changed the ruler numerous times. Rulers and ministers were in conflict and disorderly. Thus, Jin recovered its strength and seized the lands west of the [Yellow] River.

As these citations show, Qin was plagued by the same internal machinations of the hereditary ministerial families suffered by other eastern kingdoms. In the references above, we are told that on two occasions the grand ministers conspired to depose a reigning ducal lord and establish an alternative candidate. In the case of Duke Huai, the Qin ruler was militarily besieged and eventually committed suicide. Worse still, the ministers and military personnel who overthrew Chuzi went so far as to murder him and his mother, before establishing Duke Xian. These accounts show the divisive nature of the Qin ministerial elite, their ability to employ the military forces of Qin against the kingdom's ruler, and their lack of ritual respect to the ancestral authority of the Qin rulers: the latter being evidenced by their willingness to murder Chuzi and his mother. Such events weakened the central authority of the Qin ruler within his own kingdom, and, by extension, weakened the authority of the Qin vis-à-vis other kingdoms.

Yet, after this period of weakness and disorder, Qin enjoyed a successful 24-year reign under Duke Xian. Under his guidance, Qin reclaimed much of the territorial possessions formerly lost to the kingdom of Jin, and executed successful military campaigns against the kingdoms of Jin and Wei. Upon Duke Xian's death, he was succeeded by Duke Xiao. Wanting to continue the work of his predecessor, Duke Xiao was eager to find new ways of increasing Qin's strength, both internally and externally. Yet, relations with the aristocracy and the historical reminder of the past internal revolts against Qin royal authority concerned Duke Xiao.

According to the *Shiji*, Duke Xiao circulated an order calling upon bright minds with a talent for strengthening a kingdom to come to his court. We see in the order issued by Duke Xian that the political turmoil wrought by the revolts against Duke Hui and Chuzi appears to have had a direct influence on this decision to seek out foreign reformers. After discussing the "glory days" of Qin rule, Duke Xiao somberly states:

> 會往者厲躁簡公出子之不寧國家內憂未遑外事三晉攻奪我先君河西地諸侯卑秦醜莫大焉
>
> Then came the time of Li, Zao, Jian, and the turbulence of Chuzi. The kingdom was internally uneasy, and there was no leisure to pursue external affairs. The three Jin assaulted and seized our former lords' lands west of the [Yellow] River. The other lords belittle Qin, and there is no shame greater than this![8]

Duke Xiao goes on to request any person capable of improving the kingdom to come forward and advise him. This circular was sent beyond the borders of Qin and attracted the attention of a particular individual from the kingdom of Wei 衛 named, Gongsun Yang (公孫鞅, d. 338 BCE). It is during the rule of Duke Xiao, under the guidance of Gongsun Yang (hereafter Shang Yang 商鞅), that Qin government and society underwent several large-scale internal reforms.

For Shang Yang, law was the primary tool for engineering social transformation, and the transformation he envisioned was one of political unification and socio-cultural homogeneity. Shang Yang argued that the problems afflicting Qin (as well as other kingdoms) arose from the gap between current laws and social reality, heterogeneous cultural practices within an individual kingdom, corrupted administrative practices of the hereditary ministerial families, a related lack of local administrative accountability to central authority, and the ubiquity of inconsistent and unclear legal norms.

One of the first key legal issues mentioned by Shang Yang is the need for a kingdom's laws and institutions to resonate with society. Though the Qin government certainly had laws, these laws were deemed unreflective of the socio-political changes that had occurred over the years, and as such were considered incapable of functioning to maintain order or in managing and directing further social changes. The ability of ministerial families to usurp such power in the past was clear evidence of the need for maintaining effective laws to control all levels of society.

The debate recorded in the "Changing Laws," *Bian fa* 更法 chapter of the *Book of Lord Shang*, or *Shangjun shu* 商君書, is perhaps the best known articulation of Shang Yang's theory of socio-legal change. The chapter begins with Duke Xiao of Qin mulling over issues of social change and the problems of statecraft. After asking whether he should change the laws and institutions of Qin, Shang Yang replies:

> 法者所以愛民也禮者所以便事也是以聖人苟可以彊國不法其故苟可以利民不循於禮
>
> Laws are the means through which the populace is cared for; rites are the means through which affairs are efficiently managed. Thus, in the case of the sagacious person, if it strengthens the kingdom, he does not emulate antiquity; if it is capable of benefiting the populace, he does not adhere to the rites.[9]

Shang Yang confirms the importance of law and rites to the kingdom and the people, but does not concede the point that these two things are stagnant, unchanging concepts. For Shang Yang, the wisest of the wise, the sagacious person, understands the value of these two concepts for the kingdom, but also knows that to strengthen a kingdom in the present age one cannot rely upon past practices and institutions as an authoritative model for direct emulation. Shang Yang argues that social changes distinguish the past from the present, and this, in turn, necessitates a certain level of institutional fluidity in the laws and rites responsible for managing a society. Shang Yang goes on to state:

> 夫常人安於故習學者溺於所聞此兩者所以居官而守法非所與論於法之外三代不同禮而王五霸不同法而霸故知者作法而愚者制焉賢者更禮而不肖者拘焉拘禮之人不足與言事制法之人不足與論變君無疑矣
>
> So it is that commoners find solace in ancient custom, and scholars drown[10] in that which they have heard. These two are capable of filling posts and

> abiding by law; yet one cannot discuss with them that which is outside the law. The three dynasties had different rites,[11] yet still reigned as king. The five hegemons had different laws, yet still reigned as hegemons. Therefore, the knowledgeable create laws, while the ignorant are controlled by them. The worthy alter the rites; while the unworthy are ensnared by them. A person ensnared by the rites is inadequate to speak of matters with, and a person controlled by law is inadequate to discuss change with. Milord should harbor no doubts about this.[12]

Here Shang Yang clearly articulates his key principle: political and legal change must respond to social change. Rebutting the "traditionalist" scholars who claim the superiority of past precedents, Shang Yang states that it is common for simple people to become at ease with that which they find familiar and that most scholars are overly concerned with deciphering and analyzing the floods of past information to which they have access. Such people are easily overwhelmed by change, and, thus, not worthy of discussing or planning political changes. Shang Yang argues that such conformist individuals make wonderful officials, who can abide by laws and follow duties; yet, they remain incapable of envisioning change. Further, he makes the rather obvious and practical point that the rulers of previous dynasties (the Xia 夏, Shang 商, and Zhou) each maintained different rituals and the different hegemons all utilized different laws, yet this did not impede their ability to rise to power and establish long-lasting dynasties.

When read against the background of the internal problems associated with the removal of Duke Hui and Chuzi, one can view Shang Yang's argument as a veiled critique of the contemporary efficacy of former modes of quasi-feudal political control, especially control of hereditary ministerial lineages. To strengthen the kingdom, the ruler must not look solely at new methods for controlling the populace, but also keep in mind the potential dangers of a powerful hereditary aristocracy. For Shang Yang, law served as the primary centralizing institution capable of altering (or at least manipulating) the behavior of both the aristocracy and the populace.

Both the historical records in the *Shiji* and the received text excerpts from the *Shangjun shu* demonstrate that the later rulers of Qin were aware that previous socio-political institutions no longer functioned as viable means for maintaining order.[13] Much like the *Zuo zhuan* records of rulers and ministers advocating the implementation of written law, the rulers of Qin sought out alternative means of control. The changes instituted by Duke Xiao as well as by his predecessor Duke Xian, were designed to strengthen the authority of the ruler by re-centralizing control over all aspects of government and social life, at least in theory. The reforms targeted areas such as language, household divisions, hereditary titles and emoluments, and, of course, the law.[14] Underscoring this reform effort was the pivotal concept of "unity."[15] For Qin rulers, as well as those scholars typically labeled Legalists, the re-centralization of royal authority solely within the position of the ruler depended heavily upon the effective production of universal standards.[16] These standards could only maintain social and political stability if they were created under the authority of the ruler, universally promulgated throughout the kingdom and later empire, and consistently applied according to the intentions of the legislator. Any deviation in interpretation or application would be considered a usurpation of royal authority and could in turn threaten the stability of the government.

This idea linking centralization and uniformity is a common theme in much Legalist literature.[17] Most notably passages from the "Agriculture and Warfare," *Nong zhan* 農戰 and "Rewards and Punishment," *Shang xing* 賞刑 chapters of the *Shangjun shu* state:

> 凡治國者患民之散而不可摶也是以聖人作壹摶之也國作一歲者十歲彊作一十歲者百歲彊修一百歲者千歲彊千歲彊者王君修賞罰以輔壹教是以其教有所常而政有成也
>
> In general, one who rules the kingdom is apprehensive when the populace is scattered and cannot be consolidated. Therefore, the sagacious person creates uniformity to consolidate them. A kingdom with uniformity for one year shall be strong for ten years; one with uniformity for ten years shall be strong for 100 years; one with uniformity for 100 years shall be strong for 1000 years; one with uniformity for 1000 years shall be king/supreme. The ruler improves rewards and punishments to augment the unification of education. Because of this, education has constancy and the government is efficacious.[18]
>
> 聖人之為國也壹賞壹刑壹教壹賞則兵無敵壹刑則令行壹教則下聽上夫明賞不費明刑不戮明教不變而民知於民務國無異俗
>
> As for the sagacious one's governing of the kingdom, he unifies rewards, unifying punishments, and unifying education. By unifying rewards, the soldiers will have no enemy; by unifying punishments, orders will be executed; by unifying education, those below will heed those above. It is when rewards are clear there is no waste, when punishments are clear there are no executions, when education is clear there is no change. Thus, the people comprehend the people's duties and the kingdom is without divergent customs.[19]

Each example illustrates the centrality of unification to the preservation of stability and order within a kingdom. By consolidating control over the entire populace and providing clear and consistent norms of unity—laws, rewards, or education—Shang Yang believes a ruler will not only bring about an orderly society, but will be able to maintain direct control over that society. As mentioned above, there are numerous social, political, and economic areas in which the Qin instituted reforms. For the remainder of this section, I will focus on two issues viewed by Qin rulers and reform-minded Legalists as crucial targets for reform. The presence of hereditary ministerial families in the government and the dispersal of hereditary land entitlements were two key areas of non-uniformity and decentralization targeted by Qin rulers. To solve the problems associated with these two areas, the rulers restructured the Qin government creating an impersonal bureaucracy of salaried officials, and reconfigured the very landscape of Qin territories.

The removal of hereditary ministerial families from the government was an important feature of Qin institutional reforms. Historical sources state that throughout the later Warring States Period, the Qin rulers phased out hereditary titles and instituted a new ranking system based upon merit.[20] This ranking system was not necessarily hereditary, but it did bind one to the government. These ranks did not come with land entitlements, but instead were salaried at a specific rate set by the central government.

Additionally, these ranks did not guarantee one access to government posts.[21] To eradicate the negative influence of hereditary officials in the government, the Qin gradually developed an impersonal bureaucracy of salaried officials. As Herrlee Creel noted, the difference between *feudalism* and *bureaucracy*

> depends chiefly upon the locus of initiative and decision. A feudal vassal, in governing his domain, *may do* anything that he is not expressly forbidden to do. A bureaucratic official *may not properly do* anything that is not part of his prescribed function.[22]

The idea of "propriety" that Creel describes here stems ultimately from the unity of a singular source of all law, which has the power to determine standard behavior across the entire institution, as opposed to having multiple sources of authority giving rise to alternative forms of governance and resistance to centralized power. By instituting this bureaucratic system, the Qin effectively quashed the localized autonomy that ministerial families had used in the past to challenge the ruler's authority.

Yet simply replacing the aristocracy with a bureaucracy does not automatically solve all problems. A ruler cannot be everywhere at once and must delegate power to subordinates. Wary of this, the Qin rulers wanted to maintain strict control over the official behavior. This was a common problem for many kingdoms, and several scholar-statesmen attempted to provide an answer through what is commonly referred to as the practice or concept of "form and name," or *xingming* 形名.[23]

This idea, espoused by individuals such as Shen Buhai (申不害, d. 337 BCE) and Han Feizi (韓非子, d. 233 BCE), meant that government posts were created and defined by the central government (i.e., the ruler) and anyone filling such a post was required to not only fully execute his assigned tasks, but also not to *exceed* the jurisdiction of the post.[24] For example, in the "Two Handles," *Er bing* 二柄 chapter of the *Han Feizi*, Han Feizi advises:

> 人主將欲禁姦則審合形名形名者言與事也爲人臣者陳而言君以其言授之事專以其事責其功功當其事事當其言則賞功不當其事事不當其言則

罰故群臣其言大而功小者則罰非罰小功也罰功不當名也群臣其言小而功大者亦罰非不說於大功也以爲不當名也害甚於有大功故罰

When a ruler of people seeks to prohibit vileness, [he] therefore cautiously connects form and name. Form and name is when words correspond to deeds. Those serving as ministers array themselves and speak. The lord bestows tasks to them based upon their words. He exclusively uses their deeds to assess their accomplishments. If their accomplishments match their deeds and their deeds match their words then he rewards them. If their accomplishments do not match their deeds and their deeds do not match their words, then he censures them. Therefore, among the gathered ministers, if one speaks of big [deeds], yet his accomplishments are small, then he is censured. It is not the censure of a small accomplishment, but the censure of an accomplishment that does not match the name. Among the gathered ministers if one speaks of small [deeds], yet his accomplishments are great, then he is also censured. It is not displeasure towards a great accomplishment, but is due to not matching the name. The potential harm is greater than the great accomplishment, and thus he is censured.[25]

For Han Feizi, ministers should not be held accountable for their actions simply based upon the *level* of their successes. Instead, a ruler should carefully measure the outcome of a deed to what a minister specifically stated he would do. In doing so, the "name" or here named deed must match precisely with the minister's claim. Failure to live up to one's stated goal would bring about censure. More importantly, a minister would also be punished if he overstepped the jurisdiction of his position. The harm done by going above and beyond what is expected or promised is deemed more detrimental to the kingdom than any potential benefit. This provides a means for ensuring that government officials carefully executed their roles in government, but it also carefully regulates the use of royal authority that was out of necessity delegated to subordinates. Thus, according to Han Feizi, a ruler obtains a method to check the ambitions of officials.

The *Shiji* also claims that Shang Yang was influenced by the doctrine of *xingming*.[26] It is possible that such ideas influenced the Qin decision to ensure uniformity, consistency, and accountability through a heavily regulated bureaucracy. Robin Yates has produced a detailed study of the various methods the Qin government employed to control its officials. These ranged from controlling access to official positions and regulating the length of tenure in a position, to the creation of specific legal statutes dictating proper and improper performance in an official post and instituting an annual review system of bureaucratic performance.[27] Each measure taken by the Qin government was designed to ensure maximum compliance by officials with the centralized dictates of the ruler. Authority within the government was to have *one* source and all other officials were to act accordingly.

Along with the social ranking system and the establishment of an impersonal and salaried bureaucracy, Qin rulers further instituted centralized control over the kingdom by reconfiguring Qin geopolitical space. As in other kingdoms, previously the ministerial elite of Qin were able to amass localized political and military support from those regions under their direct control. This quasi-feudal arrangement allowed for the development of competing loyalties among the populace and at times allowed ministerial families to directly challenge the authority of the kingdom's ruler. In the interest of "unification," the Qin rulers reconfigured the political geography of the kingdom by employing the *jun/xian* system, or *jun xian zhidu* 郡縣制度, to bring all the lands of the kingdom under one authority. Within this system, the lands of a kingdom are divided into several large commanderies, or *jun* 郡 (similar to modern day provinces). These commanderies were administered by a governor, or *shou* 守, and his subordinates. These bureaucratic officials were salaried by the central government and were directly responsible to their superiors in the central government. They did not have loyalty towards a regional elite family, nor were they dependent upon such a family for their income. The commanderies were further subdivided into several counties, or *xian* 縣. Like officials working in the commandery offices, the officials tasked with running the county were salaried by the government and were directly responsible to their bureaucratic superiors at the commandery level.[28] Within such a system all authority was held within the central government—i.e., the ruler—and localized autonomy of ministerial elite families was circumscribed. Thus, the ability of the former ministerial elite families to amass localized power bases and potentially threaten the stability of the central government was removed.

The earliest association of a *xian* to Qin, comes from historical evidence stating that in 688 BCE the kingdom *xian*-ed (*xian zhi* 縣之) lands acquired through conquest.[29] Herrlee Creel is skeptical as to whether this initial reference indicates the beginning of the Qin practice of centralizing control over land.[30] Yet, regardless of the origins of the *jun/xian* system in the Qin, it is clear that throughout the Spring and Autumn and Warring States Periods, the Qin rulers had gradually asserted centralized control over the entire kingdom. Several quotes from the *Shiji* provide evidence for this. The "Biography of Li Si," *Lisi lie zhuan* 李斯列傳 chapter records:

> 二十餘年竟并天下尊主為皇帝以斯為丞相夷郡縣城銷其兵刃示不復用使秦無尺土之封不立子弟為王功臣為諸侯者使後無戰攻之患
>
> More than 20 years later, *all-under-Heaven* was united and the ruler was honored by becoming the August Thearch. He appointed Li Si to serve as chancellor. He flattened provincial and county walls and melted their weapons and swords so as to demonstrate these would not be again used. He caused the Qin not to bestow one *cun* of land as enfeoffments. He did not establish sons and younger brothers as kings, nor were meritorious ministers set up as feudal lords, causing not to have the worries of warfare.[31]

Additionally, the *Shiji* records Li Si commenting to the newly proclaimed emperor Qin Shi Huang Di:

今陛下興義兵誅殘賊平定天下海內為郡縣法令由一統

> Now Your Highness has mustered a righteous army and punished the barbarous and evil, pacified and settled *all-under-Heaven*. Within the boundaries of the seas, provinces and counties are established and the laws and ordinances are united from one source.[32]

Both of these quotes demonstrate the implementation of the *jun/xian* system to unify the lands of Qin, as well as the rationale for doing so. The first passage specifically links the refusal of Qin Shi Huang Di to install his sons as kings and meritorious ministers with the ability to directly control land and preclude a return of conflict. Likewise, the last passage depicts the finale of unification with a statement that *all* lands are now subsumed into the *jun/xian* system and that all laws and ordinances have a single source. The unification of land was linked to the centralization of legal authority.

The expectation of centralized control over a vast impersonal bureaucracy which was replicated on the *jun/xian* levels and held directly accountable to the central government required an intricate system of communication. Furthermore, if *unity* and *consistency* were key elements of the Qin's view of centralization, then this system of communication needed also to be capable of transmitting information accurately across vast geographic zones. And once it was received the intended audience needed to be able to comprehend the information transmitted. Thus, if the government wanted to exercise direct control over the use of powers delegated to subordinates through a rigid accountability system similar to the *xingming* system, then it needed to establish a mechanism that could accurately transmit central directives outside the parameters of the capital. Charles Sanft has demonstrated the scale of the Qin communication system, as well as the effectiveness of the Qin at utilizing various written forms as means of control.[33] Excavated evidence of these written forms comprises the subject matter of the next section. These materials demonstrate the physical form of written materials used to control official action at the local level.

Inscribing imperial legal thought: the Stele inscriptions of Qin Shi Huang Di

Before moving on to examine excavated materials reflecting the Qin goals of unifying governance and law through written forms, I will briefly mention one additional historical source of Qin legal thought. According to the *Shiji*, after Qin Shi Huang Di unified "all-under-Heaven," he embarked on a series of grand processions wherein he visited several important mountains. Here he performed various sacrifices and ordered inscriptions to be carved onto stone steles which were erected at the mountain sites. Unfortunately, the original inscriptions have not survived to the present and much of our knowledge comes from their texts as reproduced by the Han dynasty historiographer Sima Qian.[34] Though these would constitute "inscriptions," because of the lack of physical evidence,

I include their analysis in this section on "received" sources of Qin legal thought. Regardless, the purported texts of these inscriptions are important because they illustrate the ideological trend of unification, and the path to unification through universally promulgated and clearly worded laws, as well as centrally established orders of rank and position to which the aristocracy and populace were both subject.[35] Each inscription is quite lengthy and often repetitive, so I have excerpted sections from two inscriptions pertaining to law. I begin with the stele inscription placed at Mt. Tai 泰山.[36]

The August Thearch assumed His position	皇帝臨位
Created the regulations and illuminated the laws;	作制明法
…	…
The way of good rule is advanced and enacted;	治道運行
The various professions achieve their proper place,	諸產得宜
And all find rule and model.	皆有法式
…	…
His precepts and principles reach all around,	訓經宣達
The distant and near are completely well-ordered	遠近畢理
And all receive His sage will.	咸承聖志
The noble and the mean are separated and distinguished,	貴賤分明
Men and women embody compliance,	男女禮順
Cautious and respectful to their professions and duties.	慎遵職事
…	…
His transforming influence reaches without limit:	化及無窮
May [later ages] respect and follow the decrees He bequeaths	遵奉遺詔

The stele inscription from Mt. Tai offers additional information concerning the imperial rhetoric of unification espoused by the Qin government. In particular, portions of the inscription detail specific idealized notions of how the Qin emperor was able to achieve total unification and what measures were deemed essential for sustaining the unity. The inscription states that having just created the title of Huang Di, the ruler established the institutions and clarified the laws. Thus, we see again that properly attuned institutions and laws are considered to be a prerequisite for obtaining unity and order. Through these institutions and laws the methods for proper governance are promulgated, the production becomes uniform, and all people possess a standard model. Again, this is obtained via clear laws and rules being sent throughout the empire and the ability of the people to understand the laws and to comply with their dictates. The actual unification of the governmental institutions and of the laws, as well as the ability of these to sustain social and political order is entirely dependent upon their effective transfer and administration. It is only after the laws are clarified, transmitted, and received that far and near are completely well-ordered. For the Qin, effective laws required calculated construction of laws, a system of accurate promulgation, and a core group of administrators capable of consistently interpreting and applying the laws in all regions of the Qin domain.

These ideas are mirrored in a similar inscription carved at Qin Shi Huang Di's request into the cliff face of Mt. Langye 琅邪.[37]

The August Thearch created a beginning:	皇帝作始
He rectified and balanced the rules and measures	端平法度
As the guidelines for the ten thousand beings.	萬物之紀
…	…
Everywhere under vast Heaven	普天之下
He unifies the minds and integrates the wills.	摶心揖志
Vessels and implements have their identical measures,	器械一量
One uniformly writes the refined characters.	同書文字
…	…
To execute the task by responding to the times—	應時動事
This was realized only by the August Thearch!	是維皇帝
He straightens and rectifies aberrant customs,	匡飭異俗
[His influence] traversing the rivers, penetrates the lands.	陵水經地
…	…
He eliminates uncertainties, fixes the laws,	除疑定法
And all know what to avoid.	咸知所辟
…	…
The various rulings are measured and smooth.	諸治經易
Whatever one undertakes or rejects is invariably proper,	舉錯必當
There is nothing that does not conform to the scheme.	莫不如畫
…	…
The honored and the humble, the noble and the mean	尊卑貴賤
They never exceed their position and rank.	不踰次行
…	…
He regulates the tasks according to the times,	節事以時
The various professions prosper and thrive.	諸產繁殖
…	…
Joyously and merrily they received their instructions	驩欣奉教
And completely understand the rules and models.	盡知法式

Once again we see the clear progression of Qin imperial thought moving from a depiction of the emperor as *the sole source* of the methods for bringing about order to the actual characteristics of the ideal society created by those methods. The ability to unify the disparate kingdoms was made possible by the rectification of laws and their promulgation to serve as a guideline for the myriad things. This rectification of the laws included the unification of script forms and measurement devices, as well as the elimination of aberrant social customs. By fixing the laws and removing any uncertainty or ambiguity, the governing of the empire could be smoothly executed and all people would know what to avoid. Furthermore, the inscription seems to reference the anxiety over aristocratic or ministerial machinations when it states that through the promulgation and application of centralized and clearly worded laws, all people—commoner and aristocrat alike—would know their station and would not dare overstep the limits of such positions. Again, we see that law clearly was conceptualized as an effective means of controlling the populace and hereditary aristocracy alike.

Taken together, the mountain stele inscriptions of Qin Shi Huang Di (including those not covered here) support the vision of Qin imperial ideology predicated on the consistent application of centrally promulgated laws. The writings of Shang Yang and other so-called "Legalists" also prefigure the development of such a theory of socio-legal change. That said, one must understand the limitations of using received materials for the study of the distant past. They provide an important picture of how some contemporaries conceptualized the relationship between law and writing, specifically how writing could contribute to the unification and standardization of laws. The next section of this chapter examines excavated legal materials to improve our understanding of the actual historical role of writing in Qin administrative and legal thought.

Excavating Qin legal thought: a survey of archeological sources

For nearly two millennia, knowledge of Qin history was limited by a dearth of available contemporary source materials. The vast majority of post-Han scholars attempting to reconstruct Qin political, legal, or social developments found themselves necessarily restricted to analyzing the historical information recorded in Sima Qian's *Shiji* and the received editions of philosophical texts ascribed to individuals who purportedly influenced the development of Qin political thought. There are, of course, limitations to such sources. Several scholars have discussed the obvious anti-Qin bias within the *Shiji* and the problematics associated with relying upon Han historiography to reconstruct a "fair" account of the rise and fall of the Qin dynasty.[38] Similarly, the received philosophical texts ascribed to the so-called Legalists were transmitted throughout the centuries and their present form is likely the product of years of accretion and excision. The interpretation and contextualization of such texts are often conditioned by the strong commentarial (and historiographical) traditions attached to them.

The previous section examined how these philosophical and post-Qin historical sources can be used to cautiously reconstruct specific aspects of Qin legal thought. In this section, I turn my attention to contemporary Qin source materials that have been available to scholars only since the 1970s. An analysis of archeologically excavated manuscripts provides support for several characterizations of the Qin found in the received materials, while providing greater insight into specific aspects of Qin legal culture. Below I will survey a collection of epigraphic and manuscript documentation that reflects features of Qin legal theory which link together law, writing, and social/political control.

Centralized military control through writing: the tiger tallies of Qin

One issue repeatedly mentioned in historical and philosophical sources was the anxiety held by Qin rulers, and those reform-minded ministers advising them, over the devolution of the king's authority to subordinates. As shown in the previous and present chapters, several kingdoms suffered from the internal machinations of the hereditary ministerial elite. Their royal families collected large fortunes, mustered private armies, and went so far as to murder their rulers. Many of these kingdoms turned to forms of written documentation, or publicly displayed written laws in an effort to curb the growing power of ministerial families. The kingdom of Qin was no exception. Through various reforms, the Qin rulers worked to curtail aristocratic authority and establish a salary-based bureaucratic administration system. Furthermore, the Qin developed a highly effective military force, and, as such, the rulers were anxious to control the locus of military authority and power. One method for accomplishing this was to maintain absolute central control over the ability to muster and command troops. As the following example shows, writing played an important role in authorizing the use of troops.

> 甲兵之符右才(在)君左才(在)杜凡興士被甲用兵五十人以上必會君符乃敢行之燔隊事雖母(毋)會符行殹
>
> Armed forces tally. The right (portion) resides with the ruler. The left (portion) resides in Du.[39] In all cases of mustering soldiers, armored and armed, of fifty or more persons, one must unite with the ruler's tally, and only then dare to deploy them. In the event that the warning beacons [are ignited], even though one has not united the tally, deploy them.[40]

This text was inscribed on a metal object shaped like a standing tiger that measures 9.5 cm in length, 4.4 cm in height, and 0.7 cm in width. The text runs in nine lines from the head of the tiger to the back haunch. The text reads top to bottom and left to right. The text is inscribed on both sides of the artifact. The tiger can be separated into two halves and each half bears the identical text.

The tiger tally was discovered in the winter of 1975 in a small village outside of Xi'an 西安 by a peasant named Yang Dongfeng 楊東鋒. Yang apparently gave the artifact to his younger sister as a toy, and only turned it over to the authorities in 1978.[41] Because of this, there was some initial skepticism regarding the artifact's provenance and authenticity. That said, due to the numerous Qin and Han burials discovered in the vicinity of the purported discovery site and a careful comparative analysis with other tiger tallies (see below), many scholars now view the Du Tiger Tally as a genuine artifact. In addition to this tally, the *Qin Han jin wen huibian* 秦漢金文彙編 contains two more examples of inscribed tiger tallies.[42]

> 甲兵之符右才(在)王左才(在)新郪凡興士被甲用兵五十人以上必會王符乃敢行之燔隊事雖母(毋)會符行殹

> Armed forces tally. The right (portion) resides with the King. The left (portion) resides in Xin Qi. In all cases of mustering soldiers, armored and armed, of 50 or more persons, one must unite the King's tally, and only then dare to deploy them. In the event that the warning beacons [are ignited], even though one has not joined the tally, deploy them.[43]

The Xin Qi tally measures 8.8 cm in length and 3.2 cm in height. In this inscription, the ruler is referred to as "king," *wang* 王 and not "lord," *jun* 君. Because of this, scholars argue that this particular tally should be dated to between the thirteenth year of Lord Huiwen of Qin 秦惠文君 (324 BCE) when the title of *wang* was first used by Qin rulers, and the year 221 BCE when King Zheng established the title of Huang Di 皇帝, "emperor." Furthermore, the jurisdiction of this tally covers the area Xin Qi and not Du. That is, the geographic area in which the use of this tally is considered to be legitimate for the purpose of mustering armed forces is explicitly limited by the text to the area of Xin Qi. With these two exceptions, the text of the tally is almost identical with that of the Du Tiger Tally. The purpose of the next tally is similar to those of the previous two; however, its inscribed text differs in its length and terminology.

> 甲兵之符右才(在)皇帝左才(在)陽陵

> Armed forces tally. The right (portion) resides with the Emperor. The left (portion) resides in Yangling.[44]

Like the previous two inscriptions, the text of the Yangling Tiger Tally also authorizes the recipient of both halves to muster the local armed forces. It is different, however, in the title used to refer to the ruler, the jurisdictional location, and length of the text.

Although quite short, the contents of all three inscriptions provide a great deal of information from which we can infer a Qin consciousness of the efficacy of written forms to control individual behavior, as well as delineate the levels of power granted from the center to the periphery. Lothar von Falkenhausen has studied the use of tallies in the kingdom of Chu, specifically the *E jun qi* 鄂君啓 tallies.[45] These tallies, which are dated to the year 323 BCE, exempt merchants from specific tolls and taxes while conveying goods by boat or wagon through the kingdom of Chu 楚. In his study, von Falkenhausen also devotes several pages to the use of the tally—including the Qin *hufu*—within military contexts in pre-imperial China. Drawing on evidence gleaned from received textual sources such as the *Lü shi chunqiu* 吕氏春秋 and *Zhanguo ce* 戰國策, von Falkenhausen argues that central commanders or the rulers of a kingdom would retain one half of a matching set of tallies with the corresponding half residing in the specified locality of administration.[46] When the need for military action arose, the centrally held tally would be dispatched to the peripheral locality, thereby obliging the local administration to act as instructed by the tally's text. Von Falkenhausen thus reads the inscriptions found on the extant versions of military tallies and the very act of combining the two pieces of the tally as producing a military obligation owed by the peripheral locality to the central authority.[47] This use of writing and the transference of the written material from one locale to another effected the obligation of the periphery to the central authority.

I do not argue with the obligation-producing power dynamics attached to the central authority's dispatch of their half of a military tally to a peripheral locale. However, there were other important functions of the tally that should not be overlooked. The joining of two halves of the tally certainly made manifest an obligation for the peripheral administration officers to act, but it also visibly demonstrated a legitimate use of the kingdom's military forces. As mentioned above, the Qin rulers, as well as Shang Yang and Li Si, were concerned about the potential usurpation of royal authority by either the hereditary aristocracy or, after the bureaucratizing reforms, by overly ambitious government officials. Maintaining centralized control over the military was deemed to be of great importance. The requirement of joining the two halves can also be read as a control measure designed to ensure that any sizeable military force mustered within the kingdom or empire was only done under the direct command of the ruler. These tiger tallies thus demonstrate a link between the use of writing and administrative control.

The Qin central government appeared to use tiger tallies for restricting military conscription in several of its lower-level administrative districts. The counties of Du 杜 and Yangling 陽陵 were located in present day Shaanxi Province 陜西, while Xin Qi was located in present day Anhui Province 安徽. Thus the tiger form, its mirrored inscriptions, and the local administrative obligation/restriction inferred from its presence was possibly an institutionalized and uniform practice within Qin central-local administration.

Finally, the third tiger tally translated above refers to the ruler as *huang di* 皇帝 instead of *wang* 王 or *jun* 君. From this we can infer that after the consolidation of power and unification of the warring states was completed in 221 BCE, the Qin rulers continued to utilize the tally system as a method of maintaining centralized control over military forces throughout the empire. The ultimate authority to muster and command Qin imperial soldiers resided solely with the emperor, and that authority could only be transferred to government officials *via* individualized, locale-specific texts unique to each district and inscribed upon a unique platform.

The inscriptions on these tiger tallies offer additional evidence that the Qin central government made specific use of written forms and specialized media to control peripheral administration. They did so utilizing formulaic language which was consistently employed in different geographic locales. Other forms of written materials contemporary to the transition from the Qin kingdom to the Qin empire also demonstrate the continued influence of writing within Qin legal discourse.

Inscribing unity and accountability: the Twenty-sixth Year Edict inscriptions and artisan markings

The tiger tallies demonstrate a uniform method for maintaining centralized control over military forces that relied heavily on written documentation. Other forms of excavated materials also provide support for historical claims about the Qin government's policies of unification and the role of writing and law within that policy.

As shown above, when Qin Shi Huang Di consolidated his rule over the warring kingdoms, he embarked on a series of grand tours throughout his new empire. At sacred mountain sites, the emperor ordered that panegyric statements extolling the greatness and necessity of his drive to unify China be inscribed on stone steles. Several scholars have remarked that such an act demonstrates his use of the *monumental* to sanctify and legitimate his rule within the celestial realm (sacred mountains), the geopolitical realm (geographically distant mountains), and the human realm (using large visible written language).[48] Even if a person was unable to read the inscription, there would be a popular consciousness of what the inscription and location represented vis-à-vis the emperor and imperial rule. Likewise, we have a similar use of written language providing a visible representation of key tenets of Qin unification ideology. The so-called "Twenty-sixth Year Edict," *Er shi liu nian zhao* 廿六年詔 is an inscription found on a variety of platforms. The edict records:

> 廿六年皇帝盡併天下諸侯黔首大安立號為皇帝乃詔丞相狀綰灋度量則不壹歉疑者皆明壹之
>
> In the twenty-sixth year (221 BCE), the August Thearch completed the annexation of *all-under-Heaven*. The various lords and commoners were greatly pacified. [He] inaugurated the title of August Thearch. Thereupon, [he] instructed the grand councilors Zhuang and Wan: "Those laws and measurements that are not standard or are ambiguous should all be distinguished and standardized."[49]

The contents of this edict are indeed reminiscent of the inscriptions purportedly carved onto stele and placed at sacred mountains at Qin Shi Huang Di's request. The Twenty-sixth Year Edict confirms the date of 221 BCE as the date during which Qin Shi Huang Di formally completed the unification of the warring kingdoms. This act of unification, we are informed, brought peace to the various lords and commoners. More important, however, the edict claims that upon unification Qin Shi Huang Di ordered two of his grand councilors to conduct a comprehensive review of the laws and measurements of the land and to ensure they were all standardized and unambiguous.

In an act of not only geographic unification, but also of political, social, and economic unification, the emperor ordered that any and all laws or measurements that were neither standard nor clear should immediately be standardized and clarified. Supporting the statements in the *Shiji*, as well as the works attributed to Shang Yang and Li Si which describe the Qin efforts to unify all aspects of life in conquered lands, this edict provides further archeological evidence of a Qin legal theory predicated upon standardized, unambiguous law to maintain the hard won unification and that achieved this maintenance through written forms.

The placement of these inscriptions is also revealing of the efforts taken by the Qin central government to promote the legitimacy of unification through the use of public writing. The majority of these inscriptions are found on measurement implements used during the Qin to calculate weight and volumes, that is, the actual tools of measurement that the edict explicitly requires to be standardized and unambiguous. Thus, we see public writing employed by the Qin to serve several potentially *legal* functions.

This desire to centralize and standardize the units of measurement in the Qin was extremely important. Other excavated documents, such as the legal statutes recovered from the archeological site of Shuihudi (discussed below), contain numerous statutory provisions requiring that measurement devices be checked each year, as well as prescribe punishments for officials if the measurement devices they are responsible for are found to be "improper" or "inaccurate," *bu zheng* 不正.[50]

This edict, therefore, visibly represents the power, as well as the rationale, of the imperium to promulgate and regulate standardized models. Furthermore, when considered in conjunction with the Shuihudi *Xiao lü* 效律 or *Statute on Checking* provisions providing sanctions for officials if found in possession of non-standard weights and measures, the text of the edict and its location could serve as a constant visible reminder of the legal obligations of government officials to ensure that their measurement devices are consistent with the promulgated Qin standard. To that end, several measurement devices containing this inscription are also inscribed with the device's specified measurement capacity.[51] For example, on one excavated cast weight, the Twenty-sixth Year Edict is preceded by the graphs *ba jin* 八斤 or eight *jin*; on another weight the edict is preceded by the graphs *shiliu jin* 十六斤 or 16 *jin*.[52]

To non-officials who came into contact with the inscription for tax or rationing purposes, the presence of the visible text of the edict linked to the inscribed standard measurement of the device, regardless of whether or not one could fully read or comprehend the contents, could possibly convey a sense of "standardization" and that the device being used was accurate to the universal standard of the Qin.[53] Furthermore, as Sanft has argued, the use of inscriptions on government regulated items evidences the Qin conscious use of a form of mass communication to convey an image of unity.[54]

Writing, law, and unity: remonstrance in Governor Teng's letter

The above materials serve as implicit examples of the Qin use of writing as a form of control. Such materials further our understanding of the Qin belief that a written text could be used to condition the behavior of its intended audience. However, they are not the only excavated materials currently available to scholars studying the Qin dynasty, as archeological discoveries of Qin period documents over the past several decades have greatly increased our sources for understanding the ideology driving Qin territorial expansionism and cultural unification. These sources are explicitly related to the use of written law by the Qin to maintain centralized control over the actions of the increasingly expansive bureaucracy and the general populace. After examining these sources, the next two chapters will examine in detail how the Qin formulated written laws so as to produce such reactions from the intended audience.

In the 1970s at the burial site of Shuihudi 睡虎地 in Yunmeng County 雲夢縣, Hubei 湖北, archeologists excavated a Qin dynasty tomb (sealed *c*.217 BCE) of a lower-level administrative clerk named Xi 喜.[55] Among the items interred with the tomb occupant, they discovered several bundles of legal and administrative documents written on bamboo slips. One document illustrates the prevalence of the imperial rhetoric of the Qin ideology of unification through law within conquered lands. It is a copy of a letter (dated 227 BCE) dispatched from the central office of Teng 騰, the governor of the Nan Commandery 南郡 to the local government offices of all counties and districts under his jurisdiction.

The manuscript was originally placed below the abdomen of the corpse. The letter consists of eight bamboo slips which were originally bound together by three silk cords.[56] The slips measure 27.8 cm in length, 0.6 cm in width, and 0.1 cm in thickness.[57] The graphs are consistent with Qin style orthography and are written in bold black ink. Each slip contains roughly 38–40 graphs, as well as several hook-shaped punctuation markers [ㄴ].

This letter provides a unique window through which we can observe various elements of Qin legal thought and practice. In the letter, Governor Teng admonishes local officials for *not* effectively applying Qin law and for allowing the local customs of Chu to continue to influence social behavior. The Nan Commandery comprised territory that was formerly under the control of the kingdom of Chu. Those lands were incorporated into the greater Qin kingdom shortly after 278 BCE, when King Zhao of Qin (r. 305–251 BCE) dispatched General Bai Qi 白起 to invade Chu. Thus, nearly half a century later, Governor Teng writes:

> 廿年四月丙戌朔丁亥南郡守騰謂縣道嗇夫古者ㄴ民各有鄉俗其所利及好惡不同或不便於民ㄴ害於邦是以聖 [1] 王作為灋度以矯端民心ㄴ去其邪僻ㄴ除其惡俗ㄴ法律未足ㄴ民多詐巧ㄴ故後有閒令下者ㄴ凡灋律令者以教導 [2] 民ㄴ去其淫僻除其惡俗ㄴ而使之_(之)於為善殹ㄴ今灋律令已具矣ㄴ而吏民莫用鄉俗淫泆之民不止ㄴ是即灋（廢）主之 [3] 明灋殹而長邪僻淫泆之民甚害於邦ㄴ不便於民故騰為是而脩灋律令田令及為閒私方而下之ㄴ令吏明布 [4] 令吏民皆明知之毋歫於罪ㄴ今灋律令已布聞吏民犯灋為閒私者不止ㄴ私好ㄴ鄉俗之心不變ㄴ自從令丞以 [5] 下知而弗舉論ㄴ是即明避主之明灋殹ㄴ而養匿邪僻之民ㄴ如此則為人臣亦不忠矣若弗知是即不勝任ㄴ不 [6] 智殹ㄴ智知而弗敢論是即不廉殹ㄴ此皆大罪殹而令丞弗明智知甚不便今且令人案行之舉劾不從令者致以律 [7] 論及令丞又且課縣官獨多犯令而令丞弗得者以令丞聞以次傳別書江陵布以郵行 [8]

In the twentieth year (227 BCE),[58] in the fourth month, the first day of which was *bingxu* (day 23), on *dinghai* (day 24), the Governor of Nan Commandery, Teng, addresses the *sefu* of the counties and districts:

"In ancient times, ∟ the people each had their own local customs. That through which they would benefit, as well as their likes and dislikes, were not the same. Some were not convenient to the people; ∟ [some] were damaging to the state. Because of this, the sagacious (1) kings created and enacted laws and measures in order to straighten and rectify the people's hearts, ∟ to purge their eccentricities, ∟ and to eliminate their malevolent customs. ∟ The laws and statutes were inadequate, ∟ and the people were increasingly deceitful and crafty. ∟ Therefore, there were subsequently dispatched ordinances. ∟ In all cases of laws, statutes and ordinances, these were used to instruct and guide (2) the people, ∟ to purge their lewdness and eccentricities, to eradicate their malevolent customs, ∟ and to cause them to achieve proper behavior.[59] ∟ Now, the laws, statutes, and ordinances are already complete, ∟ and yet among the officials and the people no one implements them. Local customs and lewd and licentious people are not stopped. ∟ This is simply disregarding the enlightened laws of the ruler (3) and giving preference to wicked, eccentric, lewd and licentious people. This is extremely detrimental to the state. ∟ It is not expedient to the people. Therefore, I, Teng, in response to this, have amended the laws, statutes, ordinances, the arable-land ordinances, as well as the methods concerning those interfering with private matters, and have dispersed them below. ∟ I ordered officials to clearly promulgate them, (4) and have ordered officials and people both to clearly know them, and they ought not stray into guilt. ∟ Now, the laws, statutes and ordinances are already promulgated, yet I hear of violation of laws by officials and people, and those who interfere in the private matters have not been stopped, ∟ and that personal desires ∟ and village customs within their hearts have not changed. ∟ From the prefect and his assistants (5) downwards, this is known and yet it is not brought up for discussion. ∟ This is simply ignoring the enlightened laws of the ruler, ∟ and nurturing and concealing the heretical and eccentric people. ∟ If such is the case, then those serving as ministers of the people are not loyal. If they are unaware, this is simply not being successful in one's responsibilities, ∟ (6) and not being intelligent. ∟ If they are aware of it, yet do not dare to discuss it, this is simply not being honest. These are all great offenses, yet if prefects and their assistants do not clearly understand this, then this is very inexpedient. Currently, I am dispatching people to carry out investigations of this, to raise accusations towards those who do not follow the ordinances to the authorities, and to censure them in accordance with the statutes. (7) Sentences shall extend to the prefects and their assistants. Moreover, I am going to evaluate the county government offices. If one or many violates the ordinances, but the prefect and his assistants do not obtain them, then the prefect and his assistants are to be reported [to their superior]."

Transmit in sequence. Another copy is to be promulgated in Jiangling; dispatch it via post. (8)

Governor Teng's dilemma revolves around the inability (or perhaps unwillingness) of his subordinates to properly administer the laws of Qin in the conquered lands formerly belonging to the kingdom of Chu. The contents of the letter certainly portray some of the practical problems associated with the Qin government's effort to centrally administer a large geographic region, but it is Governor Teng's depiction of the role of law as a necessary tool of social unification at the beginning of the document which highlights the continued prevalence of the Qin imperial rhetoric of unification through the law.

The letter begins with a philosophical articulation of socio-legal change that resonates closely with those ideas espoused by Shang Yang. Governor Teng reminds his local subordinate officials of the purpose of law. In former times, it was the lack of consistency or uniformity of people's interests and goals which proved detrimental to state preservation and to state development. Because of this plurality, the sages enacted laws. This demonstrates the recurrent Qin idea that the implementation of law is capable of resolving problems of social disorder. Law accomplishes this by narrowing the scope of desire and benefit, and curtailing diversity or eccentricity. As a result the sages of the past produced a uniform and orderly society guided by clear laws.

The letter contains articulations of socio-legal change which are also quite similar to those advocated by Legalist philosophers, such as Shang Yang and Han Feizi. In the letter, law is conceptualized as a political tool capable of bringing about social order, and, yet, the advances and changes in society necessitate adaption of the law to reflect the changing social realities and to accommodate newly arising social needs. This situation led to the introduction of the ordinances, *ling* 令, which acted as a supplement to legal statutes.[60] Again, the implication is that the law is considered by the Qin government to be the primary means through which a ruler could effectively guide and manipulate society; however, to be efficacious, laws also had to resonate closely with social reality.

After the initial section articulates the causal link between law and social order, Governor Teng then blames the unstable condition of the counties within the Nan Commandery on the inability of his subordinates to properly and effectively apply the laws of Qin. A situation in which laws are not properly and consistently applied is simply the same as if there were no laws at all. Governor Teng's displeasure over the performance of his subordinates illustrates two main concerns. On the one hand, it clearly demonstrates a belief that the efficacy of law to promote social order is heavily dependent upon the accurate and consistent application of those laws by government administrators. The concerns of Shang Yang, Han Feizi, and Li Si over the ability of ministers and officials to undermine the ruler's authority through inconsistent or arbitrary application of law resonate quite clearly here. On the other hand, the complaint related to the prevalence of local customs that are still being practiced shows a continued Qin imperial emphasis on utilizing law to stamp out local diversity in newly conquered regions, and to pursue a uniform society predicated upon a centralized Qin socio-political paradigm.

Teng's letter also provides clear evidence of the role of writing in Qin legal culture. The contents of the letter state that the statutes and ordinances were promulgated to all offices within the Nan Commandery and there was an explicit expectation that those transmitted laws would be acknowledged (and followed) by all officials and commoners at the local level. Furthermore, Teng warns that he will dispatch auditors to review local administrative practices, particularly focused on ascertaining the success and failure of application of Qin laws and the suppression of local customs. Those found contravening their administrative duties will be subject to "censure according to the statutes," *yi lü lun* 以律論. This reference indicates that officials were accountable for proper understanding and implementation of written laws and were at the same time liable for punishments according to the laws written in statutes.

An additional document appended to Governor Teng's letter further strengthens the claim that the central government maintained an explicit expectation that its local officials were to comprehend and properly apply Qin laws. The Shuihudi editors labeled the text *Yushu* 語書, or *Discourses*, due to the presence of those two graphs on the back of Slip 15 of the manuscript. According to the editors, the document comprises seven bamboo slips and was apparently bound together with the copy of Governor Teng's letter.[61] The contents of the manuscript compare and contrast the qualities of good officials (*liang li* 良吏) and evil officials (*e li* 惡吏). The text states that "In all cases, good officials comprehend the laws, statutes, and ordinances; in handling affairs there are none who are not capable" (凡良吏明法律令事無不能殹). Such a characterization is juxtaposed to "evil officials who do not comprehend the laws, statutes, and ordinances, and do not understand how to manage affairs" (惡吏不明法律令不智事). The expectation that laws are known is clear from the fact that the first criterion mentioned for categorizing an official as good or evil is the official's comprehension of the laws of Qin. Those who are capable of completing all manner of official tasks are familiar with the law, while those who cannot comprehend the handling of affairs do not know the law. Given the rather critical and remonstrance laden content of Governor Teng's letter, the addition of the *Yushu* seems appropriate as a reminder of the central government's expectations of its peripheral bureaucracy.

Governor Teng's letter and the *Yushu* are valuable resources for understanding the administrative and legal foundation upon which the Qin desired to unify all-under-Heaven. The letter contains theoretical articulations of the purpose of law, clear evidence of the transmission of law in written form, and provides an example of an explicit expectation that the laws were to be known and followed at the local level. Likewise, within the *Yushu* one of the criteria for assessing an official is based on his knowledge of the law. These articulations clearly resonate with many of the functions of written law presented in the previous chapter through an analysis of *Zuo zhuan* passages. Laws that are clearly written, universally promulgated, and consistently applied are capable of unifying social behavior and bringing about social and political order.

Promulgating the law: local copies of legal statutes

Nearly all Warring States philosophers categorized as "Legalists" argued that in order for laws to be effective at controlling the behavior of officials and the populace, such laws not only needed to be composed in clearly understood language, they also needed be *known* to their intended audience. Leaping from philosophy to praxis, Governor Teng confirms the centrality of written law (and writing in general) to the Qin practice of social and bureaucratic control. In the Nan Commandery, written laws were intended to serve as a guideline of conduct for local officials, and to deviate from their dictates carried the potential for administrative sanction. The frustration of Teng stems from the inability of local officials to stamp out the heterodox (i.e., non-Qin) customs being practiced in former Chu territory. More importantly, the letter shows that there was an expectation from the central government authorities that legal statutes should be promulgated, copied, and transmitted with a level of accuracy that would ensure textual fidelity and interpretive consistency at all levels of the Qin administration regardless of geographic location. Thus we have implicit evidence that laws were transmitted locally and that local officials were expected to have access to them.

Additional materials from Shuihudi provide insight into the methods employed by the Qin to ensure that centrally produced written laws were efficiently and accurately promulgated throughout Qin territories. One manuscript found in the tomb of Xi, the *Eighteen Forms of Qin Statutes*, or *Qin lü shiba zhong* 秦律十八種, contains a pair of statutory excerpts providing explicit evidence of the idea that the Qin central government maintained an expectation that centrally promulgated legal statutes could be accurately distributed from the center to the distant periphery.

> *Qin lü shiba zhong*—Slip 186
> 縣各告都官在其縣者寫其官之用律　　　內史雜
>
> Counties shall each inform those offices in their county to write the statutes used by their offices. Miscellanea of the *Nei shi*

When this statutory excerpt is read against the background of Qin theories of law, as well as the contents of Governor Teng's letter, the central government's purposive use of writing and law as a means to control local level administrators becomes clearer. First, the excerpt from the *Miscellanea of the Nei shi* on Slip 187 demonstrates that each individual office within the county seat was expected to maintain a collection of legal statutes specifically related to such an office. From this simple passage we can confirm a few key features about the availability of legal statutes at the local level. Within each county there likely existed a "master" copy of all the Qin statutes received by that county. This statutory article requires that personnel within the individual county offices are "to write" or "to copy down," *xie* 寫, those statutory provisions *used* by their office. Therefore we know that local officials below the rank of county magistrate had access to these master copies. Furthermore, we know that such officials were capable of comprehending which statutes were pertinent to their government function, and were capable of copying specific statutes. Lastly, local officials were *aware* that within the plethora of Qin legal statutes there were specific statutes dictating the proper (and improper) conduct within their posts. Laws were clearly being written, and indeed re-written, to directly control each office.

This evidence supports the argument that Qin legal statutes were composed and promulgated to the periphery with the expectation that they would be accurately transmitted and consistently read and implemented at the local level. It is not likely, however, that the Qin capital dispatched legal statutes directly to *every* county. It is more plausible, and the contents of Governor Teng's letter support the claim, that legal statutes were transmitted from the center to the commandery, and then on down to the individual counties. Once in the counties, individual departments then excerpted the relevant statutes for their posts. Considering the Qin expectation that law be universally applicable and consistently applied, however, this system of transmission, copying, and recopying did hold the inherent possibility of textual corruption. If statutory language varied from county to county or commandery to commandery, then there would be no way of ensuring the universality and consistency of Qin legal practice throughout the kingdom or empire. Another excerpt from the *Qin lü shiba zhong* contains hints as to a procedural mechanism designed to limit the dangers of textual corruption.

> *Qin lü shiba zhong*—Slip 199
> 歲讎辟律於御史　　　尉雜
>
> Annually, compare compiled[62] statutes with the Chief Censor. Miscellanea of the Commandant

Like the previous passage, this excerpt is quite short; however, its contents provide important insight into procedural features of the Qin legal system designed to accommodate statute-based administrative and populace regulation. According to this passage, each year officials are required to compare the collected statutes with those of the *Royal Secretary*. If properly practiced, we could then argue that the Qin government had in place a procedure to ensure that the *text* of local copies of legal statutes was accurate to within a year. This simple passage resonates with a passage recorded in the "Establishing Distinctions," *Ding fen* 定分 chapter of the *Shangjun shu* wherein Shang Yang states:[63]

> 法令皆副置一副天子之殿中爲法令爲禁室有鋌鑰爲禁而以封之內藏法令一副禁室中封以禁印及入禁室視禁法令及禁剟一字以上罪皆死不赦一歲受法令以禁令
>
> Laws and ordinances should all be copied. Place one copy in the temple of the Son of Heaven. For laws and ordinances construct a forbidden chamber. There should be a lock and key to make it forbidden, and seal it. Inside, store one copy of the laws and ordinances. The forbidden chamber is to be sealed using a forbidding seal. If ever [anyone] enters the forbidden chamber to view the forbidden laws and ordinances as well as forbiddingly excises

> one character or more are all punished by death without clemency. Once a year [officials] receive the laws and ordinances that accord with the prohibited ordinances.

This passage from the *Shangjun shu* provides a more comprehensive illustration of what is merely hinted at in Slip 199. In this chapter, Shang Yang advises Duke Xiao of Qin on ways of maintaining centralized control over the bureaucracy. When discussing the kingdom's laws, Shang Yang advises that a master copy be made and stored in the temple of the Son of Heaven. Furthermore a forbidden chamber should be constructed, and a copy of the laws and ordinances should be sealed away inside. Shang Yang thus devises a control mechanism for testing the accuracy of other copies of laws and ordinances. When laws are to be examined on a yearly basis, the central government possesses a "true" copy that has been sealed away unaltered. While I do not wish to over-read elements of the *Shangjun shu* into the Slip 199 excerpt, one cannot help but notice some similarities that lead to the conclusion that there did exist a procedural mechanism within the Qin administrative system for evaluating the accuracy of local copies of Qin legal statutes and ordinances. This system would have required something similar to a control copy of the statutes that could be used to evaluate local copies.

Taken together the excerpts found on Slip 187 and Slip 199 demonstrate that—at least in theory—Qin legal statutes were expected to be available to local officials. Each office within the county seat was required to maintain a copy of those statutes and ordinances pertaining to the functions of said offices. This shows that written laws were dispatched throughout the kingdom and later empire, and that there existed an official practice of copying statutes at a sub-county level (i.e., individual county administrative units). Furthermore, Slip 199 provides evidence that the Qin central government was conscious of the potential for the texts of statutes to be corrupted during the dual processes of transmission and copying. To combat this problem, the local statutes were required to be compared to a centralized "master" copy held in the office of the Royal Secretary. For the officials of Qin to be universally subject to the same laws and to consistently apply them to others, the actual text of the laws needed to be accurately transmitted and maintained.

Additionally, we can infer from these two excerpts that the Qin rulers also understood one of the main hazards of a statute-based legal system: the danger that law and social reality could become overly divorced from each other. As mentioned by Shang Yang, Han Feizi, and others, one primary underlying factor determining the efficacy of statutes to maintain socio-political order is the law's resonance with actual social conditions. A common research theme in several socio-legal studies examines the erosion of statutory "relevance" over time and the methods devised by various legal systems to accommodate social and legal changes.[64] By requiring local offices to engage the "master" text of statutes held at the county level, those officials would not only be conscious of the changing expectations of the central authorities, but would also likely have continuing access to any direct changes to the law which might be received. Likewise, the text of Slip 199 could also indicate a procedural check not just of the textual accuracy of the statutes vis-à-vis a centralized standard, but also an evaluation of how up-to-date the local statute collections are. When officials are held liable for whether their actions conform to the dictates of the statutes, access to accurate and up-to-date copies of such statutes is crucial. The text of Slip 199 indicates an expectation that local statutes were up-to-date for at least a year.

The annual checks, if carried out, would ensure that current statutes would be accessible and applicable in all the local counties. Other excavated manuscripts from Qin demonstrate that officials were quite conscious of carrying out their duties according to the statutes. Below I analyze some examples of how this anxiety influenced the very language of local administration.

In accordance with the law: statutory regulation of official action

Governor Teng's letter reminds officials that they are responsible for correctly applying the laws of Qin and further warns that failure to do so would result in them being "censured according to the statutes," *yi lü lun* 以律論. Likewise, the excerpts from the *Qin lü shiba zhong* demonstrate that the central government explicitly required Qin statutes to be available for officials and that there existed (at least in theory) a legislated procedural mechanism for ensuring that locally maintained statutes were accurate and up-to-date. We thus see the accessibility of these statutes and the expectation that such written documents were to serve as a guideline for correct official behavior. This reflects the concerns of various Warring States philosophers such as Shen Buhai, Shang Yang, Han Feizi, and Li Si, all of whom considered the key to successfully governing a kingdom to be the effective control of the aristocracy or bureaucracy through clear and universally promulgated laws.

The idea of *xingming* 形名 mentioned earlier illustrates how Warring States Period philosophers formulated an expectation of behavior by which official conduct was judged as either correct or aberrant. It is possible that the extant Qin laws represent the translation of the idea of *xingming* into written form, wherein laws pertaining to specific offices and actions were promulgated and those officials in such posts were responsible for acting within the statutory limits prescribed by law. One's official function was defined by written law (or a set of laws) and one's advancement or censure was determined by how well one's actions were judged to conform to the statutes.[65] The criteria informing this were centrally controlled, thus circumventing the ability of ministers and lower officials to shirk their responsibilities or to usurp royal authority.

Both the expectation of central authorities and the anxiety of local officials related to the proper conduct of local officials as defined by statutes are further evidenced in formulaic administrative phrases meant to convey either a desire for conformity to statutory dictates or to demonstrate one's compliance with them. Two of the most common phrase types found in Qin statutory and administrative language demonstrating this are: "in accordance with the statutes (and ordinances)," *ru lü* (*ling*) 如律(令) and "carry out these matters in accordance with the statutes (and ordinances)," *yi lü* (*ling*) *cong shi* 以律(令)從事.[66]

> *Falü zachao* 法律雜抄—Slips 1–2
> 任灋(廢)官者為吏貲二甲 • 有興除守嗇夫叚佐居守者上造以上不從令貲二 [1] 甲 除士吏發弩嗇夫不如律及發弩射不中尉貲二甲 [2]
>
> One who employs a permanently dismissed officer to serve as an official is fined two suits of armor. • When there is a muster [of troops], appoint a provisional *sefu* and temporary assistants; anyone of *shangzao* rank or higher who does not follow the ordinances is fined two (1) suits of armor. • If the appointment of military officers and crossbow *sefu* does not accord with the statutes, as well as when the crossbowmen's shots do not hit the mark, the commandant is fined two suits of armor. (2)

This example, taken from an eclectic text comprising several statutory excerpts, demonstrates the Qin government's expectation that laws and ordinances would directly guide official behavior. When discussing the muster of troops and the installation of provisional local officials to manage county affairs, the statutory excerpt clearly provides that anyone caught not acting in accordance with the ordinances will be fined two suits of armor. Likewise, the subsequent line provides a punishment of two suits of armor for the county commandant if military officers and *sefu* of crossbowmen are appointed "not in accordance with the statutes," *bu ru lü ling* 不如律令. These passages provide evidence that laws were expected to be available to their intended audience and that audience was expected to act accordingly or suffer punishment.

> *Qin lü shiba zhong*—Slips 137–138 partial
> 凡 [137] 不能自衣者公衣之令居其衣如律然 … [138]
>
> In all cases wherein (137) one is unable to clothe themselves, the government clothes them. Order them to work off the equivalent of their clothing in accordance with the statutes. (138)

In Slips 137–138, we have a statute dictating what must be done with government conscripts who are fulfilling their debts or fines to the government through labor. If such individuals are unable to clothe themselves, the government offices are required to ensure that they are sufficiently clothed. The government, however, does not provide convict laborers with provisions free of charge. In this example, those provided with government issued clothing are to work off their value "in accordance to the statutes." Here again, we see a statute dictating specific actions to officials (i.e., those required to provide clothing) and a subsequent reference to additional statutory provisions prescribing action to other individuals mentioned in the present excerpt (i.e., those who receive government issued clothing). Written laws are being used to regulate the behavior of specific officials, as well as dictate the behavior of those individuals under their control.

As mentioned in the introduction of this book, the Shuihudi legal statutes serve as the primary source material for this study; however, they are by no means the only legal statutes dated to the Qin that have been uncovered in recent years. In 1989, archeologists discovered several fragments of Qin legal statutes buried with the occupant of Tomb 6 in Longgang 龍崗, Yunmeng County, Hubei 湖北. The editors of the Longgang bamboo slips believe the tomb occupant was a lower Qin official named, Bi Si 辟死. This name is mentioned on a wooden tablet found in the tomb. The tablet records what appears to be part of a trial record, wherein Bi Si was originally found guilty and sentenced to serve as a *chengdan* 城旦, possibly in the Forbidden Gardens. His case was reviewed and the decision was overturned. The Assistant Prefect and a scribe ordered that Bi Si's sentence be expunged and ordered him to be released.[67] After this, the editors postulate that Bi Si served in an official capacity as the warden of the gardens.[68]

This career scenario is used to explain why the contents of the Longgang statutory material focuses on issues related to the maintenance of the Forbidden Gardens, such as forestry and animal husbandry.[69] Unfortunately, these bamboo slips were not well preserved and only small fragments, typically upper portions of slips, remain today. It is for this reason that I make limited use of these materials throughout this book. Despite their fragmentary nature, however, several graphs and phrases are visible on the remnant portions of the bamboo slips. Perhaps not surprisingly, even these scant traces of text provide further evidence of bureaucratic control through references to performing specific actions in accordance to written statutes.

> Longgang—Slip 117
> 田不從令者論之如律□□□□□□□□□□□
>
> fields. Those not following the ordinances, censure them in accordance to the statutes …
>
> Longgang—Slip 8
> 制所致縣道官必復請之不從律者令丞□□□□□□□□□□□
>
> missive (?)[70] once received, the county and district offices must again request advice for the matter. Those not following the statutes, the Magistrate and Assistant

Both of these fragments demonstrate the centrality of statutes and ordinances in governing officials working in local administration. The short piece of Slip 117 provides that a specific matter—likely related to fields—is governed by an ordinance; however, failure to carry out the provisions of this ordinance is to be censured "according to the statutes." Again we see the expectation that official actions are to conform to the parameters set out by written laws. In this instance an ordinance. This excerpt further demonstrates the interconnectedness of two different legal documents as tools of bureaucratic control. It is plausible that the ordinance mentioned in Slip 117 merely provides the action (or inaction) expected of an official without specifically listing a censure for noncompliance, while a separate statute contains the specific punishment corresponding to such contravention. Likewise, Slip 8 requires a specific action to be taken by county officials upon the receipt of a formal official document. Although the remaining text is lost, it is conceivable that any failure to execute the dictates of this text fully in accordance with the statutes would have resulted in some form of administrative censure. Both fragments demonstrate that written texts are expected to provide a blueprint for action and if these blueprints were not followed, then additional texts contained applicable punishments.

Administration in accordance with the statutes: Liye documents

The central government's expectation that officials fully comply with the dictates of the statutes and ordinances even influences the language of bureaucratic communication. Newly discovered Qin administrative documents from Liye 里耶 also provide evidence of centralized control over government officials via direct and indirect reference to legal statutes and ordinances.[71] Such references further demonstrate that legal statutes/ordinances were available at the local level and that higher authorities expected these laws to govern the actions of officials and the local populace. The Liye administrative documents were uncovered in a large cache at the bottom of a well located in the Qin county seat of Qianling 遷陵, a part of Dongting Commandery 洞庭郡. Although the Liye materials have not been completely published, those manuscripts that have been reveal a heavy use of the formulaic phrasing similar to *ru lü ling* or *yi lüling cong shi*, as well as several direct citations of legal statutes and ordinances. For example, in Wang Huanlin's initial study of 31 Liye manuscripts, 18 documents contained a phrase explicitly requiring a specified action be carried out in accordance with the statutes and ordinances. The Liye corpus contains several different types of administrative documents ranging from family registers to notations of the arrival and departure of official post. Many of the Liye documents fall into the category of what I term "archive" texts in that they represent a final copy of several communications between counties or between central and local authorities.[72] Most of these archive texts record attempts to clarify potential administrative problems and a portion of the communication (typically from a higher authority) explicitly orders actions to be taken to rectify a situation. These explicit orders often require action to take place in accordance with the statutes and/or ordinances. For example:

Liye—J1(16)5[73]
Front 正面 (seven lines)

(1) 廿七年二月丙子朔庚寅洞庭守禮謂縣嗇夫卒史嘉假卒史谷屬尉令曰傳送委輸必先悉行

In the twenty-seventh year, in the second month the first day of which was *bingzi*, on the day *gengyin*, Governor Li of Dongting informed the county *sefu*, the martial scribe Jia, the acting martial scribe Yu, and the commandants: The ordinance states: "When conveying and transferring, one must first fully employ

(2) 城旦舂隸臣妾居貲贖債急事不可留乃行徭今洞庭兵輸内史及巴南郡蒼

wall and grain-pounders, government slaves both male and female, and debtors. For urgent matters that cannot be delayed, only then employ corvée laborers." At present, Dongting weaponry is to be transferred to Neishi, as well as Ba, Nan Commandery, and Cang

(3) 梧輸甲兵當傳者多即傳之必先悉行乘城卒隸臣妾城旦舂鬼薪白粲居貲贖

Wu. The transfer of armor and weaponry requires many to serve as transporters. If transporting them, you must first fully employ those *cheng chengzu*, government slaves both male and female, wall builders and grain-pounders, *guixin* and *baican*, debtors,

(4) 債司寇隱官踐更縣者ㄴ田時殹不欲興黔首嘉谷尉各謹案所部縣卒徒隸居

robber catchers, *yinguan*, *jian gen*. It is the planting season. I do not wish to muster the black-headed ones. Jia, Yu, Wei each carefully examine the county seats' department registers of militiamen, government slaves, debtors,

(5) 貲贖債司寇隱官踐更縣者薄有可令傳甲兵縣弗令傳之而興₌黔₌首₌興黔首可

robber catchers, *yinguan*, and *jian gen*. If there are those capable of being ordered to transport armor and weaponry and the county does not order them to transport them, but one instead musters the black-headed ones; or if the muster of black-headed ones can be

(6) 省少弗省少而多興者輒劾移縣₌縣亟以律令具論當坐者言名X泰(太)守府嘉

minimized, but is not minimized; or if one can minimize, yet increases the muster, then the county should immediately censure those liable in accordance with the statutes and ordinances. For those liable inform their names and sentences to the Governor's office. Jia,

(7) 谷尉在所縣上書嘉谷尉令人日夜端行它如律令

> Yu, and the commandants in their counties report. Jia, Yu, and the commandants order a person to day and night swiftly dispatch (this message). All else should be in accordance with the statutes and ordinances.

In document J1(16)5, Governor Li of Dongting Commandery 洞庭守禮 sends a message to the county officials and military officials reminding them of the ordinances, *ling* 令, requiring that local officials first employ several classes of prisoners, debtors, and government slaves to transport materials before issuing a summons for compulsory labor among the general populace. He then acknowledges that there is a need to transport military equipage from Dongting to other commanderies, but warns his officials that because it is planting season they should follow the above-mentioned ordinance and not disturb the local population with a summons for compulsory labor. Anyone caught contravening this should be swiftly censured in accordance with the statutes and ordinances.

This particular document demonstrates the use of written law as a method of bureaucratic control on several levels. First, we have the partial text of an ordinance directly cited in a document that was dispatched from the central authority of a commandery to outlying counties. In many ways, this document is reminiscent of the letter sent by Governor Teng of the Nan Commandery to the county officials under his jurisdiction reminding them of their duty to follow and employ the laws of Qin. In the present case, however, Governor Li explicitly cites an ordinance that his subordinates are required to follow. This demonstrates an assumption by higher officials that written laws could be accurately transmitted, as well as properly comprehended and applied by local officials.[74] This further implies an assumption by Qin officials that a law written, transmitted, and understood could in turn directly condition the actions of an individual if it carried with it a level of penal liability.

This liability could also work both ways: top-down and bottom-up. That is, the inclusion of the ordinance quotation can also be read as a measure employed by Governor Li to increase the authority and seriousness of the document's orders for which he too was partially liable. Agriculture was extremely important for the Qin economy and for government taxation, so any disruption that would negatively affect the production of agricultural products would be bad not only for the local officials, but also for the governor who was responsible for the failings of those under his authority. Portions of the Shuihudi *Xiao lü* manuscript mentioned above provide evidence of various levels of liability for supervisors based on the actions of their subordinates. In this particular document, Governor Li is ordering his subordinates to undertake a rather labor intensive task of transporting military equipment from one commandery to several others. Thus, by including the text of the pertinent ordinance, Governor Li is reminding his subordinates—via writing—of the legal guidelines governing the execution of such actions and ensuring that they clearly understand the *legal* responsibility of the orders and the actions.

On a second, and related, level we see the written text of the ordinance directly influencing the bureaucratic language employed in the message sent by Governor Li. Compare the ordinance which Li cites and the subsequent order to his subordinates:

> Ordinance:
>
> 傳送委輸必先悉行城旦舂隸臣妾居貲贖債急事不可留乃行徭
>
> When conveying and transferring, one must first fully employ wall and grain-pounders, government slaves both male and female, and debtors. For urgent matters that cannot be delayed, only then employ corvée laborers.
>
> Governor Li:
>
> 即傳之必先悉行乘城卒隸臣妾城旦舂鬼薪白粲居貲贖債司寇隱官踐更縣者田時殹不欲興黔首
>
> If transporting them, you must first fully employ those *cheng chengzu*, government slaves both male and female, wall builders and grain-pounders, *guixin* and *baican*, debtors, robber catchers, *yinguan*, *jian gen*. It is the planting season. I do not wish to muster the black-headed ones.

The language of this ordinance makes it clear that the central government does not wish to conscript labor from the general populace unless it is absolutely necessary. There is a desire by central officials to keep local populations within their own commanderies working towards agricultural production. The ordinance provides that the local governments should completely exhaust all "official" laborers available to them before engaging the local population. In fact, the local population should *only* be conscripted in cases of absolute urgency when the transportation cannot be delayed. Governor Li's language reflects the intention of the ordinance. He states that the counties within his jurisdiction should first completely utilize all those individuals who owe service to the government. Interestingly, Governor Li extends the list of potential candidates for transport duty by naming several other categories of individuals who owe government service. Again, the true reason behind the ordinance, the protection of the general populace engaged in agriculture is evident when Li states that "It is planting season. I do not wish to muster the black-headed ones." The language of these two passages is quite similar so we see the direct influence of the language of a legal text conditioning the language of an administrative text.

On another level, Governor Li orders that any official found to be acting in contravention of this ordinance is to be censured in accordance with the statutes and ordinances. Once again this phrasing implies that officials have access to the relevant legal documents to properly censure another official and that the text contained within those documents specifically outlines a course of action. Thus, the ordinance and additional written texts prescribe further actions to take if the originally prescribed act is not properly carried out. Both levels here are indicative of the use of writing to create/delegate authority and to prescribe specific action.

The text of J1(16)5 demonstrates that written laws were considered to be viable means of controlling official behavior at all levels. Governor Li's actions of placing the text of the ordinance into his letter and the way in which the text of the ordinance influenced the language of his message indicates that written law was efficacious at influencing upper level officials, or at the very least they were conscious of their own liability to written laws. The requirement that all officials act in accordance with the ordinances and statutes demonstrates a shared belief that the actions of multiple officials at different hierarchical bureaucratic levels could be conditioned by written texts.

Additional examples of the requirement that official acts conform to the dictates of statutes and ordinances are found in Liye documents J1(9)1 through 12. Each tablet contains a series of correspondences between two counties and the central offices of the Nan Commandery. These documents record attempts by Yangling County 陽陵縣 to discover the whereabouts of 12 debtors working off their government debts in another county. After repeated attempts by Yangling authorities to locate these individuals fail, the central offices of the Dongting Commandery finally locate the debtors in Qianling County 遷陵縣. The central offices command the assistant prefect of Qianling to report the required information to Yangling authorities. In doing so, they are ordered to "carry out this matter in accordance with the statutes and ordinances," *qi yi lü ling cong shi* 其以律令從事.

Liye—J1(9)1
Front 正面 (six lines):

(1) 卅三年四月辛丑朔丙午司空騰敢言之陽陵宜居士五(伍)毋死有貲餘錢八

In the thirty-third year, fourth month—of which the first day was *xinchou*—on the day *bingwu*, the Minister of Works, Teng, dares to state: Wu Si, a commoner of Yiju Village in Yangling County, has a remaining pecuniary fine of 8,064 cash.

(2) 千六十四毋死戍洞庭郡不智(知)何縣署 • 今為錢校券一上謁言洞庭尉令

Wu Si is deployed for military service in Dongting Commandery, but it is not known to which county or service unit. • Now we have made one monetary contract to be sent up with a request for the Commandant of Dongting to order

(3) 毋死署所縣責以受(授)陽陵司₌空₌[司空]不名計問何縣官計年為報

the county of Wu Si's deployment locale to collect [the fine] and hand it over to the Yangling Minister of Works. The Minister of Works does not name Wu Si on the register and asks the said that is, unknown county with authority over the register to append the unit's yearly register in response.

(4) 已訾其家=[家]貧弗能入(納)乃移戍所報署主責發敢言之

[We] have already admonished his household. The household is poor and unable to remit it; thereupon we transfer the contract of debt to the locale of military service deployment. Report back with notification from the overseer of debt indicating he opened the document. I dare to state this.

(5) 四月己酉陽陵守丞廚敢言之寫上謁報=[報]署金布發敢言

In the fourth month on day *jiyou*, the Aide of Yangling, Chu, dares to state: What is written is sent up requesting a response. Report back with notification from the finance official indicating he opened the document. I dare to state

(6) 之 / 儋手

this. / Handled by Dan.

Back 反面 (five lines):

(1) 卅四年六月甲午朔戊午陽陵守慶敢言之未報謁追敢

In the thirty-fourth year, sixth month—of which the first day was *jiawu*—on day *wuwu*, the *shou* of Yangling, Qing, dares to report this: You have yet to respond. We request you pursue it. I dare to

(2) 言之 / 堪手

state this. / Handled by Kan.

(3) 卅五年四月己未朔乙丑洞庭叚(假)尉[illegible]謂遷陵丞陽陵卒署遷

In the thirty-fifth year, fourth month—of which the first day was *jiwei*—on day *yichou*, the provisional Commandant of Dongting, X, told the Aide of Qianling [County] that the conscripts of Yangling [County] are deployed in Qian

(4) 陵其以律令從事報之當騰=[騰] / 嘉手 ● 以洞庭司馬印行事

ling. Let it be that the matter is handled in accordance with the statutes and ordinances. Report on it. This warrants transmission by post-horse. / Handled by Jia. ● Use the seal of the Dongting Minister of Horses to carry out the matter.

(5) 敬手

Handled by Jing.

This example (one of 12 published to date) provides a window into the potential breakdown of administrative channels between two county jurisdictions. Qin statutes require that each county submit annual reports on its residents to the commandery and these reports were likely then forwarded to the Qin capital. These reports also include records of those individuals owing a government debt and the amount of that debt which was worked off through labor during the year. In the Liye documents, we see the anxiety of the officials of Yangling over their inability to act in accordance with the statutes serving as the catalyst for this stream of correspondence. Once the commandery authorities were able to determine the location of those "missing" individuals, the officials of Qianling were commanded to report the necessary information to Yangling in accordance with the statutes, *yi lü ling cong shi* 以律令從事. Thus, we see the actions of Yangling officials predicated on a desire to conform with the dictates of the statutes. Likewise, the command issued by the governor of Dongting to the Qianling County officials explicitly required them to act as prescribed in the statutes and ordinances.

One final wooden board further demonstrates the Qin government's desire to centralize control of not only the actions of its bureaucracy, but to also unify and regulate the very language of government. The partially damaged text of board J1(8)455[460] consists of a list of bureaucratic terms previously used by officials and their new government mandated equivalencies.[75] The text is composed in two registers: an upper register (A) containing 25 legible or semi-legible entries, and a lower register (B) containing 31 legible or semi-legible entries. As many of the entries replace the term *wang* 王with *huang di* 皇帝, we can say this board clearly dates to a period after 221 BCE when King Zheng took the title of Huang Di.

> *Liye*—J1(8)445—excerpts
> Register B
> Line 6
> 以王令曰以皇帝詔
>
> For "in accordance with the King's orders" say "in accordance with the Emperor's edicts.
>
> Line 20
> 王游曰皇帝游
>
> For "Royal Procession" say "Imperial Procession."
>
> Line 21
> 王獵曰皇帝獵
>
> For "Royal Hunt" say "Imperial Hunt."
>
> Line 22
> 王犬曰皇帝犬
>
> For "Royal Hounds" say "Imperial Hounds."

As noted earlier, the Qin sought to unify language, script, measures, and laws as an expedient means of consolidating and maintaining centralized control over its own territories, as well as new territories recently incorporated via conquest. Furthermore, as mentioned above, it is believed that Qin rulers attempted to directly control the use of specific words and orthographies through the establishment of taboo characters, *bihui* 避諱. The graph *zheng* 正 was replaced with *duan* 端 since the First Emperor's given name was *zheng* 政. This is used to explain the switch from *zheng yue* 正月 to *duan yue* 端月 in Qin texts, as well as the switch from *li zheng* 里正 "canton chief" to *li dian* 里典. Yet with the increased availability of excavated Qin source materials, the extent to which this taboo was actually enforced has been called into question by several scholars. Several of the texts found at Shuihudi, Liye, and Longgang make varied use of *zheng*/*duan* or *zheng*/*dian* substitutions. It does not seem that the taboo was overly enforced during the later stages of the Qin kingdom and during its dynastic period. From this, we can question both the authenticity of Sima Zhen's seventh century CE claim, as well as the ability of the Qin government to effectively impose such proscriptions.[76]

As Olivier Venture argues, however, the Liye document J1(8)455[460] represents one way in which the Qin government attempted to ensure uniformity in government by regulating the very language used by officials.[77] As shown above in the text of J1(16)5, the language of the ordinance requiring specific local officials to fully utilize all available government personnel for transport duty before conscripting from the general populace appears to directly influence the language employed by Governor Li in the orders to his subordinates. The present example, however, explicitly provides a series of terms that officials are required to use.

All of the Liye examples provide a window through which we can view the detail to which the Qin government attempted to centrally regulate its vast bureaucracy on the level of the individual official, as well as on an intercommunication level between officials. The past practices of localized administrative autonomy, seen by Shang Yang and other "Legalists" as one of the primary sources of conflict within a kingdom, were in theory stamped out by a fairly rigid system of written administrative statutes. The consistent reference to written statutes and ordinances demonstrates the expectation that local officials should have access to those laws related to inter-county administration and should abide by such laws. Failure to do so, would likely result in some form of official censure. Once again, we see an explicit use of written law as a tool of control.

Law, writing, and control over commoners

Before leaving the excavated materials, I wish to briefly consider the use of legal and administrative writing to control the general population. Much of my analysis to this point has focused on the role of written law as a means of controlling the Qin bureaucracy, yet it should be remembered that Shang Yang, Han

Feizi, Li Si, and Qin rulers were also concerned with establishing centralized control over the entire populace.[78] In connection with the last section, the requirement to "act in accordance with the statutes" applies not only to government officials. True, many scholars when discussing the concept of *xingming* and its practice in pre-imperial and early imperial China tend to focus on its application to bureaucrats; however, the concept also applies to the general populace, particularly those members employed by the government.

We know from historical texts that the Qin and Han dynasties required corvée labor service from the general populace. This typically involved standard military requirements for males, as well as a corvée service requirement of one month per year for males and possibly females. In his analysis of artisans in early China, Anthony Barbieri-Low both directly and indirectly demonstrates how the Qin government's use of artisans not only illustrates the ability of the Qin government to control the general populace on a massive scale, but also the ways in which written laws and other forms of written texts were employed as a means to control the behavior of the conscripted laborers as well as those managing them.[79]

Control over the populace began with "registration," or *fu* 傅. The Qin embarked on a massive registration program designed to account for all individuals within the borders of the kingdom and later empire. Such a register would be essential for managing not only human resources, but also managing other tax liabilities. From excavated materials, it appears that under Qin rule males were registered between the ages of 15 and 17 years of age.[80] Once registered, one's suitability for government service was also prescribed by the statutes. Hulsewé, Yates, and Barbieri-Low all note that the excerpts from the *Statute on Granaries*, *Cang lü* 倉律, found in the *Qin lü shiba zhong* manuscript indicate that the height of a person partially determined the type of statutory labor he or she would be assigned to carry out.[81] Thus we see statutes employed to control the registration of individuals and producing specific obligations for them.

Yet again, the Liye corpus of local administrative documents provides new insight into the reach of state control, particularly in the area of universal registration. Several documents discovered at the excavation site have been characterized by archeologists as household registration ledgers, *huji* 戶籍. These ledgers record the names, sex, ages, and ranks of all members of individual households within the jurisdiction of Qianyang County.

Liye Household Registration Ledger—K17[82]

南陽戶人荊不更黃▫	Huang X ranked *bugeng* of Jing; registered in Nanyang
子不更昌	Adult son Chang ranked *bugeng*
妻曰不實	Wife called Bu Shi
子小上造悍	Minor son Han ranked *shangzao*
子小上造▫	Minor son X ranked *shangzao*
子小女規	Minor daughter Gui
子小女移	Minor daughter Yi

This ledger records the primary householder's name, rank, and the area in which he was registered. This information is followed by information concerning those family members registered as part of his household. It includes one adult son named Chang, who given his age and rank would be liable for military service and corvée labor. The name of the primary householder's wife is given, and this is followed by four entries of household minors: two sons and two daughters. Thus, we have evidence that Qin local government was capable of maintaining accurate records of not only population numbers, but also details of that population relevant for military/labor service, as well as taxation. Several such register ledgers were discovered in pits around the excavation site, as well as within Well 1 itself. Yet, we also have evidence that these statistics were centrally valued by higher levels of administration.

Liye—J1(8)553 [552]

卅二年遷陵積戶五萬五千五[百]卅四

Thirty-second year, Qianling compiled households: 55,534.

This tablet indicates that the county of Qianling compiled the total number of households in their jurisdiction and forwarded this information to higher authorities. As such, we can argue that population control was centrally regulated via a universal household registration system maintained at the local level and annually reported to the central government.

With registers available at each county, officials could ensure that those individuals with tax, military, or labor requirements would be called up as expected. Once called to service, a laborer was obligated, just like an official within the bureaucracy, to act in accordance with the statutes and ordinances. Another legal text from the Shuihudi corpus, the *Questions and Answers on Laws*, or *Falü dawen* 法律答問, contains a series of questions attempting to disambiguate the meaning of specific legal terms and phrases. Two passages concern laborers who failed to perform their required duties. In the first passage, a person who "does not report when required to assemble," *bu hui* 不會, is considered to be a "vagrant," *jiang yang* 將陽, and should be punished with 50 lashes. The second passage clarifies the difference between "evading service," *bushi* 逋事 and "failing statutory service," *fa yao* 乏徭 mentioned in legal statutes.[83] The response states that one who does not report once called to service is considered to be evading service, while one who does report but absconds while traveling to the work place is considered to have failed their statutory service. Thus, failure to perform obligatory services in accordance with the statutory provisions warrants punishment.

Similarly, the quality of work done while performing one's corvée labor is also subject to punishment according to the statutes. In the *Qin lü shiba zhong*, an excerpt from the *Statute on Corvée Labor*, *Yao lü* 徭律, provides that if earth walls are ordered to be built, but the quality is so bad that they collapse within one year, then the *si kong* and overseers of construction are liable for a penalty and their "conscripts are to be ordered to re-build them. [This] ought not be calculated as statute labor," *ling qi tu fu tan zhi wu ji wei yao* 令其徒復垣之勿計爲徭.[84] We see the legal text prescribing quality-based expectation applied to the work of corvée laborers (the *ming* 名 of *xingming*) and failure to adequately perform or meet the quality expectation (*xing* 形) leads to a punishment. In this instance, the punishment meted out is for those convicted to re-build the collapsed walls without having those labor hours count towards their statutory labor quota.

Writing and law were also combined to not only control corvée laborers, but also non-corvée laborers working in government workshops by regulating the quality standards of the items produced. It will be remembered that the edict inscriptions placed on government regulated items, such as weights and other measuring devices, are an important source for understanding how writing was used to produce and convey centralized authority. Just as inscriptions on measuring devices conveyed the fact that officials tasked with using such items were liable for maintaining their accuracy, other forms of inscriptions illustrate that the artisans employed to produce such items for government use were also held liable for their quality. Anthony Barbieri-Low has demonstrated that the use of writing as a means of centralized control over production quality extended beyond officials and can be found as a mechanism producing accountability at lower levels of society, particularly those involved in the mass production of standardized and regulated items.[85] This is supported by statute excerpts in the Shuihudi corpus relating to production and artisans. These excerpts demonstrate a governmental expectation over quality.

> *Qin lü shiba zhong*—Slip 98
>
> 爲器同物者其小大短長廣亦必等
>
> When producing the same type of item, the smallness/largeness, shortness/highness, and width must all be equal.

To ensure accountability and that individual artisans' *ming* 名 or task matched his or her *xing* 形 or output, the Qin required artisans to inscribe the items they produced—particularly metal items such as weapons or lacquered items—with their names and often the location or workshop where the item was produced.[86] Although the statute excerpt translated above does not explicitly provide a punishment for artisans, we can assume that if a faulty item were produced in a workshop, then just as wall-builders were liable for the construction of faulty walls, artisans could be liable for sanction if they failed to produce items that met the Qin government's quality standard. The name/location inscription would directly link the liable artisan to the faulty product.

Barbieri-Low argues that this practice demonstrates that a functional level of literacy was not only required by their profession, but was expected by the government. Drawing on William Harris's term "craftsman literacy," Barbieri-Low illustrates the ways in which "a sizable proportion of skilled craftsmen gain and transmit literacy at a functional level that enables them to carry out their craft and its related business functions."[87] However, unlike some scholars who see the increase of literacy among the populace (or at least non-elite) as having a liberating effect, Barbieri-Low thus argues that craftsman literacy was instead a control mechanism directly linking artisanal accountability to quality control measures instituted by the central government.[88] So again we see the Qin government regulating the behavior of commoners via writing and law.

Conclusion

The debates over the introduction of written law during the Spring and Autumn Period were not simply born of attempts to eliminate social unrest and to control the general populace. Those kingdoms considering the implementation of public written laws were often plagued by governmental instability partially brought about by the semi-feudal practices allowing hereditary ministerial families carrying out the governance of the kingdom to amass a great deal of autonomy. Written law was seen by the Qin central government to be a viable tool for regulating the aristocracy, ordering the administration of the kingdom, and controlling the general populace. However, the use of writing to effect a form of centralized control over subordinates was not necessarily innovative during the Eastern Zhou period. We have several examples of investiture inscriptions dating to the Western Zhou period that record the Zhou king providing written copies of orders to his officers. Written forms, therefore, have a long history of being implemented as tools for controlling government officials. For the early and mid-Eastern Zhou periods, a primary concern for rulers was eliminating the autonomy of government administrators. By utilizing written law, these rulers were able to create public standards of behavior for all persons in a kingdom.

The historical records and philosophical texts associated with Qin portray the kingdom as one suffering from socio-political problems akin to those of other kingdoms. Powerful ministerial families were able to amass enough support to directly disobey the orders of the ruler, or, worse yet, were able to amass enough local military support to stage coups against the Qin ruling family. The Qin rulers were influenced by various statesmen each advocating the need to reform the kingdom's laws and institutions to better reflect the changing socio-political conditions. As a result the Qin initiated several reforms to limit the direct autonomy of ministerial families and to restrict their ability to amass such strong local support. The introduction of the *jun/xian* system undercut the landed autonomy of government ministers and made the lands directly subject to centralized control. Those employed as officials in these areas were directly responsible to the central authority of the ruler and not to local elites. To successfully carry out such transformations, statesmen and philosophers influencing Qin policy argued for the implementation of universally promulgated and consistently applied laws. Official posts were dictated by central authorities and the correctness or incorrectness of their actions was determined by law. The autonomy of the previous era was replaced by a fairly rigid reward-and-punishment bureaucratic structure that ensured no official would be able to amass sufficient power to usurp royal authority. To accomplish this, laws needed to be clearly worded, accurately conveyed, and consistently applied, and harsh punishments needed to follow any and all contraventions.

These extant records have been subjected to intense scrutiny over the centuries as contemporary evidence from Qin was not available; however, with the archeological discoveries of the twentieth century, we now have a great deal of textual evidence available to reassess the interaction of writing and law in the formulation of methods for enhancing and maintaining centralized bureaucratic control. Much of this evidence, formed of inscriptional and manuscript materials, provides insight into the ways in which the Qin government actually utilized written forms as tools of administrative control. Inscriptions on metal objects such as tiger tallies and various measurement devices confirm the claims of the historical tradition in ascribing the use of writing and written law as means of standardizing behavior of officials. Furthermore, bamboo manuscripts demonstrate the prevalence of the Qin understanding of socio-legal change and of the role of written law in effecting changes and controlling individual behavior. Laws were composed in written form and transmitted throughout the kingdom and later empire, and both historical and excavated materials confirm that there was an assumption, or even expectation, in the upper levels of Qin bureaucracy that written laws could be accurately transmitted and implemented consistently. The Liye materials demonstrate that this expectation was evident even in the language of administrative communication.

From this evidence we see the intended *function* of written law to be an administrative resource capable of controlling official behavior and, simultaneously, maintaining centralized control over the functioning of the Qin government at the local level. The next two chapters will consider the second big issue arising from a statute-based legal system, the *form* of legal statutes. The intended function of a law is meaningless if it cannot be conveyed in such a way as to influence or condition the audience to interpret the law in the way desired by those who drafted it. As such, the remainder of the book will focus on the way in which the Qin drafters of laws actually composed the written text.

Notes

1 See, for example, Cao Lüning, *Qin Lü Xin Tan* (Beijing: Zhongguo she hui ke xue chu ban she, 2002); Hainian Liu, *Zhanguo Qindai Fazhi Guankui* (Beijing: Falu chuban she, 2006); Michael Nylan, "The Rhetoric of 'Empire' in the Classical Era in China," in *Conceiving the Empire: China and Rome Compared*, ed. Achim Mittag and Fritz-Heiner Mutschler (Oxford: Oxford University Press, 2008), 39–66; Charles Sanft, *Communication and Cooperation in Early Imperial China: Publicizing the Qin Dynasty* (New York: SUNY, 2014).

2 Yuri Pines, Lothar von Falkenhausen, Gideon Shelach, and Robin D.S. Yates, eds., *Birth of an Empire: The State of Qin Revisited* (Berkeley: Global, Area, and International Archive, University of California Press, 2014), 11–34; Liu, *Zhanguo Qindai Fazhi Guankui*, 322–363.

3 The term "Legalist" is an anachronistic category developed by Han historiographers. It is often applied to scholar-statesmen of the Warring States Period who advocated a mode of governance reliant on bureaucratic techniques that included strict centralized laws and harsh punishments. They were not necessarily a self-identified group, yet modern scholars still use the term heuristically. See Kidder Smith, "Sima Tan and the Invention of Daoism, 'Legalism,' 'et cetera,'" *Journal of Asian Studies* 62, no. 1 (2003): 129–156.

4 For analysis of the similarities between the Qin and other kingdoms, see Teng Mingyu, "From Vassal State to Empire: An Archaeological Examination of Qin Culture," in *Birth of an Empire: The State of Qin Revisited*, ed. Yuri Pines, Lothar von Falkenhausen, Gideon Shelach, and Robin D.S. Yates (Berkeley: Global, Area, and International Archive, University of California Press, 2014), 71–112; Lothar von Falkenhausen, *Chinese Society in the Age of Confucius (1000–250 BC): The Archaeological Evidence* (Los Angeles: Cotsen Institute of Archaeology, University of California, Los Angeles, 2006).

5 For more on Sima Qian's sources of Qin history, see Yuri Pines, "Biases and Their Sources: Qin History in the Shiji," *Oriens Extremus* 46 (June 2005): 10–34; Yuri Pines, "The Messianic Emperor: A New Look at Qin's Place in China's History," in *Birth of an Empire: The State of Qin Revisited*, ed. Yuri Pines, Lothar von Falkenhausen, Gideon Shelach, and Robin D.S. Yates (Berkeley: Global, Area, and International Archive, University of California Press, 2014), 258–279.

6 *Shi ji*: 5.199.

7 *Shi ji*: 5.200.

8 *Shi ji*: 5.202.

9 *Shang zi* (Sibu congkan ed.): 1.1a–1.2b. For references to the *Shangjun shu* I will cite the Sibu congkan edition; however, my translations are based upon the text and annotations found in Zhu Shizhe, *Shangjun shu jiegu dingben* (Taipei: He Luo tushu chuban she, 1975). For this passage see p. 2.

10 Zhu interprets *ni* 溺, "to drown or be addicted to" as meaning *huo* 惑, "to be misled or perplexed." I retain the original meaning of "to drown" in my translation. The primary argument of Shang Yang is that such people are easily overwhelmed and cannot therefore be employed to innovate, but only ordered to follow.

11 Older editions of the *Shangjun shu* contain the phrase 三代不同道而王 "three dynasties maintained different *paths* yet reigned as kings." Most scholars, however, believe that the graph *dao* 道 is a later corruption and the text should be read as *li* 禮, "rite." This is followed in most editions, including Duyvendak's earlier English translation. See Jiang Lihong, *Shangjun Shu Zhuizhi* (Beijing: Zhonghua shuju, 1986), 4; J.J.L Duyvendak, *The Book of Lord Shang: A Classic of the Chinese School of Law* (London: Probsthain & Co., 1928), 171; Zhu Shizhe, *Shangjun shu jiegu dingben*, 2.

12 *Shangjun shu jiegu ding ben*, 2–3. *Shang zi* (Sibu congkan ed.): 1.1a–1.2b.

13 The need for social and political institutions to adapt to changing times is noted by several scholars. See, for example, Liu, *Zhanguo Qindai Fazhi Guankui*, 334–338.

14 Robin D.S. Yates, "State Control of Bureaucrats under the Qin: Techniques and Procedures," *Early China* 20 (1995): 331–365; Sanft, *Communication and Cooperation in Early Imperial China*; Liu, *Zhanguo Qindai Fazhi Guankui*, 330–334.

15 Michael Loewe, "China's Sense of Unity as Seen in the Early Empires," *T'oung Pao* 80 (1994): 6–26.

16 Liu, *Zhanguo Qindai Fazhi Guankui*, 338–341.

17 For several studies noting the link between centralized authority and uniformity, see Zhengyuan Fu, *China's Legalists : The Earliest Totalitarians and Their Art of Ruling*, New Studies in Asian Culture (Armonk, NY: M.E. Sharpe, 1996), 57–66; Geoffrey MacCormack, "The Legalist School and Its Influence upon Traditional Chinese Law," *Archiv Für Rechts-Und Sozialphilosophie* 92 (2006): 71–72; Sanft, *Communication and Cooperation in Early Imperial China*, 58–60.

18 Zhu, *Shangjun shu jiegu dingben*, 14. *Shang zi* (Sibu congkan ed.): 2.9b.
19 Zhu, *Shangjun shu jiegu dingben*, 59. *Shang zi* (Sibu congkan ed.): 4.4b.
20 For an initial study combining historical sources as well as materials from Shuihudi (discussed below), see Liu, *Zhanguo Qindai Fazhi Guankui*, 145–160.
21 Again, with the discovery of more excavated manuscripts we are beginning to understand the methods of training and appointment for officials. For a brief analysis, primarily focused on Han excavated materials, see Robin D.S. Yates, "Soldiers, Scribes, and Women: Literacy among the Lower Orders in Early China," in *Writing and Literacy in Early China: Studies from the Columbia Early China Seminar*, ed. Feng Li and David Prager Branner (Seattle: University of Washington Press, 2011), 343–360.
22 Herrlee Glessner Creel, *What is Taoism? And Other Studies in Chinese Cultural History* (Chicago, IL: University Of Chicago Press, 1970), 134–135.
23 John Makeham, "The Legalist Concept of Hsing-Ming: An Example of the Contribution of Archaeological Evidence to the Re-Interpretation of Transmitted Texts," *Monumenta Serica* 39 (1991 1990): 87–114.
24 Numerous Han dynasty texts attribute the doctrine of *xingming* to Shen Buhai; however, as Herrlee Creel observed, the remnant fragments related to the text of Shen Buhai do not contain the term at all. It is clear that Shen Buhai was exceedingly interested in methods for controlling ministers and other government officials, but *xingming* is not explicitly referenced in any extant passage attributed to him. See Herrlee Glessner Creel, *Shen Pu-Hai: A Chinese Political Philosopher of the Fourth Century B.C.* (Chicago, IL: University Of Chicago Press, 1974), 119–124.
25 *Han Feizi* (Siku quanshu ed.): 2.8.
26 The *Shiji* states that "Yang, in his youth, enjoyed the study of *xingming*" *Yang shao hao xingming zhi xue* 鞅少好刑名之學 (*Shiji* 68: 227). In this passage the graph *xing* 刑 (OCM *gêŋ) is used instead of *xing* 形 (OCM * gêŋ). Scholars note that in this context one could simply read *xing* 刑 as a loan for *xing* 形. Alternatively one could argue that the meaning is for *punishments and names* to match. Similar to the idea of proportional correspondences found in *xingming* 形名, Shang Yang advocated that for punishments to be properly applied they must specifically match the "named" deed or offense. Either way, the idea of proportional correspondences is central. See, for example, Leo S. Chang and Wang Hsiao-po, *The Philosophical Foundations of Han Fei's Political Theory* (Honolulu: University of Hawai'i Press, 1986), 57–69; Makeham, "The Legalist Concept of Hsing-Ming."
27 Yates, "State Control of Bureaucrats under the Qin."
28 Through scant references in the historical literature, as well as more detailed evidence from excavated manuscripts, we know that there were additional subdivisions below the *jun* and *county* levels. Evidence from Longgang, Shuihudi, and Liye illustrates the use of sub-county bureaucratic units of *xiang* 鄉 or canton, and *li* 里 or hamlet. These units were subsumed within the overall geopolitical structure, and loyalty and accountability were directed towards the center and not to local figures. See Hsing I-tien, "Qin-Han Census and Tax and Corvee Administration: Notes on Newly Discovered Materials," in *Birth of an Empire: The State of Qin Revisited*, ed. Yuri Pines, Lothar von Falkenhausen, Gideon Shelach, and Robin D.S. Yates (Berkeley: Global, Area, and International Archive, University of California Press, 2014), 155–186; Hou Xiaorong, *Qindai Zhengqu Dili* (Beijing: Shehui kexue wenxian chuban she, 2009), 60–113.
29 *Shiji* 5: 16–17.
30 Creel, *What Is Taoism?*, 144.
31 *Shiji* 87: 2546.
32 *Shiji* 6: 236.
33 Sanft, *Communication and Cooperation in Early Imperial China.*
34 There are a total of seven inscriptions mentioned in the *Shiji*, though only six inscriptions are recorded. See Martin Kern, *The Stele Inscriptions of Ch'in Shih-Huang: Text*

and Ritual in Early Chinese Imperial Representation (New Haven, CT: American Oriental Society, 2000), 2–6. These inscriptions have been studied by numerous scholars in China and the West. For Chinese studies, see Rong Geng, "Qin Shi Huang Ke Shi Kao," *Yanjing Xuebao* 17 (1935): 125–171; Wu Fuzhu, *Qin Shi Huang Ke Shi Kao* (Taipei: Wen shi zhe, 1994). For a comprehensive study in English, see Kern, *The Stele Inscriptions of Ch'in Shih-Huang.*

35 Several scholars have argued that although the inscriptions are only known via Han dynasty sources, the language and rhetoric of the purported passages does seem to reflect Qin political, social, and legal attitudes. As such, they can be cautiously utilized to reconstruct aspects of Qin thought. When compared to the excavated materials examined below, the likelihood of their veracity is increased. See Kern, *The Stele Inscriptions of Ch'in Shih-Huang*, 155–196; Sanft, *Communication and Cooperation in Early Imperial China*, 64–65.

36 *Shiji* 6: 243. This translation and the one below both follow Kern, *The Stele Inscriptions of Ch'in Shih-Huang*, 17–24.

37 *Shiji* 6: 245–247. See also, Kern, *The Stele Inscriptions of Ch'in Shih-Huang*, 25–34.

38 Pines, "Biases and Their Sources: Qin History in the Shiji."

39 Scholars believe that Du is likely the former area of the kingdom of Du Bo 杜伯 that was annexed by the Qin during the reign of Duke Wu (r. 697–678 BCE), and renamed Du *xian* 杜縣 or Du County. There is still a Du Village located roughly 2 km from the reported discovery site of the tally. See Hei Guang, "Xi'an shijiao faxian Qinguo Du hufu," *Wenwu* 9 (1979): 93.

40 It is believed that this tally dates to the mid- or late fourth century BCE. See Chen Zhaorong, *Qin xi wenzi yanjiu* (Taipei: Zhongyang yanjiu yuan lishi yuyan yanjiu suo, 2003), 256.

41 Chen Zunxiang, "Du Hufu Zhenwei Kaobian," *Wenbo* 9 (1985): 29.

42 For a general survey of all extant Qin tiger tallies, see Chen Zhaorong, *Qin xi wenzi yanjiu*, 252–263.

43 Sun Huizu and Xu Gefu, eds., *Qin Han jinwen huibian* (Shanghai: Shanghai shudian, 1997), 1.

44 Ibid., 2.

45 Lothar von Falkenhausen, "The E Jun Qi Metal Tallies: Inscribed Texts and Ritual Contexts," in *Text and Ritual in Early China*, ed. Martin Kern (Seattle: University of Washington Press, 2005), 79–123.

46 Ibid., 86–87.

47 Ibid., 86.

48 Such arguments can be found in Kern, *The Stele Inscriptions of Ch'in Shih-Huang*; Pines, "The Messianic Emperor"; Sanft, *Communication and Cooperation in Early Imperial China*, 79–90.

49 Numerous examples of this inscription can be found in Sun and Xu, *Qin Han jinwen huibian*, 4–19.

50 One of the *Statute on Artisans*, *Gong lü* 工律, excerpts found in the *Qin lü shiba zhong* manuscript requires measurement devices of counties and of workshops to be corrected each year without fail. Slip 100 (縣及工室聽官為正衡石纍斗桶升毋過歲壹). Additionally, several articles from the *Xiao lü* manuscript provide detailed punishment scales for various levels of inaccuracy among measurement devices. See Chapter 4 for more details.

51 For analysis of volume and weight measuring devices in the Qin, see Qiu Guangming, ed., *Zhongguo lidai duliangheng kao* (Beijing: Kexue chuban she, 1992), 188–207 and 348–397. For an earlier study of the size, shape, construction, and inscriptions of Qin dynasty weights, see Wu Hung, "Qin quan yanjiu," *Gugong jikan* 4 (1979): 33–47.

52 See Sun and Xu, *Qin Han jinwen huibian*, 12–14.

53 This is not to imply that the inscriptions were not intended to be read. I merely point out that we cannot assume universal literacy among all those individuals who might have come into contact with such an implement.

54 Sanft, *Communication and Cooperation in Early Imperial China*, 74–76.

55 In this chapter I will reference several manuscripts from this corpus; however, I will save an in-depth paleographic analysis of the excavated materials for the next chapter. For more information on the site, see Yunmeng Shuihudi Qin mu bianxie zu, ed., *Yunmeng Shuihudi Qin mu* (Beijing: Wenwu chuban she, 1981).

56 An additional text known as the *Yushu* 語書 or *Discourses* is believed to have been appended to this letter. This text outlines specific characteristics associated with being a "good official" or "bad official."

57 Yunmeng Shuihudi Qin mu bianxie zu, *Yunmeng Shuihudi Qin mu*, 12–16.

58 The letter does not provide the name of the ruler whose "twentieth year" is listed. Gao Min 高敏 and Hou Xiaorong 后曉榮 both draw on traditional histories which state that Nan Commandery was established in 278 BCE after the Qin defeat of Chu forces in the area. This date of 278 BCE coincides with the twenty-ninth year of King Zhao's reign and after Zhao the only Qin ruler to reign for 20 years or more is King Zheng (Qin Shi Huang Di). The editors of the manuscript also note that the month/day (四月丙戌朔丁亥) also corresponds to the twentieth year of King Zheng's reign. See Gao Min, *Shuihudi Qin jian chutan* (Taipei: Wanjuan chuban she, 2000), 23; Hou Xiaorong, *Qindai Zhengqu Dili*, 396–397; Shuihudi Qin mu zhujian zhengli xiaozu, *Shuihudi Qin mu zhujian*, 13–14.

59 The phrase 使之_(之)於為善殹 is slightly awkward; however, the Shuihudi editors argue that the initial *zhi* 之 refers to "the people," while the repeated *zhi* should be read as part of *zhi yu* 之於 "to arrive at" or "obtain."

60 Anthony J. Barbieri-Low and Robin D.S. Yates, *Law, State, and Society in Early Imperial China: A Study with Critical Edition and Translation of the Legal Texts from Zhangjiashan Tomb No. 247* (Leiden: Brill, 2015), 70–76.

61 The Shuihudi editors note that the binding markers at the top of the *Yushu* are slightly lower than those of Governor Teng's letter. Due to this, they posit that the two manuscripts were originally produced separately and only later joined together.

62 As noted by Hulsewé, the binomial phrase *bi lü* 辟律 is not found in any received text. Following the Shuihudi editors, Hulsewé translates the phrase as "penal statutes." While this is a possible reading, I suggest reading the graph *bi* as "compiled" similar to the usages found in the *Zuo zhuan* passages noted in Chapter 1. Thus, the review is of those *compiled* statutes (e.g., non-originals which are copies) held in each office or by individual officials. See A.F.P. Hulsewé, *Remnants of Ch'in Law* (Leiden: E.J. Brill, 1985), 90.

63 Zhu, *Shangjun shu jiegu dingben*, 93. *Shang zi* (Sibu congkan ed.): 5.12b.

64 See, for example, Roger Cotterrell, *The Sociology of Law*, 2nd ed. (Oxford: Oxford University Press, 1992), chap. 2; Lawrence M. Friedman, "Legal Culture and Social Development," *Law and Society Review* 4, no. 1 (1969): 29–44; Lawrence M. Friedman, *Law and Society: An Introduction* (Englewood Cliffs, NJ: Prentice-Hall, 1977), chap. 2; Alan Watson, *The Evolution of Law* (Baltimore, MD and London: Johns Hopkins University Press, 1985), 98–112.

65 Robin Yates has carried out an extensive survey of the bureaucratic mechanisms employed by the Qin to maintain a tight grasp on official actions. Nearly all his reconstructions are based upon excavated legal statutes, thus strengthening the *use* of written legal statutes as a tool for control. See Yates, "State Control of Bureaucrats under the Qin."

66 I have bracketed the word *ling* 令 because it does not occur in all cases of these phrases. Often only the word *lü* 律 is used in such formulations.

67 Zhongguo wenwu yanjiu suo and Hubei sheng wenwu kaogu yanjiu suo, eds., *Longgang Qin jian* (Beijing: Zhonghua shuju, 2001), 144–145.

68 Ibid., 7.

69 Dating the Longgang manuscripts is difficult, yet there are some clues to give a rough range of 223 BCE to just after the unification by Qin in 221 BCE. One slip fragment (#98) contains the date 廿四年正月甲寅 which corresponds to year 24 of King Zheng's reign or 223 BCE. Furthermore, Slips 15 and 16 contain the title *huang di* 皇帝. Zhongguo wenwu yanjiu suo and Hubei sheng wenwu kaogu yanjiu suo, *Longgang Qin jian*, 7.

70 The editors of the Longgang Qin manuscripts argue that the graph *zhi* 制 should be read as the end of a proceeding sentence the slip for which is now lost. Given the content of this particular passage, the editors believe that the previous section likely referenced a specific type of official document. Zhongguo wenwu yanjiu suo and Hubei sheng wenwu kaogu yanjiu suo, *Longgang Qin jian*, 74.

71 For an English language overview of the Liye find, see Robin D.S. Yates, "The Qin Slips and Boards from Well No. 1, Liye, Hunan: A Brief Introduction to the Qin Qianling County Archives," *Early China* 35–36 (2012–2013): 291–329. Only one volume of the Liye corpus has been published to date, as well as a small number published in the original archeological report, *Liye fajue baogao*. Robin Yates notes that the study of Liye materials is made difficult by the variant numbering sequences of the wooden tablets used in the *Liye fajue baogao*, the *Liye Qin jian* vol. 1, and the *Liye Qin jiandu jiaoyi* vol. 1. The *Liye fajue baogao* utilizes a numerical sequence that lists the Well number (*jing* 井=J), the excavation level number, and the tablet number. So J1(9)16 represents: Tablet 16 found at level 9 of Well no. 1. When the *Liye Qin jian* vol. 1 was finally published the editors dropped the JX designator since the other wells on site did not yield further tablets. They used a system that only signified the excavation level and tablet number (e.g., 8–455 as Tablet 455 from level 8). As Yates notes, the editors also used different numbers for the photograph plates. For example, the photograph of Liye tablet 8–455 is labeled #460. Chen Wei and the editors of the *Liye Qin jiandu jiaoyi* vol. 1, number their transcriptions according to the photograph number. In short, to properly work with (and cite) the Liye materials, one needs access to the photographs and both sets of transcriptions. For this chapter, I have utilized as full a citation as possible: e.g., J1(8)455 [460] represents Tablet 455 found at level 8 in Well 1 and pictured on plate 460.

72 I would like to thank Professor Donald Harper for drawing this feature to my attention.

73 This translation is based on the work of Wang Huanlin 王換林 and the editors of the *Liye fajue baogao*. For the photographs and transcriptions, see Hunan sheng wenwu kaogu yanjiu suo, *Liye fajue baogao* (Changsha: Yuelu shushe, 2006), 192–193; Wang Huanlin, *Liye Qinjian jiaoku* (Beijing: Zhongguo wenlian chubanshe, 2007), 104–112. This document has not been published in the official *Liye Qin jian* series, so I do not give the plate number.

74 McKitterick makes a similar argument for the use of written correspondence with legal import for medieval Europe. The written word assumed a level of comprehension with its intended audience and that the audience would be able to act accordingly. See Rosamond McKitterick, *The Carolingians and the Written Word* (Cambridge: Cambridge University Press, 1989).

75 Again noting the frustration of working with the Liye materials, I provide a full notation of the board number including Well number, excavated level number (X), board number, and photo plate number [x]. The transcription of this board can be found at Hunan sheng wenwu kaogu yanjiu suo, ed., *Liye Qin jian*, vol. 1 (Beijing: Wenwu chuban, 2012), 33; Wei Chen, ed., *Liye Qin jiandu jiaoyi*, vol. 1 (Wuhan: Wuhan daxue chuban, 2012), 155–157.

76 See, for example, Mansvelt Beck, "The First Emperor's Taboo Character and the Three Day Reign of King Xiaowen: Two Moot Points Raised by the Qin Chronicle Unearthed in Shuihudi in 1975," *T'oung Pao* 73 (1987): 69–72.

77 Olivier Venture, "Caractères Interdits et Vocabulaire Officiel Sous Les Qin: L'apport Des Documents Administratifes de Liye," *Études Chinoises* 30 (2011): 92–93.

78 I mention lower ranks of society in this section; however, the primary focus of my book concerns the function of written law as a means of control over the Qin bureaucracy and how this intended function influenced the physical and linguistic forms of such laws.

79 Anthony J. Barbieri-Low, *Artisans in Early Imperial China* (Seattle: University of Washington Press, 2007), 214–217.

80 From the records of the *Bian nian ji* 編年記, we know that the tomb occupant, Mr. Xi, was born in 262 BCE and was first registered at 17 *sui* 歲 (246 BCE). See A.F.P. Hulsewé, "Some Remarks on Statute Labour during the Ch'in and Han Period," *Orientalia Venetiana* 1 (1984): 198–199; Robin D.S. Yates, "Social Status in the Ch'in: Evidence from the Yun-Meng Legal Documents. Part One: Commoners," *Harvard Journal of Asiatic Studies* 47, no. 1 (1987): 203–219.

81 *Qin lü shiba zhong*, slips 49–52. See Hulsewé, *Remnants of Ch'in Law*, 31; Barbieri-Low, *Artisans in Early Imperial China*, 214.

82 Hunan sheng wenwu kaogu yanjiu suo, *Liye fajue baogao*, 204 and plate 37.

83 Hulsewé, 167.

84 *Qin lü shiba zhong*, slips 116–117. See also Hulsewé, 63–64.

85 Anthony J. Barbieri-Low, "Craftsman's Literacy: Uses of Writing by Male and Female Artisans in Qin and Han China," in *Writing and Literacy in Early China: Studies from the Columbia Early China Seminar*, ed. Li Feng and David Prager Branner (Seattle: University of Washington Press, 2011), 370–400.

86 Barbieri-Low, *Artisans in Early Imperial China*, 74–75.

87 Barbieri-Low, "Craftsman's Literacy," 373.

88 Ibid., 389. Barbieri-Low's argument utilizes the work of Claude Lévi-Strauss, who argued in *Tristes Tropiques* that "the primary function of writing, as a means of communication, is to facilitate the enslavement of other human beings." See Claude Lévi-Strauss, *Tristes Tropiques*, trans. John Russell (New York: Criterion, 1961), 292 as cited in Barbieri-Low, "Craftsman's Literacy," 397–398.

4 The anatomy of a Qin Legal Statute Part I

Introduction

The previous chapters focused on the development and evolution of theories of writing and law in early China. Through an examination of specific *Zuo zhuan* 左傳 passages, Chapter 2 highlighted some of the earliest evidence of a discourse related to the establishment of a legal system predicated upon written law in pre-imperial China. Decentralization and a loss of control over the ministerial aristocracy combined with a growing consciousness of the value of *written* forms to transcend geography, time, and individual status, led to increased calls among some kingdoms for the use of public written laws to serve as a centralized standard of conduct for both the aristocracy and the populace. In Chapter 3, I turned my attention to the kingdom of Qin, specifically the extant sources, both historical and excavated, that allow us to reconstruct a general understanding of the nexus of law, society, and writing in Qin legal theory. Historical and philosophical records demonstrate that the Qin government suffered many of the same administrative maladies which afflicted the kingdoms mentioned in the *Zuo zhuan*. Ministerial machinations, usurpations, and regicide gave rise to government reform movements meant to curb the power and authority of the ministerial aristocracy. Underpinning these reform policies was a philosophical tradition that emphasized strong centralized rule, a closely controlled bureaucracy, and a heavily regulated populace. For over a century, Qin ministers such as Shang Yang 商鞅 and Li Si 李斯 each advocated the use of centrally drafted, clearly worded, universally promulgated, and consistently applied legal regulations. Written law was considered to be the primary means through which a kingdom could regain and subsequently maintain socio-political order. A review of several types of excavated Qin textual materials, dated prior to and just after political and geographic unification in 221 BCE, further demonstrated the ubiquity of administrative and populace-based control via textual materials. Official action was regulated by written statutory provisions, formulaic documentation, and annual reviews. Individual members of the Qin population were confronted with public textual materials conveying the rationale for unification and providing hallmarks of credibility for items regulated by universalized Qin standards. Writing, law, and control were firmly intertwined by the time of Qin unification.

The remainder of the book examines the extant legal statutes of Qin from the Shuihudi 睡虎地 corpus. I will ask the question, how does one compose a written law that can be read, interpreted, and applied in a manner consistent with the original intention of its author/drafter? The present chapter and subsequent chapter will examine in detail the codicological and linguistic features of extant legal statutes discovered in Tomb 11 at Shuihudi, Hubei 湖北 Province. The purpose will be to determine the extent to which Qin normative theories of how law ought to function were physically translated into the actual production of the very texts designed to carry out that function.

The present chapter first introduces the primary excavated sources for analyzing Qin legal statutes, the Shuihudi corpus. Then, I go on to examine various physical features of the manuscripts, which demonstrate awareness of the need for a material document capable of being altered to accommodate legal changes and of being easily read and properly applied by those tasked with its implementation. This "form and function" analysis is accomplished by analyzing the orthographic and calligraphic features of the legal statutes (or statutory extracts), media-based implications of composing the text on bamboo slips, and the use of orthographic and non-orthographic forms of punctuation.

Forms and functions

The intended audience and function of a text can directly influence the physical production of the document bearing that text. This is clear today, just as it was in the past. For example, newspapers are considered a form of textual ephemera and, as a result, are produced on relatively inexpensive and non-durable paper materials. The relationship between the economics of production and the facts that newspapers are produced daily and are typically read by the audience on the day of their production but not often afterwards (apart from the avid researcher) influences the medium used and physical form of newspapers. Likewise, books purchased by a library are often re-bound with more durable coverings as it is understood that such books are likely to receive more use than individual, private copies. As such, their physical forms need to be more durable so as to maintain their structural integrity through continued use. These are modern examples of how newspaper publishers and libraries produce or alter the physical appearance of textual material in order to accommodate the *functional* aspects of that text.

Earlier examples drawn from medieval European history also demonstrate how the consciousness of the function of a text influenced their physical production. For example, the common *Book of Hours* was used as a text of personal meditation throughout the day for many Christians. Because this genre of book was intended to be personal, frequently used, and transportable, most editions are small and replete with various devices (clips, chains, or bracelets) to facilitate carriage. Likewise, books belonging to great rulers were often ostentatiously ornamented externally with jewels, gold encasements, and ivory, and internally with colorful illuminations often highlighting specific positive attributes or feats of the ruler. Editions of the Bible utilized by missionary monks for pedagogic purposes often contain large pictures or elaborated illuminated initials to provide a visible reference for a potentially illiterate target audience.[1] In each of these examples, the intended function of the text influenced to a certain degree the physical form of the manuscript.

It is clear that today, just as in the past, the *function* of text (be it the common usage of such a text or the desire to elicit from the audience a specific reading) directly influenced the physical features of the textual document. Such considerations affected the medium used to support the text, the physical size of the text document, the spatial layout of the text, the script used, and the presence and style of supporting imagery. The following sections draw on this kind of "form and function" analysis to explore the physical features of individual legal statutes and compilations of statutory articles in the Qin corpus discovered at Shuihudi.

Three main texts: *Xiao lü*, *Qin lü shiba zhong*, and *Qin lü zachao*

This section details the principal codicological features of the three primary manuscripts that will be examined in this chapter and the next. The purpose is to present the physical attributes of legal materials and to consider the implications of such attributes against the background of Qin legal theory. I ask how the physical attributes of the manuscripts influence the capacity of their texts to properly convey the legislative intentions of the Qin government, as discussed in Chapter 3.

Xiao lü 效律

The *Statute on Checking* or *Xiao lü* will be the focal manuscript of this chapter and the next, yet its analysis will be supplemented by reference to the *Eighteen Varieties of Qin Statutes*, *Qin lü shiba zhong* 秦律十八種, and the *Miscellaneous Transcriptions of Qin Statutes*, *Qin lü zachao* 秦律雜抄. The reason for my emphasis on the *Xiao lü* is twofold. First, the manuscript has an archeological provenance. As indicated in the previous chapter, the manuscript was discovered in the tomb of a county-level official of the Qin. Due to the duties of the interred official in life, as described in the *Recorded Annals*, *Biannian ji* 編年記, the *Xiao lü* likely represents a functional document utilized by the interred individual during his lifetime.[2] As such, this text represents a form of legal manuscript that a county-level Qin official would likely be required to engage in the course of his daily official duties.

Second, unlike the *Qin lü shiba zhong* and *Qin lü zachao*, the *Xiao lü* manuscript is the closest form of a "complete" Qin statute with an archaeological provenance that has been published. That is, the manuscript contains what appears to be nearly complete statutory text or at least a substantial portion of a statutory text, whereas the *Qin lü shiba zhong* and *Qin lü zachao* are compilation texts of excerpted statutory articles.[3] The length and content-focus of the *Xiao lü* allows one to make more generalized and systematic statements about the physical and linguistic attributes of Qin legal statutes. So what do the codicological features of the *Xiao lü* manuscript tell us about the production and dissemination of legal statutes at the county level?

The title, *Xiao lü*, is derived from two sources. First, the recto side of the initial bamboo slip contains the graph, *xiao* 效, meaning "to check, inspect, or audit." Additionally, the verso side of the initial bamboo slip contains the phrase, "being the Statute on Checking for general offices as well as counties," *wei du guan ji xian xiao lü* 為都官及縣效律. From this we can infer that the bamboo manuscript was likely rolled from textual end to beginning and could be stored so that the title of the manuscript would be visible on the outside of the initial slip. Furthermore, a reader could examine the first slip of the manuscript and know its source, audience, and general textual contents without having to unroll the entire document. The linguistic and reader-interface implications of this use of titling are dealt with in more detail in the next chapter.

The text of the *Xiao lü* is composed on a total of 60 bamboo slips. The slips appear to have been carefully prepared with the tops and bottoms of the individual slips squared off.[4] Each slip measures approximately 27 cm in length and 0.6 cm in width. Photographs taken of the manuscript reveal that the bamboo slips were originally bound together by three silken cords. The remnant traces of lines from the cords are clearly visible, as well as three sets of binding notches or *qikou* 契口 found approximately 1.3 cm from the base (bottom), 13.5 cm from the base (middle), and 1.3 cm from the top.

The existence of the binding notches not only allows us to reconstruct how the manuscript was physically formed, but it also allows us to postulate *when* the text was placed upon the manuscript medium. A key question asked of almost all early Chinese manuscripts is whether or not there is evidence that the manuscript was "first written, then bound," *xianxie houbian* 先寫後編 or "first bound, then written," *xianbian houxie* 先編後寫. For the *Xiao lü* manuscript, it appears the medium was first prepared and bound, and then the text of the statute was written down. Evidence for this comes from the fact that the graphs of the manuscript fit neatly within the margins of the upper and lower binding notches. Furthermore, there is a visibly wider vertical gap between graphs separated by the middle binding notch. Most graphs of the manuscript are vertically separated by 0.3–0.4 cm of space; however, there is often 0.6–0.8 cm of space between graphs sitting immediately above and below the central binding notch. It thus appears that whoever wrote this document did so within the physical confines of predetermined margins created by the binding devices used to physically construct the manuscript.

The *Xiao lü* text consists of several hundred legible graphs. Because the composer of this particular manuscript began writing on a fresh slip at the beginning of a new statutory article, the number of graphs written upon each slip varies from six to 33. That said, those slips that are "filled" with text typically contain 24–30 graphs. One reason for this discrepancy arises from the composer's narrowing of the gap between graphs if the number one [1] is present. That is, the gap between two graphs is narrower if one of the graphs is the numerical graph "one," *yi* 一. The sanctions mentioned in this text are often phrased as *one* or *two* suits of armor or shields, thus there are ample occurrences of bamboo slips having higher numbers of graphs. On average, however, each graph is separated from the other graphs by roughly 0.3–0.4 cm.

The graphs were written by brush in black ink, with clear bold strokes. Scholars studying the evolution of the Qin script, and particularly that of the Shuihudi corpus, believe that the script form used in these excavated documents represents a stage in the transition from seal script, *zhuan shu* 篆書 to what develops into the dominant script form of the subsequent Han dynasty, the clerical script, *lishu* 隸書.[5] The use of this quasi-clerical script—perhaps better understood as Qin clerical script—to compose the legal documents of the Shuihudi corpus has implications for our understanding of measures taken to ensure textual and interpretive consistency during the transference of legal knowledge and the production of the legal manuscripts within Qin legal culture.

Several scholars have emphasized an apparent level of "conservatism" in the calligraphic and orthographic Qin script forms. This characterization is supported by the remarkable similarities of the Qin script of the Spring and Autumn and early Warring States Periods to those forms found on extant materials from the late Western Zhou period. During this same time other polities, particularly those kingdoms in the east, were in the process of developing strong regional calligraphic and orthographic styles.[6] The conservative script form was labeled by Qiu Xigui as the standard form of Qin writing, better known as seal script; however, scholars as early as the Han dynasty noted the existence of an alternative script form that developed in Qin and eventually became what is known as the clerical script.

Both the *Hanshu* 漢書 and the preface to the *Shuowen jiezi* 說文解字 state that to accommodate the Qin desire to standardize script forms, as well as meet the needs of an increasingly document-based bureaucracy, a form of clerical script was developed.[7] For Han scholars, this development of a specialized Qin script was viewed as a direct response to the demands of the increasingly complex Qin administrative system.

Examining the extant Qin materials dated to the Spring and Autumn and the Warring States Periods, Qiu Xigui has argued that the Qin clerical script more likely developed out of a popular form of the Qin script. Through various sundry applications a "daily use" version of the standard Qin script form gradually evolved through the simplification of many seal character forms. This simplification involved the rounding of sharp angular edges of standard graphs, the shortening of longer strokes, and quite often deletion of specific strokes or sets of strokes in individual graphs.[8]

To make his point about the transformations that produced the clerical style script, Qiu Xigui highlights the orthographic changes to the character element *shui* 水, "water," in Qin excavated materials. Qiu notes that earlier graphs incorporating a water element tended to write the component in a more complex form []. The water component was later simplified in bamboo texts as three strokes [氵], and is considered by Qiu to be representative of a "proto-clerical" style orthography. The strength of Qiu Xigui's argument is illustrated by comparing formal and proto-clerical orthographies of the graph for law, *fa* 灋. On monuments and official items, such as weights and measurement tools, the graph is written in a formal seal orthography. The water component is written in its more complex form. This can be compared to the graphic form more closely associated with the clerical script mentioned by Qiu Xigui. In this form, the water component is simplified to [氵].

The extant Qin manuscripts from Shuihudi, as well as those of Qingchuan 青川, Fangmatan 放馬灘, Longgang 龍崗, Liye 里耶, and the Yuelu Academy corpus 岳麓書院秦簡 contain remarkably similar versions of this Qin clerical script—though with some slight variation—leading many scholars, such as Qiu Xigui, to consider Qin clerical script used in these manuscripts to be representative of a transitional (i.e., evolving) script phase that would later become the standardized clerical script of the Han dynasty.

The use of the Qin clerical style script for legal and administrative documents does tell us something about the compositional intent of these particular documents. The type of graphic style used conformed to a style of graph that was easy to write and that was gaining prominence as *the* administrative orthography. The fact that several other legal and administrative documents employ similar graphic forms demonstrates the ubiquity of the Qin clerical graphic form for administrative purposes. It further allows us to postulate that an official writing in this script in Location A would be able to transmit that textual document to another official in Location B and have that official read and interpret the text in a similar manner. While the use of the more stylized and complex seal script was still present in later bronze inscriptions (most notably weapons), the clerical script was becoming more visibly common to Qin administration. Having documents written in a common script potentially ensured that texts would be read consistently given the familiarity of the script to officials throughout the empire.

Qin lü shiba zhong 秦律十八種

The *Qin lü shiba zhong* or *Eighteen Varieties of Qin Statute* is an eclectic document comprising 110 individual excerpts drawn from 18 different Qin legal statutes. The manuscript was discovered on the right side of the tomb occupant. It is one of the longest extant legal manuscripts from early China. The document does not have a visible title; therefore, the editors named the manuscript, *Qin lü shiba zhong*, based on its textual contents. Although the overall text lacks a title, each statutory excerpt ends with direct reference to the title of the original "complete" statute from which it was excerpted. Furthermore, regardless of how few graphs are placed on the final bamboo slip of an excerpt, the reference title of the original statute is always located somewhere below the middle binding marker. In terms of reading and function, this practice could be understood as a quick referencing tool designed to facilitate quick perusal of the manuscript to determine which, if any, of the excerpts are pertinent to the issue confronting the official.

The 110 statutory excerpts are written on 202 bamboo slips. Each excerpt is self-contained and, like the *Xiao lü*, a fresh bamboo slip is used to begin a new excerpt. Each bamboo slip measures on average 27 cm in length and 0.5 cm in width. Similar to the *Xiao lü* manuscript, photographs of the *Qin lü shiba zhong* reveal that it too was originally bound by three sets of leather or silken cords. Three sets of binding notches are clearly visible 0.9 cm from the top, 13.8 cm from the top, and 1.0 cm from the base of the manuscript. Unlike the *Xiao lü*, however, the photographs reveal that the text was written upon the bamboo slips prior to the manuscript being bound. Evidence for this is found in several instances where the remnant traces of the binding cord overlap with graphs located in the middle and the bottom of the manuscript. Interestingly, while many graphs come close to the upper binding marker, the upper binding cord and notch rarely overlap any graphs.

Like the *Xiao lü* manuscript, the graphs of the *Qin lü shiba zhong* are written with brush strokes of black ink. There is less consistency, however, in the graphic size and spacing between graphs. While the slips average 35 graphs per bamboo slip, several slips contain over 45 graphs. Furthermore, the space between graphs ranges from 0.4 cm to 0.1 cm, and in a few extreme cases the lower and upper portions of two vertically separated graphs nearly touch. That said, despite the discrepancy in size, each graph is clearly written and the calligraphic and orthographic styles of the graphs correspond closely to the Qin-style clerical script employed in the *Xiao lü* manuscript.[9]

Qin lü zachao 秦律雜抄

The *Qin lü zachao* or *Miscellaneous Transcriptions of Qin Statutes* is another compilation text consisting of 26 statutory excerpts written on 42 bamboo slips. In many ways, it is quite similar to the *Qin lü shiba zhong*. Both are compilations containing a series of statutory extracts for which the source statute is visibly referenced. Both utilize a variety of punctuation style markers and spatial organization techniques to facilitate accurate and rapid use. And both manuscripts are written in Qin clerical style script. The two manuscripts also differ in many ways, however.

The *Qin lü zachao* was physically located between the legs of the tomb occupant. The bamboo slips averaging 27.8 cm in length and 0.6 cm in width which comprise the *Qin lü zachao* are slightly longer and wider than those of the *Qin lü shiba zhong*. Additionally, whereas the *Qin lü shiba zhong* maintains a clear distinction between individual statutory excerpts by using blank space and starting new excerpts on a new bamboo slip, the *Qin lü zachao* textual excerpts are presented in a running style and are only distinguished by [•] markers. Although both manuscripts employ clerical style scripts, the calligraphy and arrangement of the *Qin lü zachao* are neater than the *Qin lü shiba zhong*. Each graph is clearly written and consistently spaced. Related to this feature, the photographs of the manuscript support the argument that the *Qin lü zachao* was written after the physical manuscript was bound with binding cords. Like the *Xiao lü*, there is a clear increase in space between the lower and upper portions of graphs separated by the binding cord. Furthermore, there are two instances where it appears that a graph was "squeezed" into the existing space above the binding marker. Because of this, I argue that the text of the *Qin lü zachao* was written onto the bamboo slips after the slips had already been bound.

To summarize, all three manuscripts evince physical features which would facilitate consistent reading and interpretation by any individual possessing the basic level of Qin scribal training, such as the tomb occupant Xi. The compact size of the manuscripts is possibly indicative of personal use. The use of the commonly understood administrative "clerical" script demonstrates that a person with a basic understanding of the Qin script could *read* any of the three manuscripts. That is, within the Qin government different officials would be able to read and comprehend the same document because of its orthographic styling. Before turning to the use of punctuation, one additional physical feature needs to be considered: the implications of the relationship between legal thought and the preferred writing platform of bamboo slips.

Composite texts and bamboo slips

The use of bamboo slips as the preferred medium for legal statutes—at least the legal statutes appearing to be personal versions found in the Shuihudi tomb—can tell us something about the relationship between written law and legal theory in Qin China. In this section, I briefly argue that, at least in theory, the manuscript medium of bamboo slips and the composite nature of legal statutes in Qin China jointly facilitated the maintenance of accurate legal statutes and the production of compilations of legal excerpts for specific functions.

First, as seen in the previous chapter, a key requisite for producing efficacious law, at least from the perspective of Qin legal theory, is that in order for the law to be effective in maintaining social order it must resonate with the prevalent socio-political circumstances. Therefore, a legal culture needs certain institutional mechanisms in place which ensure a level of legislative flexibility when confronted with changing conditions that potentially curtail an extant statute's functional efficacy. Another related requisite is the maintenance of textual accuracy of individual statutes which have been transmitted in written form across large distances and subsequently copied and/or re-copied. If laws are miscopied, then the Qin government's requirement for consistency of interpretation and application would have become impossible. A statutory excerpt analyzed in the previous chapter provides that:

Example 4.1—*Qin lü shiba zhong*—Slip 199
歲讎辟律於御史　　　尉雜

Annually, compare compiled statutes with the Chief Censor. Miscellanea of the Commandant

The potential relationship between this statutory article and the decision to use bamboo slips as a medium for producing legal statutes and statutory excerpts can be interpreted as follows. First, the requirement that compiled statutes were to be audited for accuracy on an annual basis meant that the possessor of the statutes needed a way to alter statutory provisions that were deemed inaccurate. Manuscripts comprised bamboo slips bound with leather or silken binding cords would be much easier to amend or correct than those produced on bolts of silk or placards of wood. Various utensils certainly existed to make small amendments to the latter forms of manuscript; however, the continued risk of confusion and the need for larger scale alterations could prove quite problematic for a scribe using such writing platforms. By using bamboo slips, the scribe could simply unbind and remove the bamboo slips containing the inaccurate provisions. The space available for the corrected provision would not be an issue regardless of the size of the correction. If the number of graphs in the correction corresponded to the excised provision, then the scribe could simply remove the affected slip or slips. If, however, the corrected provision substantially altered the size of the statutory article, then the entire article could be excised and rewritten. Most Qin statutory articles run one to four bamboo slips and this would be significantly easier to rewrite and rebind, than, for example, scraping off large sections of text from a wooden placard and attempting to squeeze in the newly amended provision to the restricted space available. With bamboo slips, one could accurately and clearly introduce the newly corrected statutory provision into the overall text with minimal disruption to the overall structure of the manuscript. Furthermore, if one were to need to rewrite the entire manuscript, there is the increased potential for incorrect transcribing of the manuscript's text. Likewise, as laws changed or were altered centrally, a scribe could easily alter one or a series of affected slips, re-bind the manuscript, and use the bulk of the previous manuscript.

The second implication of the purposive use of bamboo slips for legal statutes is the potential production of editable compilation texts. One of the most interesting features of early Chinese manuscript culture that has come to light since the increased discovery of excavated manuscripts is the apparent composite nature of many early texts. Excavated manuscript versions of the *Laozi* 老子 and the *Yijing* 易經, for example, possess different arrangements from their received counterparts. As written documents, these two works consist of short articles, each possessing a level of inter-textual independence. When transcribed onto the medium of bamboo slips, the short article format allows the individual textual units to be positioned and repositioned based on interest and need. As part of a larger argument on the componential nature of early Chinese texts, William Boltz has argued that the different organizations of the *Yijing* demonstrate a level of randomness; however, this randomness should not be construed as indicative of a lack of internal order, but is simply evidence that these various arrangements represent alternative logics or functional purposes.[10] In terms of law, particularly written law, the utilization of a compositional structure for legal statutes wherein individual articles are constructed to possess a level of inter-textual independence allows an official to potentially transcribe only those elements of a statute relevant to his government position.[11] Evidence for such a potential practice could be inferred from the following provision:

> Example 4.2—*Qin lü shiba zhong*—Slip 187
> 縣各告都官在其縣者寫其官之用律　　內史雜
>
> Counties shall each inform those offices in their county to write the statutes used by their offices. Miscellanea of the *Nei shi*

As shown, the use of bamboo slips to copy officially sanctioned legal statutes would have greatly facilitated the correction of inaccurate texts or the updating of individual portions of statutory articles without the need to rewrite the entire text or a substantial portion of it and with minimal disruption to the physical form of the manuscript. Furthermore, as will be shown in the next chapter, Qin legal statutes were composed of numerous individual statutory articles. These individual articles could be excerpted from the overall text of the statute and be used to produce compilation texts based on the needs of the particular official. If those needs changed, then the compilation text would be easily altered by adding additional bamboo slips or removing bamboo slips which had become irrelevant. The remainder of this chapter will focus on the extremely important visible device of punctuation that was utilized by the individual who composed the Shuihudi legal documents to ensure that the textual units of the manuscripts were *read* properly.

Law, writing, and punctuation

Punctuation is a ubiquitous linguistic device used in writing today for the purposes of facilitating desired readings of textual materials. But how important is punctuation in the context of the law? Furthermore, in early China where the use of punctuation devices was limited, were such devices considered important as guides for textual interpretation?

In 2002, a Canadian company, Rogers Communication Inc., signed a multi-year deal with another company, Aliant Inc., for the use-rights to telecommunications service poles. The drafters for Rogers believed they had constructed a contract locking in a fixed rental rate for five years with an option for additional multi-year extensions which would also retain the same fixed rental rate. To Rogers' surprise, in 2005 Aliant suddenly cancelled the contract and raised the rental rates, a move that would cost Rogers an estimated 2.13 million dollars in additional rental charges.[12]

The lawyers of Aliant cited page seven of the original contract which stated that the agreement "shall continue in force for a period of five years from the date it is made, and thereafter for successive five year terms, unless and until terminated by one year prior notice in writing by either party."[13] Aliant claimed that, based on the rules of English grammar, the inclusion of the second comma after the phrase "successive five year terms," did allow the cancellation conditions to apply not only to the successive terms, but also to the initial five-year period. Rogers claimed that was not their original intention and that Aliant was intentionally mis-reading the text. Rogers wanted the cancellation clause to apply only to the successive five-year terms, not the initial five years. The Canadian Radio-television and Telecommunications Commission (CRTC), however, sided with Aliant, stating that according to the rules of proper grammar, the inclusion of the comma does allow the termination of the contract with a one-year notice.[14]

The intent of this brief excursus into modern contract law is merely to show that punctuation can play an extremely important role in the interpretation of written legal texts, and, by extension, its use must be carefully considered when composing such documents. In general, any written text lacks agency. Once it leaves the hands of its author the original textual meaning is subjected to a variety of interpretations formulated by its readers as they engage with the written words. Such interpretations can potentially misrepresent the author's intended meaning or worse completely alter it.

This phenomenon poses serious problems when composing written law and legal documents, the purpose of which is to convey clear, unambiguous meaning to any person reading the text. As such, their drafters, as well as the authors of most genres, must employ specific "strategies that are meant to produce effects, dictate a posture, and oblige the reader."[15] Within a legal context, such strategies are employed so that interpretative variability and textual ambiguity are minimized resulting in a written document capable of accurately transmitting information and meaning between the sender/author and receiver/reader without the physical presence of the sender. Authors of many genres utilize a variety of conventions to accomplish this, such as a common orthography, standard layout, common word choice and syntax, as well as punctuation.

Defining punctuation in the West: value for the Chinese context?

The use of punctuation within written texts has developed into an essential feature of modern Western orthography and syntax. The historian Julian Brown discusses the development of Western punctuation forms beginning with ancient Greek *paragraphos*[16] to the more recognizable period [.], comma [,], semi-colon [;], colon [:], and question mark [?]. Specifically, he traces the evolution of punctuation's function within western Europe from a heavily elocutionary role (i.e., as a guide to proper oral reading, such as notes of intonation or pause found in hymnals or recitation manuals) to that of a syntactic marker designed to aid reading, but not necessarily reading-aloud.[17]

The earliest forms of punctuation found in medieval western European manuscripts are typically divided by modern paleographers into two systems known as "punctuation by *distinctiones* and punctuation by *positurae*."[18] Within the former system, words of a text written in *scriptura continua* (i.e., a continuous stream of text wherein individual words are not separated by space) were disambiguated by placing a penned dot, or *punctus*, between words. Such early texts were intended to be read aloud; therefore the *punctus* was typically placed to separate individual words which could have been confused (i.e., jointly read) thereby facilitating correct readings. The vertical alignment of the *punctus* vis-à-vis the written letters (i.e., low, median, high) came to indicate the strength of a pause when reading aloud.[19] Within the Insular region, the Anglo-Saxon and Irish readership of Latin-based Christian texts required a higher level of visual indication of correct reading than did their Latin-derived linguistic contemporaries, such as the Spanish, French, and Italians. This necessity for further disambiguation led to the development of word separation and an increased syntactic function of the *punctus*.[20]

The *distinctiones* system of punctuation was a simple method of clarifying meaning (distinguishing words) and vocalization (oral pause). Punctuation is rarely used in early English legal statutes; however, whenever punctuation was necessary scribes often employed the *punctus* which was primarily attached to vocalized portions of written legal documents. By CE 1066, however, there is ample evidence of the *punctus* functioning within legal texts, such as the *Domesday Book*, solely as a syntactic marker disambiguating sentences or phrases.[21] Here, the distinction between correct and incorrect readings held legal consequences for the parties involved, and as a result *punctus*-based markers were added to ensure the reader interpreted the written text properly and consistently.

The *distinctiones* system of punctuation remained in use until the late twelfth century CE, and its use partially overlapped with the other system known as punctuation by *positurae*. This system emerged during the late eighth century CE and is distinguished from *distinctiones*—which indicated pause strength by the height of a single mark form—by its use of multiple symbol types to indicate the strength of a pause, as well as correct intonation when reciting. For example, the *punctus interrogativus* indicated a particular length of pause, a particular vocal intonation, and a dual semantic value of a sentence end and that the previous sentence was an interrogative.[22] Thus, the diverse symbols within the *positurae* system evinced specialized oral and semantic values.

As time progressed, the social function of written texts evolved. Along with this evolution one can see similar alterations in the function of punctuation. Noting these changing roles, M.B. Parkes writes that during the late medieval period

> the manifestation of language had begun to acquire a new status which was more independent of that of its spoken counterpart. Just as pauses had indicated phrasing in oral delivery, which would bring out the meaning of a text, so in manuscripts from the end of the seventh century onwards punctuation came to be used as a signal to the eye of the silent, and thus to facilitate the communication of the message of a text.[23]

Through an examination of two manuscript editions of Bede's *Historia ecclesiastica gentis Anglorum*—one from the mid-eighth century and the other from the mid-eleventh century—Parkes notes that when the later edition is compared to the earlier edition, one clearly sees an increased use of punctuation and an increased number of punctuation forms. He argued that the eleventh century "addition of further marks to the repertory of punctuation" to the earlier edition, which only sparingly utilized a few *punctus* markers, "provided new signals which enabled a reader to apprehend the relationships between these elements, and to appraise their function in communicating the sense of the text."[24] For Parkes, the difference in the use of punctuation evident in these two manuscripts demonstrates that by the time of the later edition punctuation was

> no longer merely a guide to the oral performance of the written word but has already become an essential component of the written medium, which contributes directly to the reader's comprehension of the message of the text. More subtle notation has made possible more secure interpretations of a text.[25]

Though punctuation certainly maintained its elocutionary function as an indicator of proper vocalization within certain medieval texts, one sees, however, a gradual transition as the syntactic and semantic functions of punctuation marks as guides to comprehending the correct meaning of a given text become increasingly emphasized.[26]

This evolution in the form and function of punctuation in Western contexts produced numerous, ongoing academic debates over the "true" definition of punctuation. Simply put, one side retains a continued emphasis on the historical and present day link between punctuation's elocutionary and syntactic roles, while the other side is primarily interested in the syntactic/semantic importance of punctuation. One's stance on these debates dictates both how one conceptually defines punctuation and how one studies its development and use within a particular context.

Noting the historical development, as well as the ongoing debates between the elocutionary and syntactic schools of thought over the "true" function of punctuation, Julian Brown advocates a rather wide, umbrella definition of punctuation as "the use of spacing, conventional signs and certain typographical devices as aids to the understanding and correct reading, both silently and aloud, of handwritten and printed texts."[27]

Brown's rather broad, catch-all definition of punctuation is quite useful when comparing the variety of non-Western writing conventions serving various syntactic functions analogous to Western punctuation. It allows for consideration of both elocutionary and syntactic functions of punctuation. The importance of punctuation in Brown's definition has less to do with determining its link to orality and more to do with its function as a visual guide indicative of a correct reading (whether oral or silent). Furthermore, the definition does not restrict the scope of inquiry to mere orthographic forms of punctuation. That is, one can also consider page layout, spacing features, and even the shape of the media used as contributing a syntactic-punctuation function to the text.

Few studies emphasize the importance of "virtual" punctuation. This oversight would fail to consider, for example, the syntactic value of the layout *per cola et commata* in St. Jerome's edition of the Bible.[28] Nor would the formatting and blank space utilized by the ancient Greeks when inscribing written laws onto public architecture be considered a "true" form of punctuation intended to aid the reader in clearly and unambiguously comprehending the meaning of the inscribed laws. Relatedly, by construing the definition of punctuation so as to include only orthographic forms, one is unable to consider the potential influence that the text's foundation medium might have on the conscious employment of spatial strategies to ensure a proper or intended reading. Indeed, a broad understanding of punctuation as a visual tool intended to aid the reader in comprehending the text s/he is reading (silently or aloud) is a valuable way of approaching early Chinese punctuation.

The problematics of Chinese punctuation

Punctuation in premodern China is a rather complex subject, and one typically frustrated by a dearth of scholarly attention. It is further problematized by the conventional assertion that modern or true punctuation was introduced via the West, and became systematically representative of grammatical syntax only after the Chinese began using Western printing techniques and orthographic conventions.[29] This is perhaps due in part to the apparent lack of orthographic forms of punctuation in most woodblock print editions of texts comprising the traditional Chinese corpus. Most students of classical Chinese at some point confront the daunting and frustrating task of reading unpunctuated Song dynasty texts and learning the useful practice of sentential parsing, *duanju* 斷句. This training in classical/literary Chinese further reinforces the conventional knowledge of a lack of punctuation by emphasizing the syntactic role of grammatical particles, *xuci* 虛辭, in disambiguating sentential form and context.[30] Upon closer examination, however, one finds evidence of particular orthographic forms serving a syntactic-punctuating function within a variety of texts from the early, medieval, and late imperial periods.

The forms and functions of punctuation found in the Qin Shuihudi corpus, particularly those within the legal manuscripts, have yet to receive a systematic analysis. Past scholars have certainly noted the presence of various orthographic forms of punctuation, yet such attention is commonly made with an ambivalent attitude towards the interpretative value of such markings when attempting to understand the form and function of a legal statute.[31] Indicative of an approach which minimizes the syntactic/interpretive value of punctuation marks, Derk Bodde claimed that the "dots" of the Shuihudi legal texts should only be understood as the most rudimentary markers of sentence division and that it would be a stretch to even consider such markings to be "proto-punctuation."[32] Furthermore, the primary attention of scholars, particularly paleographers, is focused on the purely orthographic forms and little has been said of the interpretive implications of both orthographic and non-orthographic punctuation.[33]

The remainder of this chapter examines the forms and functions of orthographic and non-orthographic punctuation found in the legal manuscripts of

Shuihudi with specific reference to the *Xiao lü* manuscript. The purpose is twofold. The first is to systematically examine the various forms of punctuation found in legal statutes of Qin and to ascertain what linguistic functions they served. The second aim is to consider what specifically the presence of punctuation in such manuscripts can tell us about the conscious use of embedded visual aids for reading, and the production of complex texts designed to be consistently interpreted by multiple readers.

Punctuating the law in Qin legal culture

The legal manuscripts of the *Shuihudi* corpus contain four different types of early Chinese punctuation (one spatial and four orthographic): blank space, titles, the bold black dot [•], the double horizontal marker [=], and the hook-shaped or "L" marker [∟].

Though each of these punctuation forms serves specific syntactic functions, some can be functionally interchangeable. For example, blank space is used to separate topically distinct textual units in the texts of the *Xiao lü* and *Qin lü shiba zhong* manuscripts, yet the bold black dot serves the same function in the *Qin lü zachao* manuscript. Such a phenomenon is not uncommon in other manuscript cultures. Javier Calle-Martin and Antonio Miranda-Garcia note that European Renaissance punctuation practices evidence a high level of arbitrariness over the orthographic form and its syntactic function. Furthermore, despite the increased use of printing during the Elizabethan age (r. CE 1558–1603) in England, Calle and Miranda show that within legal texts of the period, punctuation forms have a relatively high level of interchangeability. That is, one punctuation form may be used for a variety of functions in a single document or within a single document two or more punctuation forms might be used to serve the same syntactic function. For example, within legal warrants a period, comma, semi-colon, or virgule [/] were interchangeably used to distinguish enumerated units of a sentence.[34]

In the analysis below, I will focus primarily on those punctuation forms found in the *Xiao lü* manuscript: blank space, the double horizontal marker, and the hook-shaped marker.[35] As mentioned in the previous chapter, the *Xiao lü*

Table 4.1 Punctuation statistics for the *Xiao lü* manuscript

Type	*Total # of examples*	*# of slips containing example*	*Percentage of ms containing examples (based on # of slips)*
Written and/or blank space	52	41	68.3
Blank space	28 (?)	28	46.6
Written punctuation (total)	24	16	26.6
[=] marker	13	8	13.3
[∟] marker	10	7	11.6
MS title	1	1	1.6

manuscript comprises 60 bamboo slips. Of these slips, 41 utilize some form of punctuation, while 16 specifically use a written form of punctuation. The bold black dot does not appear in the manuscript, but comparative reference will be made to it where necessary.

Blank space disambiguating individual textual units

Blank space is perhaps one of the oldest punctuation devices utilized in early Chinese manuscript culture. Oracle bone inscription, *jiagu wen* 甲骨文, examples dating to the mid- and late Shang dynasty indicate the employment of blank space to disambiguate individual, and often times independent, textual units inscribed upon the same medium.[36] This use of blank space to distinguish individual textual units continued on a variety of media through the Warring States Period,[37] and later Qin and Han dynasty examples of this phenomenon are commonly found in legal and administrative texts written upon bamboo slips and wooden placards.

For the legal manuscripts contained within the Shuihudi corpus, blank space is utilized to form two distinct textual layouts, both of which serve a similar syntactic function of disambiguating individual textual units. The first layout design [Text End+Blank Space+Source Title+Blank Space] is employed throughout the legal manuscript entitled *Qin lü shiba zhong*.[38] In this manuscript, the individual statute excerpts (consisting of one or multiple bamboo slips) form discrete textual units. This is indicated through the use of blank space in conjunction with a source title for each excerpt.[39] After the last graph of a textual excerpt, a space roughly equivalent to three to five character spaces is left blank. This blank space is followed by a record of the source title. Any remaining space on the bamboo slip coming after the source title is also left blank and the subsequent independent, textual excerpt then begins on a new bamboo slip.

This particular use of blank space in the *Qin lü shiba zhong* performs two disambiguative functions. First, the space between the excerpted text and the source title indicates to the reader the end of the excerpted text and that the graph or phrase following the blank space is referencing the excerpt source. That is, the blank space syntactically functions as a text segmenting device indicating to the reader a distinction between the "body of the text" and its sub-/title. Second, the blank space left after the source title clearly indicates the *complete* end of the independent textual unit (inclusive of source title), and signals that the text found on the subsequent bamboo slip belongs to a separate textual unit to which it does not necessarily have any topical or contextual association.

Like the *Qin lü shiba zhong*, the physical and textual layout of the *Xiao lü* manuscript makes extensive and consistent use of blank space to disambiguate independent textual units. Each textual unit represents an individual legal article of which 30 comprise the overall statute. The text of these legal articles can run from a single bamboo slip to as many as five bamboo slips. Similar to the *Qin lü shiba zhong*, in the *Xiao lü* the end of an individual textual unit is indicated by leaving the remainder of the bamboo slip blank and beginning the subsequent textual unit/legal article at the top of a new bamboo slip.

Example 4.3 Illustration of the use of blank space + title to disambiguate individual legal articles in the *Qin lü shiba zhong*—Slips 63–65

Excerpt source:	*Jin bu lü*		*Cang lü*
Slip #:	*65*	*64*	*63*
	乃發用之百姓市用錢美惡雜之勿敢異　　金布	官府受錢者千錢一畚以丞令印印不盈千者亦封印之錢善不善雜實之出錢獻封丞令	畜雞離倉用犬者畜犬期足猪雞之息子不用者賣之別計其錢　　倉

When comparing Examples 4.3 and 4.4, it is clear that the interpretive implications of the use of blank space as a form of punctuation differ slightly between the manuscripts of the *Xiao lü* and the *Qin lü shiba zhong*. The latter text is an eclectic assemblage of textual excerpts from different legal statutes. Within such a legal document, blank space works in conjunction with a source title, thereby serving a dual syntactic function of distinguishing the main body of the textual excerpt from the source title and distinguishing textually, and potentially categorically, independent statute excerpts from each other. Related to this last point, the layout of the manuscript contents assists in signaling (a) the eclectic and incomplete nature of the individual excerpts, and (b) that additional information on a given topic may be

Example 4.4 Illustration of the use of blank space to disambiguate individual legal articles in the *Xiao lü*

Art. #	*FOUR*			*THREE*		*TWO*	*ONE*
Slip #	*7*	*6*	*5*	*4*	*3*	*2*	*1*
	分升一 以上升不正廿分升以上黃金衡纍不正半銖以上貲各一盾	上鈞不正四兩以上斤不正三銖以上半斗不正少半升以上參不正六	斗不正半升以上貲一甲不盈半升到少半升貲一盾半石不正八兩以	不正二升以上貲一甲不盈二升到一升貲一盾	衡石不正十六兩以上貲官嗇夫一甲不盈十六兩到八兩貲一盾桶	官嗇夫冗吏皆共償不備之貨而入贏	為都官及縣效律其有贏不備物值之以其價多者罪之勿纍
# of graphs	28	28	28	19	27	15	24

found in the original source statute.[40] In contrast, the *Xiao lü* manuscript contains a single legal statute comprising 30 distinct legal articles. Within this type of legal document, blank space (*sans* source title) merely serves a singular function of disambiguating individual, yet categorically related (i.e., not fully independent) legal articles which together form a larger, integral text.

From this we can conclude that when composing, and/or copying, a written text comprising single or multiple written legal statutes (or statute excerpts), this particular Qin scribe often employed blank space to *visually* distinguish individual textual units.[41] Furthermore, depending on the type of legal document (e.g., a single legal statute or an eclectic assemblage of excerpts), blank space could also function to indicate the existence of a categorical, symbiotic relationship between individual textual units, or when combined with individualized source titles, a lack thereof. A similar practice of using blank space is noted in the earliest written laws of ancient Greece. Excavated legal statutes inscribed on marble bricks were commonly written in the "boustrophedon" style. That is, the initial line of the statute was written right to left. Upon coming to the end of the brick medium, the second (lower) line was written left to right, and so on. In an excavated law from Dreros, the initial provision is written in three lines of boustrophedon style, and the third line of text (written left to right) only takes up half of the available space. Instead of using the remaining space, the mason moved down and began a fourth line (restarting the left to right direction) to indicate the start of a new provision. The mason also distinguished the two separate provisions by adding a special sign (⧖) to the beginning of the fourth line.[42]

Dreros Boustrophedon style and multi-provision text

[=] mark indicating **hewen** *(ligature) and* **chongwen** *(duplication)*

One of the most common forms of written punctuation found in the Shuihudi corpus is the [=] marker. These markers, composed of a parallel set of two small horizontal lines, are frequently placed at the bottom right of the graph being modified. The presence of such marks indicates that the graph to which they are attached should be read as either a *hewen* or a *chongwen*. I argue that both usages are present in the *Xiao lü* manuscript, and examples drawn from the text are discussed below.

Hewen fuhao 合文符號

In early Chinese manuscript culture, the placement of a [=] marker as a *hewen fuhao* functions to signify to the reader that the *single* written character under which the marker is positioned actually represents *two* distinct characters and words. There are two varieties of its usage. In the first, the *hewen* graph is actually two graphs written jointly [e.g., 卡= (上下)]. In the second usage, a single graph represents two distinct words, one of which is orthographically embedded within the *hewen* graph [e.g., 夫= (大夫)].[43] Examples of [=] indicating a *hewen* are found in several early Chinese texts dating as far back as Western Zhou bronze inscriptions, and the recent stream of publications of Warring States Period bamboo documents from the kingdom of Chu 楚 contain a high frequency of the [=] marker serving a similar function.[44] On the other side of the historical spectrum, numerous examples of [=] indicating a *hewen* reading in medieval Chinese manuscripts demonstrate both the continued use of *hewen* graphs in Chinese manuscript culture, as well as the continued function of [=] as its orthographic indicator of a specific syntactic/semantic reading.[45]

Although the Shuihudi corpus contains several examples of *hewen* graphs [the most common being 夫= (大夫)], the *Xiao lü* manuscript, however, contains only a single graph contentiously argued to represent a *hewen* compound. An analysis of this graph and its [=] marker demonstrates that the use of punctuation markers in early Chinese manuscripts does not always facilitate the reading of a passage by modern scholars. The graph occurs twice (or thrice) on the same slip. Below I will offer two transcriptions and translations based on the two possible readings of the graph *lü*, ⿰方⿱𠂉衣.

Example 4.5—*Xiao lü*—Slip 41, Article 18
(A)
甲⿰方⿱𠂉衣札贏其籍及不備者入其贏⿰方⿱𠂉衣_(旅衣)札而責其不備⿰方⿱𠂉衣_(旅衣)札

With armor, if suit component scales exceed their register, as well as when they fall short, take in the excess suit component scales; but, charge the shortage of suit component scales.[46]

(B)
甲⿰方⿱𠂉衣(旅旅)札贏其籍及不備者入其贏⿰方⿱𠂉衣_(旅旅)札而責其不備⿰方⿱𠂉衣_(旅旅)札

When parts of a suit of armour or scales are in excess of their register as well as when they are short, the excess parts and scales are to be entered, whereas parts and scales that are short are charged.[47]

There is some disagreement over the precise reading of this particular article. Much of the debate stems from ambiguity over the meaning of the graph ⿰方⿱𠂉衣 and the syntactic/semantic function of the [=] marker in relation to it. Li Xueqin argues that the two graphs ⿰方⿱𠂉衣 and their corresponding [=] markers should be understood as *hewen*, or orthographic composite, graphs representing [⿰方⿱𠂉衣-(旅衣)]. Li states that

> with the armor of ancient times, that which was worn on the upper body was referred to as *upper lü*, *shang lü* 上旅; that which was worn on the lower body was referred to as *lower lü*, *xia lü* 下旅; and armor scales were referred to as *zha* 札.[48]

Li and the Shuihudi editors are insistent upon a *hewen* reading of ⿰方⿱𠂉衣 due to its componential structure, but neither explains what 旅衣札 actually means, how it is different from 旅, or the potential relevance of the missing [=] marker after the first instance of the graph. Furthermore, the *baihua* 白話 translation of the passage made by the Shuihudi editors does not reflect the *hewen* reading as they only mention 旅札.[49] That is, their modern translation only considers this article to be discussing the scales for suits of armor.

Alternatively, Hulsewé, acknowledges the graph to comprise two parts *yan* 㫃 and *yi* 衣, yet reads the graph as simply representing the word *lü* 旅, "a piece of a suit of armor." Like Li Xueqin and the Shuihudi editors, Hulsewé also supports his reading by reference to the *Zhouli* 周禮 in which the graph 旅 indicates two separate sections (upper and lower) of a single suit of armor.[50] Hulsewé argues that all three ⿸㫃衣 graphs should have a corresponding [=] marker, but for some unknown reason the marker was omitted from the first instance of the graph. For the editors and Hulsewé, the [=] marker is not indicative of a *hewen*, but instead should be read as a *chongwen* marker. That is, the marker would indicate to the reader that the graph ⿸㫃衣 = should be read not as [⿸㫃衣 = (旅衣)] but as [旅=(旅旅)]. Therefore, the first *lü* graph should represent an upper or lower component of a suit of armor, while the second *lü* should be understood as the leading graph in the bi-syllabic compound *lüzha* 旅札 or "armor scale." Additionally, Hulsewé notes that the initial phrase *lüzha* lacks a [=] marker. In his opinion, this represents a scribal mistake and one should read all three instances as having a conjoined [=] marker.

The reading of Hulsewé is perhaps strengthened if one takes into account Qin orthography related the graph *lü* 旅. An examination of several instances of the graph 旅 in the Shuihudi corpus and subsequently discovered Qin manuscripts demonstrates a rather common Qin practice of writing the graph *lü* 旅 as ⿸㫃衣. As such, one could potentially follow Hulsewé and not to read the graph ⿸㫃衣 in conjunction with a [=] marker.

This debate demonstrates the difficulties posed by Qin orthographic and punctuation practices for modern day paleographers. Other texts in the Shuihudi corpus, however, do contain clear examples of [=] markers serving to indicate a *hewen* reading of a particular graphic form.

Example 4.6—*Qin lü zachao*—Slip 7—*hewen* marker [=]
●故夫_[大夫]斬首者遷

A former *dafu* who severs heads is to be banished.

Example 4.7—*Qin lü zachao*—Slip 9—*hewen* marker [=]
●驀_[驀馬]五尺八寸以上不勝任奔摯不如令縣司馬貲二甲令丞各一甲

With riding, if horses that are five *chi* eight *cun*[51] or above are not suitable for service, or when running their trappings are not in accordance with the ordinances, then the county Minister of Horses is to be fined two suits of armor. The Prefect and his assistants are each to be fined one suit of armor.

Example 4.6 contains one of the more common *hewen* usages in the Shuihudi corpus. Here the single graph *fu* 夫 is used in conjunction with a [=] marker to indicate that the graph should be read as *da fu* 大夫. The reader would register the meaning of the *hewen* from the fact that the graph *da* 大 is contained within the orthography of the graph *fu* 夫.

This punctuation convention is made clearer when we consider the *hewen* found in Example 4.7. Here the graph *mo* 驀 is followed by the [=] marker from which the reader can, with the help of context, comprehend that this individual graph represents two graphs. The *Shuowen jiezi* 說文解字 gives the meaning of *mo* 驀 as "to mount or ride a horse," *shang ma ye* 上馬也. The graph *mo* consists of two components: *mo* 莫, from which the graph derives its pronunciation, and *ma* 馬 providing a semantic association to "horse," *cong ma mo sheng* 從馬莫聲.[52] Given the context of this statute article which involves the measurements of something, reference to trappings for riding and to the Minister of Horses 司馬, the reader would thus interpret the [=] marker to indicate that the graph *mo* 驀 should be read as a *hewen* for *mo ma* 驀馬 "When riding, horses…" This is indeed the process followed by the editors of the Shuihudi corpus and Hulsewé.[53]

In terms of reading clarity and the potential for legal ambiguity, the use of a *hewen* demonstrates that a reader/user of this manuscript and this particular legal article would need to be familiar with the construction and placement of *hewen* graphs as a scribal practice within Qin legal texts.[54] The reader would need to comprehend that *hewen* graph A_indicates graphs/words A+B or that complex *hewen* graph C_indicates graphs/words A+B.

Chongwen fuhao 重文符號

The other syntactic use of the [=] marker is as an indicator of a *chongwen* reading. That is, the mark, when placed under a *chongwen* graph, indicates that this particular graph should be *read* twice, even though it is only *written* once [e.g., 令_ (令令)]. In such an instance, one can make an argument for an economy of both space and time, as a single graph is used to represent two words.[55] The use of *chongwen* graphs dates as far back as Shang dynasty oracle bone inscriptions, and evidence of its continued use within Chinese manuscript culture can be found during the medieval period and later.[56] The Shuihudi corpus contains multiple examples of *chongwen* graphs, and the *Xiao lü* manuscript makes frequent use of *chongwen* signifiers for single graph repetition, as well as multi-graph phrase repetition.[57]

> Example 4.8—*Xiao lü*—Article 8, Slip 17
> 官嗇夫免縣令_(令)人效其官_(官)嗇夫坐效以貲大嗇夫及丞除
>
> When the *sefu* of the office is dismissed, the County **Prefect_ orders** another person to verify/check his **office_**. The sefu of the **office** is liable for the fines resultant of check. The grand *sefu* and his assistant are exempt

In this example, the [=] serves as a duplication marker indicating the repetition of the two graphs *ling* 令 and *guan* 官. To understand the meaning of the duplication, however, the reader cannot simply rely upon the [=] marker. The context of the repetition is necessary to understand the specific meaning of each graph that is repeated. In the first case, for example, the repeated graph is *ling* 令. Its initial usage is as the final graph in the binomial official title *xianling* 縣令 or "County Prefect." The *ling* component of the compound is indicated for duplication [=], yet the duplicated graph does not syntactically represent a noun, but instead is to be read in the verbal form as *ling*, "to order." So the duplication marker in this particular instance indicates to the reader that the single graph of a binomial compound is to be repeated. Then, the reader must take context into account in order to understand that the repeated graph should be read as a *verb*.

The second usage of [=] indicates that the graph *guan* 官 is to be repeated. Here the initial graph is a noun *guan* meaning a specific county office which another person, sent by the County Prefect, is ordered to verify/check. This graph is followed by the duplication marker. In this case, the repeated graph 官 also refers to the specific county office, yet it is linked in a tri-character phrase which modifies the type of *sefu* (i.e., 官嗇夫, the *sefu* of the aforementioned office). Thus, when combining the [=] marker with the context, it becomes clear to the reader that the duplicated graph refers in both instances to the county office specified at the beginning of the article. In the second instance, however, the syntax is slightly different as the *guan* is qualifying the type of *sefu*. In each of the examples from this particular passage, the [=] marker certainly signals to the reader that the graph should be duplicated, yet it remains for the reader to infer any change in syntax or meaning from the context of the duplicated graph. One could possibly argue that the use of such a marker could potentially increase ambiguity if the intended meaning of the duplicated graph was not clearly indicated from context.

Example 4.9—*Xiao lü*, Article 13, Slip 33
其有所疑謁縣_嗇_夫_(縣嗇夫)令人復度

If there exists that which is doubtful, report to the **County_** ***se_fu_***. The **County** ***sefu*** will order another person to re-measure

Here the three duplication markers are utilized to indicate a tri-character noun phrase comprised of the graphs *xian* 縣, *se* 嗇, and *fu* 夫. As with the sequential use of [=] in bi-character compounds, the reader of this sentence would have to determine whether or not the phrase should be read as AABBCC or ABCABC. The commonality of the phrase and the context of the sentence would likely aid the interpretive process.

The use of [=] markers for common bi- or tri-character compounds would not be overly problematic; however, some legal texts within the Shuihudi corpus do contain a few rather extreme examples of the use of *chongwen* markers for sentential or phrasal repetition. In such instances, the reader must correctly interpret the lengthy duplicated phrase as ABCDEABCDE or AABBCCDDEE.[58]

Example 4.10—*Qin lü zachao*, Slip 38–39—phrasal repetition with the [=] marker
●捕盜律曰捕人相移以受爵者耐●求盜勿令=送=逆=為= 它= (令送逆為它令送逆為它)事者貲二甲

●The statute on Arresting Thieves states: "Those transferring arrested persons in order to receive rank are to be shaved. ● Thief catchers ought not

> be **ordered to escort or receive on behalf of others**. Those who **order [them] to escort or receive on behalf of others** are to be fined two suits of armor.

The [=] marker within Qin legal manuscripts performs several functions. On the one hand, it can represent a *hewen* graph. The inclusion of such a graph would necessitate a consciousness of specific writing conventions in the reader/user of the text. Such a reader would need to understand which graph(s) were represented by the *hewen* and which words those graphs indicated.

On the other hand, when representing a *chongwen* graph, the [=] marker would need to signal to the reader several layers of information. First, which graphs are to be replicated? Second, in what order should these duplicated graphs be assigned? Third, the [=] marker would signal that a consideration of the duplicated graph's context is necessary to determine whether or not there is a semantic shift in the meaning of one of the duplicated graphs? When combined with the fact that the [=] marker is also used for the *hewen*—replete with its interpretive requirements—we can say that while the use of the marker does attempt to facilitate the reading of a manuscript, it also conveys limited information, the rest of which relies upon the knowledge of the reader.

Sentential and phrasal segmenting indicated by [∟] markers

The third and final form of punctuation that I will discuss is the [∟] or hook-shaped marker. This type of punctuation marker is commonly found in a variety of early Chinese manuscript media ranging from Eastern Zhou bronzes and Warring States politico-philosophical bamboo manuscripts, to Han dynasty legal and administrative texts written on bamboo slips or wooden placards.[59] This marker was typically employed within the Warring States Period bamboo manuscripts to disambiguate distinct textual components within a larger textual unit. As such, it often indicates an internal distinction between different topics, sentences, or phrases.

> Example 4.11—*Cao Mie zhi chen*, Slips 6–10—[∟] marker indicating internal distinctions[60]
> 莊公曰昔池胉語寡人曰 [6 partial] 君子得之失之天命∟今異於而言∟ 曹蔑曰 [7] 亡以異於臣之言君弗盡∟臣聞之曰君 [8b] 子以賢稱而失之天命∟以亡道稱而沒身就死亦天命不然君子以賢稱害有弗 [9] 得以亡道稱 害有弗失∟ … [10 partial][61]
>
> Duke Zhuang said, "Previously, Chi Bo informed this deficient person saying (6) 'Whether a junzi obtains them or loses them is mandated by Heaven.' ∟ Now this differs from your words." ∟ Cao Mie said, (7) "There is nothing that differs from your servant's words. Milord has not exhausted it. ∟ I have heard it said that, when a junzi (8b) is said to be worthy, yet loses it, [it] is mandated by Heaven. ∟ When [a junzi] is said to be without

> the Way, yet lives a full life before dying, [it] is also mandated by Heaven. If it were not so, how else could a junzi said to be worthy not (9) obtain it and [one] said to have lost the Way not lose it?" ㄴ (10)

Within this dialogue between Duke Zhuang of Lu (魯莊公, r. 693–662 BCE) and his minister Cao Mie, excerpted from a Warring States Period Chu bamboo manuscript,[62] we find repeated usage of the [ㄴ] marker to disambiguate smaller, individual textual units within a larger composite textual unit. In this case, the larger composite textual unit comprises two individuals speaking to one another. The text of their dialogue includes narrative phrasing, the speakers' direct speech, as well as internal direct quoting of the speech of other individuals not present. It appears that the [ㄴ] marker was employed in conjunction with narrative phrasing to curtail any misreading and directly indicate breaks in speaker and speech. For example, Duke Zhuang is speaking to Cao Mie, then quotes a line from Chi Bo, and then returns to his own speech. The markers indicate that what Cao Mie is currently saying is different from the words of Chi Bo. When the Duke finishes quoting Chi Bo's speech the [ㄴ] marker is inserted to indicate that it is Duke Zhuang stating "Now this differs from your words." Yet another [ㄴ] follows this sentence indicating that a new speaker is being introduced, Cao Mie.

A lack of consistency in usage within Warring States Period bamboo manuscripts, however, poses a clear challenge to overly definitive postulations concerning a systemic or predictable use of [ㄴ] markers. Even with the Cao Mie manuscript, there are locations within the text where one would *expect* to find a [ㄴ] yet it is not there. Within Qin administrative and legal documents, however, one finds a great deal more consistency and predictability of usage.

Several [ㄴ] markers are employed in the manuscripts of the Shuihudi corpus.[63] In the *Xiao lü* manuscript, this marker occurs on seven slips for a total of ten marks written.

> Example 4.12—*Xiao lü*—Article 3, Slips 3–4—[ㄴ] segmenting topic-sentences
> 衡石不正十六兩以上貲官嗇夫一甲不盈十六兩到八兩貲一盾ㄴ桶不正二 升以上貲一甲不盈二升到一升貲一盾
>
> If the *heng-dan*[64] is not accurate by 16 *liang* or more, then fine the office's *sefu* one suit of armor. If not fully 16 *liang* to eight *liang*, then fine one shield. ㄴ If the *tong* is not accurate by two *sheng* or more, then fine one suit of armor. If not fully two *sheng* to one *sheng*, then fine one shield.

In this example, the [ㄴ] marker functions to segment two topically distinct sentences of a singular textual unit, both constructed as complex conditional sentences. The first topic is the *heng-dan* and two potential weight discrepancies are listed and connected to two distinct penal sanctions. The [ㄴ] marker is placed after the final apodosis and before the initial protasis of the new conditional sentence topic, the *tong* measurement device. Such a usage would be analogous to a full stop period [.] in modern orthography. The *Xiao lü* contains other examples of this practice.

> Example 4.13—*Xiao lü*—Article 4, Slips 5–7—dual function of the [∟] mark segmenting topic-sentences and enumerative dependent protasis clauses
> 斗不正半升以上貲一甲不盈半升到少半升貲一盾∟半石不正八兩以 上鈞不正四兩以上∟斤不正三銖以上∟半斗不正少半升以上∟參不正六分升一以上∟升不正廿分升一以上∟黃金衡纍不正半銖以上貲各一盾
>
> If the *dou* is not accurate by one-half *sheng* or more, then fine one suit of armor. If not fully one-half *sheng* to one-third *sheng*, then fine one shield.∟ If the half-*dan* is not accurate by eight *liang* or more, the *jün* is not accurate by four *liang* or more,∟ the *jin* is not accurate by three *zhu* or more,∟ the half-*dou* is not accurate by one-third *sheng* or more,∟ the *can* is not accurate by one-sixth *sheng* or more, ∟ the *sheng* is not accurate by one-twentieth *sheng* or more, ∟ weights of a gold balance are not accurate by a half-*zhu* or more, then for each fine one shield.

In Example 4.13, the marker [∟] is extensively used and performs two distinct syntactic functions. The first function is similar to that of Example 4.12. The marker separates two different topic-sentence textual units. The initial sentence concerns the *dou* measuring device and provides two different measurement discrepancies with particularized sanctions for each discrepancy. The marker is placed after the apodosis of the final conditional clause related to the *dou* and then the protasis of the new conditional sentence begins. Within this next extraordinarily long sentence, the [∟] signifies individual dependent clauses of a single, yet very complex conditional sentence. Each segmented textual unit represents an individualized protasis with distinct measurement discrepancies linked to distinct measurement devices (i.e., 半石, 鈞, 半斗, 參, 升, and 黃金衡纍); yet all are dependent upon the final apodosis, *zi ge yi dun* 貲各一盾 which completes the conditional sentence by providing a single sanction applicable to the discovery of a discrepancy in any of the attached cases.

Though it is clear that in the *Xiao lü* manuscript the [∟] marker functions to disambiguate individual textual segments within a single legal article, it is, however, quite difficult to ascertain whether these marks were originally composed within the government circulated *ur* statute or were merely added by the scribe/user as reader marks meant to facilitate the use of this particular manuscript.[65]

It should be noted, however, that while I argue that these markers are used to disambiguate textual segments more consistently than what we find in Warring States Chu manuscripts, there are some indications that this overall consistency may have some limitations. For example, in Example 4.13, one would expect to find a [∟] marker separating the discussion of half-*dan* 半石

measuring devices with the *jün* 鈞 device; however, it is missing. This could either indicate that the scribe placed all the [ㄴ] markers and simply did not place one here, or that the scribe omitted a [ㄴ] marker from the original that was being copied. Until we have another copy of this particular statute, it will be difficult to determine.

Regardless of the original source of the markers, it is clear that their placement does facilitate an accurate (i.e., author intended) reading of the text by segmenting topically different conditional sentences as well as demarcating multi-protasis topical phrases linked to a singular apodosis.

Comparative contributions from Liye administrative documents

The above analysis of the *Xiao lü* manuscript provides clear evidence of a conscious use of specific orthographic and spatial means to improve readability and to ensure consistency in interpreting the legal statute. Yet to argue that the Qin consistently assigned specific functions to specific forms of punctuation in legal/administrative documents via a narrow focus on a single legal manuscript (or even a group of manuscripts discovered within a single archaeological context) is quite open to criticism. One needs to compare the *Xiao lü* to other Qin manuscripts in order to show that such punctuation practices were not merely the idiosyncratic scribal habits of the individual charged to carry out the dictates of this specific document. In the above analysis, I made limited reference to other legal documents found within the Shuihudi corpus, as well as a few comparisons to Qin statutory materials found at other sites. Unfortunately, most of these other archaeological finds of Qin manuscripts provide little of comparative value. The legal materials discovered in these finds, such as excerpts of statutes, are much too fragmentary to sustain a detailed examination of the form and function of punctuation within an individual document. The situation changed, however, with the discovery of a massive cache of Qin administrative documents excavated from a well in Liye County 里耶縣, Hunan 湖南 in 2002.[66] Below, I will provide a brief codicological overview of the Liye administrative documents, and will then proceed with an examination of their use of punctuation markers.

The majority of manuscripts excavated from Well 1 (井1) are written upon long rectangular wooden tablets. These average 23 cm long, with a few longer tablets. The widths of the tablets are far from standardized and range from 1.3 cm to over 5 cm. Wang Huanlin 王煥林 believes that this width variation is due to the practice of using one tablet for one affair. Thus, if an issue needed to be recorded, but the required number of graphs was low, a thinner piece of wood could be used.[67] There are some problems with this hypothesis as many of the Liye manuscripts published to date contain large amounts of blank space, making it difficult to assume that this particular document was chosen after considering the space requirements for the text to be written.

The medium used is primarily wood from Chinese fir trees (*shan mu* 杉木; *Cunninghamia lanceolata*) or Chinese pine trees (*song mu* 松木; *Pinus armandii*).

The wood is hard with very fine grains that run from top to bottom of the document. Previously excavated Qin manuscripts from the site Shuihudi, contain instructions for the Minister of Works 司空 to select certain trees with wood that are conducive for writing with ink and to "square them," *fangzhi* 方之. It further states that if trees are unavailable, then reeds can be woven together to form a writing surface.[68]

Most of the Liye manuscripts are classified as administrative documents pertaining to the mundane affairs of a single county called Qianling 遷陵 located in the Dongting Commandery 洞庭郡. While such a discovery might not compare to the splendor of the Chu bamboo manuscripts containing philosophical texts, the Liye material has already made a tremendous impact upon our knowledge of the historical development of early imperial administration. The Liye materials, consisting of administrative documents in the form of communications on

Table 4.2 Liye J1(9)1

Front	*Back*
卅三年四月辛丑朔丙午司空騰敢言之陽陵宜居士五毋死有貲餘錢八 千六十四毋死戍洞庭郡不智何縣署●今為錢校券一上謁言洞庭尉令 毋死署所縣責以受陽陵司=空=不名計問何縣官計年為報 已訾其家=貧弗能入乃移戍所報署主責發敢言之 四月己酉陽陵守丞廚敢言之寫上謁報=署金布發敢言 之╲儋手	卅四年六月甲午朔戊午陽陵守慶敢言之未報謁追敢 言之╲堪手 卅五年四月己未朔乙丑洞庭叚尉觿謂遷陵丞陽陵卒署遷 陵其以律令從事報之當騰=╲嘉手●以洞庭司馬印行事 敬手

various county-level affairs, allow us to once again reevaluate how the Qin state actually functioned by giving us the ability to compare the normative aspects of statutory law with the more "realistic" issue of the practical application.

Of primary importance for the present chapter, the Liye corpus contains many lengthy documents permeated with a variety of orthographic and non-orthographic forms of punctuation. Furthermore, many of the texts appear to be duplicates of "standard form" administrative documentation. That is, many of the texts are archival records of administrative or legal cases and are written in a standard format. In a collection of several documents on a particular type of administrative issue, the main differences one finds are the names of people involved or a few specific facts particular to the case being reported. These records were clearly intended to be retained for future reference, and, as such, the scribes charged with compiling or transcribing them utilized various forms of punctuation to serve rather systematic syntactic functions in an effort to ensure the future readability of these archival documents. Below, I will provide one example drawn from the Liye corpus. This example will illustrate administrative conventions of punctuation usage for Qin government documents.

Translation of Liye document J1(9)1

Example 4.14—J1(9)1
Front 正面 (six lines):

(1) 卅三年四月辛丑朔丙午司空騰敢言之陽陵宜居士五(伍)毋死有貲餘錢八

In the thirty-third year, fourth month—of which the first day was *xinchou*—on the day *bingwu* (day 6), the Minister of Works, Teng, dares to state: Wu Si, a commoner of Yiju Village in Yangling County, has a remaining pecuniary fine of 8064 cash.

(2) 千六十四毋死戍洞庭郡不智(知)何縣署 ● 今為錢校券一上謁言洞庭尉令

Wu Si is deployed for military service in Dongting Commandery, but it is not known to which county or service unit. ● Now we have made one monetary contract to be sent up with a request for the Commandant of Dongting to order

(3) 毋死署所縣責以受(授)陽陵司=空=[司空]不名計問何縣官計年為報

the county of Wu Si's deployment locale to collect [the fine] and hand it over to the Yangling Minister of Works. The Minister of Works does not name Wu Si on the register and asks the said (that is, unknown county) with authority over the register to append the unit's yearly register in response.

(4) 已訾其家=[家]貧弗能入(納)乃移戍所報署主責發敢言之

We have already admonished his household. The household is poor and unable to remit it; thereupon we transfer the contract of debt to the locale of military service deployment. Report back with notification from the overseer of debt indicating he opened the document. I dare to state this.

(5) 四月己酉陽陵守丞廚敢言之寫上謁報=[報]署金布發敢言

In the fourth month on day *jiyou* (day 9), the Aide of Yangling, Chu, dares to state: What is written is sent up requesting a response. Report back with notification from the finance official indicating he opened the document. I dare to state

(6) 之 / 儋手
this. / Handled by Dan.

Back 反面 (five lines):
(1) 卅四年六月甲午朔戊午陽陵守慶敢言之未報謁追敢

In the thirty-fourth year, sixth month—of which the first day was *jiawu*—on day *wuwu* (day 25), the *shou* of Yangling, Qing, dares to report this: You have yet to respond. We request you pursue it. I dare to

(2) 言之 / 堪手

state this. / Handled by Kan.

(3) 卅五年四月己未朔乙丑洞庭叚(假)尉觿謂遷陵丞陽陵卒署遷

In the thirty-fifth year, fourth month—of which the first day was *jiwei*—on day *yichou* (day 7), the provisional Commandant of Dongting, X, told the Aide of Qianling [County] that the conscripts of Yangling [County] are deployed in Qian

(4) 陵其以律令從事報之當騰=[騰] / 嘉手 ● 以洞庭司馬印行事

ling. Let it be that the matter is handled in accordance with the statutes and ordinances. Report on it. This warrants transmission by post-horse. / Handled by Jia. ● Use the seal of the Dongting Minister of Horses to carry out the matter.

(5) 敬手

Handled by Jing.

Analysis of punctuation in the Liye manuscripts

The example translated above is representative of a series of 12 documents found in Well 1, all of which concern ascertaining the location of prisoners from

Yangling serving their labor sentences in Qianling. Each of the 12 manuscripts contains a multi-layered series of communications between the counties of Yangling and Qianling and the central authority of the Dongting Commandery. Initial inquiries and requests originated in Yangling and were conveyed to the central authority of Dongting Commandery. The central authority determined that the prisoners were assigned to Qianling County, and subsequently forwarded the inquiries/requests from Yangling to Qianling, along with orders dictating the required response. As such, the textual contents of the manuscripts discovered in Well 1 are, in a sense, archival documents maintained at the Qianling county seat and they are composite texts containing several interrelated texts that were, however, composed at different times and for different recipients. In an effort to disambiguate the various internal textual units for future readers, the scribe producing this final manuscript document made conscious use of multiple forms of both orthographic and non-orthographic punctuation. Those punctuation forms commonly employed are blank space, [=] markers, [•] or [■] markers, and the diagonal or virgule marker [/].

Maintaining a clear distinction between chronologically different communications within a composite administrative text would be quite important. Each new communication contains a chronological heading; however, the scribes managing these documents further disambiguated the individual texts by employing a spatial strategy emphasized by blank space. In terms of layout, this means that once the text of a communication being copied ended, the scribe began the text of the subsequent communication at the top of the medium, regardless of whether or not space remained after the previous communication.

Although the materiality of the Liye documents differs from the Shuihudi documents—the former are composed on single blocks of wood, not a composite medium of multiple bamboo slips like the latter—a format and layout comparison between Liye and Shuihudi manuscripts, like the *Xiao lü* and *Qin lü shiba zhong*, shows a similar pattern of utilizing blank space and beginning subsequent texts on a fresh line. Thus we see that the use of blank space to disambiguate complex, multi-text documents was a common feature of Qin administrative practice.

In the Liye example above, the [=] marker is employed several times to indicate a *chongwen* reading of various graphs. The most common is the simple duplication of an individual graph, such as 家 or 報.

The [•] or [■] markers are used to indicate topic shift within an individual communication. In J1(9)1, lines 1 and 2 describe the primary subject of the communication. An individual of a certain name, from a certain village in Yangling, is currently working off a pecuniary fine owed to the Yangling government; however, the Yangling county seat does not know where this person has been assigned to satisfy this debt through labor. Having provided the pertinent data, the perspective of the text then shifts to a recounting of "present" actions of the county seat. This shift is indicated by the [•] marker. Thus, the two sentences on either side of the [•] marker are interrelated; however, the marker functions to clearly indicate a shift from the facts of the administrative problem to the actions taken in response by the government office of Yangling.

This use of [•] markers to disambiguate distinct, but interrelated, text written in a continuous, unbroken format is common in other Qin manuscripts, including legal texts from Shuihudi.

> Example 4.16—*Qin lü zachao*, Slips 38–39
> •捕盜律曰捕人相移以受爵者耐•求盜勿令₌送₌逆₌為₌ 它₌事者貲二甲
>
> •The statute on Arresting Thieves states: "Those transferring arrested persons in order to receive rank are to be shaved. • Thief catchers ought not be ordered to escort or receive on behalf of others. Those who order [them] to escort or receive on behalf of others are to be fined two suits of armor.

This passage from the *Qin lü za chao* was analyzed earlier because of its use of *chongwen* [=] markers. In this instance, however, the [•] marker is important. Like the Liye documents, the use of [•] marker here distinguishes different sections of text. The first usage distinguishes the initial sentence that directly quotes the *bu zei lü* from the previous excerpt contained in the manuscript, while the second marker indicates a distinction between the two sentences, both of which come from the *buzei lü*. We can, therefore, say that the composer of this text took care to ensure that the reader would not confuse the beginnings of the *buzei lü* excerpts with other statute excerpts, and further distinguished individual excerpts from the same statute. Similarly, in the Liye context, the use of [•] provides a clear indication of interpretive/topical distinction between two sentences without using blank space, which is commonly used to indicate in these documents separate communications or texts that are being jointly transcribed into a single document.

Lastly, the Liye documents make use of the diagonal slash or virgule [/]. This orthographic form is not found in the legal manuscripts of the Shuihudi corpus; however, it is a common feature in administrative documents from both the Qin and Han periods.[69] In the Liye examples above, the [/] marker indicates a complete stop to a communication and is commonly followed by phrase X *shou* (X 手) which records the name of the scribe who handled/processed (手) this particular communication.[70] In J1(9)1, for example, we see that after the initial communication ends on line 6 (front), there is a virgule followed by the name of a scribe, Dan 儋. A response is dispatched and recorded in this document. This particular communication ends on line 2 (back) and yet another virgule is written and followed by the name of the responsible scribe named Kan 堪. Finally, the last communication—which includes the final orders of what action is to take place—is transcribed. Following this final communication, at the bottom corner of the wooden placard we see the final virgule followed by the name Jing 敬. Jing appears to be the last person involved in the processing of these communications, and is possibly the individual who transcribed the placards in this series.[71]

The use of the virgule indicates two things to the reader. First, it indicates where the contents of individual communications end at this point. Second, it provides a reference to the individual government official who processed this particular document. If a question arose over the contents of the communication, one could—in theory—track down Mr. Dan. Additionally, for the modern researcher, the frequent inclusion of scribal names provides empirical evidence that can be used to further our understanding of the individuals who produced and processed textual documents in early China.

From the above analysis of the Liye examples, it is clear that Qin scribes employed a variety of both orthographic and non-orthographic forms of punctuation in an attempt to compose/copy multi-layered complex documents into a format that was "reader-friendly." In doing so, they utilized several forms of punctuation, the functions of which correlate closely to those examples found in the Shuihudi legal materials. This observation lends some credibility to an argument that "readability" and elements of a shared scribal culture were consciously linked during the composition of complex texts.

Form and function of punctuation in Qin legal statutes

Within Western contexts, the development and increased use of orthographic and non-orthographic forms of punctuation within various literary genres indicates a heightened desire of composers, scribes, and/or readers to ensure precise and consistent comprehension/interpretation of textual materials. Regardless of the oral or silent-reading engagement by the reader, the overall function of punctuation was "to resolve structural uncertainties in a text, and to signal nuances of semantic significance which might otherwise not be conveyed at all, or would at best be much more difficult for the reader to figure out."[72] Recitation texts or hymnals required precise and consistent pronunciation and enunciation, while non-oral texts, such as the Bible or legal registers, required consistent interpretation of textual meaning by a range of potential audiences.

For early China, various forms of punctuation were also employed to facilitate precise and consistent interpretation of textual materials. Within the context of administrative or legal documents, the previous chapters demonstrated the Qin desire to universally promulgate consistently interpreted and accurately applied laws. To ensure the success of this policy, strict liabilities were levied against Qin officials who failed to properly carry out their assigned duties or who failed to conduct their affairs "in accordance with the written statutes and ordinances," *ru lü ling* 如律令. This necessitated the production of accurate and reader-friendly copies of those statutes and ordinances pertaining to one's specific government office. The Shuihudi manuscripts examined in this chapter demonstrate that effort was made to ensure accurate readings of the legal statutes (or statute excerpts). Yet, this does not necessarily mean that the Qin central government produced *ur* statutes replete with punctuation which was subsequently distributed throughout the growing empire and diligently copied by scribes and officials.

Parkes warns that when studying punctuation in Western manuscripts one should always be cautiously aware that "[p]unctuation is and always has been a personal matter."[73] By this, Parkes means that it is difficult to assess whether or not punctuation found in extant manuscripts are (a) indicative of a greater, systematic scribal convention of punctuation, (b) representative of the idiosyncratic habits of a particular composer, scribe, or reader of a specific manuscript, or (c) reflect punctuation or format features of a preexisting *ur* text. Similarly, Matthias Richter warns that when dealing with Warring States Period bamboo manuscripts one should not assume that the presence of punctuation within a particular text necessarily represents an indication of a general scribal practice. That said, the frequent use of punctuation markers that serve fairly consistent functions does seem to indicate that there was developing a more standardized use of punctuation within legal and administrative documents.

From the above analysis we can make the following tentative conclusions. First, the presence of punctuation within the *Xiao lü*, and related Shuihudi manuscripts, certainly illustrates a conscious effort to clearly highlight areas of interpretive importance and to condition the reader to comprehend a specific, targeted *reading* of the textual passages. Second, both the forms of the punctuation and their functions found in the *Xiao lü* manuscript are fairly consistent with the forms and functions of punctuation found in other legal manuscripts of the Shuihudi corpus. Lastly, the similarities in punctuation form and function of the *Xiao lü* manuscript and those found in the administrative documents of the Liye corpus seem to indicate the existence of a common set of scribal punctuation conventions for ensuring accurate reading of government documents by different individuals, particularly documents related to government administration and legal administration. Because of this, it would be likely that most educated Qin officials would be able to read Xi's copy of the *Xiao lü* manuscript and accurately comprehend its meaning.

Punctuation was clearly a valuable method through which Qin authors or copyists increased the consistency of targeted interpretations of specific texts. It is, however, only one method. The next chapter will consider the various linguistic or composition-based strategies employed by Qin drafters of legal statutes to produce texts that would be consistently interpreted and applied. Through a detailed analysis of the textual contents of the *Xiao lü* manuscript, the next chapter will analyze multiple linguistic levels of legal drafting ranging from word choice and legal definition to complex enumerative protasis clauses and inter-/intra-statute cross-referencing.

Notes

1 Christopher De Hamel, *A History of Illuminated Manuscripts*, 2nd ed. (London: Phaidon Press, 1994), chaps. 1, 2, and 6.
2 For an analysis of Xi's life as seen in the *Biannian ji*, see Chapter 1.
3 The editors of the Shuihudi corpus believe that the manuscript's length, content, and the inclusion of an individual statutory title on the back and front of Slip 1 indicates that this is a "head-to-toe" complete Qin legal statute. See Shuihudi Qin mu zhujian zhengli xiaozu, ed., *Shuihudi Qin mu zhujian* (Beijing: Wenwu chuban she, 1990), 69.
4 Hsu Fu-chang, *Shuihudi Qin jian yanjiu* (Taipei: Wen shi zhe, 1993), 174–177.

5 Qiu Xigui, *Chinese Writing*, trans. Jerry Norman and Gilbert L. Mattos (Berkeley: The Society for the Study of Early China and the Institute of East Asian Studies, University of California, 2000), 105.
6 Ibid., 98.
7 For an examination of this belief, or at least the idealized accounts of Qin script reform found in Han texts, see Imre Galambos, *Orthography of Early Chinese Writing: Evidence from Newly Excavated Manuscripts* (Budapest: Eötvös Lorand University, 2006), chap. 2.
8 Qiu Xigui, *Chinese Writing*, 106–107.
9 Sun Hong, *Qin jian du shu yanjiu* (Beijing: Beijing daxue chuban she, 2009), 42–43.
10 William Boltz, "The Composite Nature of Early Chinese Texts," in *Text and Ritual in Early China*, ed. Martin Kern (Seattle: University of Washington Press, 2005), 54.
11 For more on the inter- and intra-textual relations among statute and statutory articles, see Chapter 5.
12 Cited in Grant Robertson, "Comma Quirk Irks Rogers," *Globe and Mail*, 2006, www.theglobeandmail.com/report-on-business/article838561.ece.
13 Ibid.
14 Ibid.
15 Roger Chartier, *Forms and Meanings: Texts, Performances, and Audiences from Codex to Computer* (Philadelphia: University of Pennsylvania Press, 1995), 1.
16 A horizontal line placed under the initial words of a new topic, see T. Julian Brown, *A Palaeographer's View : The Selected Writings of Julian Brown* (London: Harvey Miller, 1993), 80.
17 Ibid., 79–85.
18 Raymond Clemens and Timothy Graham, *Introduction to Manuscript Studies* (Ithaca, NY: Cornell University Press, 2007), 82.
19 Ibid., 83–84.
20 M.B. Parkes, *Scribes, Scripts, and Readers: Studies in the Communication, Presentation and Dissemination of Medieval Texts* (London: Hambledon Press, 1991), 1–18.
21 David Mellinkoff, *The Language of the Law* (Eugene, OR: Wipf & Stock Publishers, 2004), 159–160.
22 Clemens and Graham, *Introduction to Manuscript Studies*, 85.
23 M.B. Parkes, *Pause and Effect: An Introduction to the History of Punctuation in the West* (Berkeley: University of California Press, 1993), 69.
24 Ibid.
25 Ibid., 69–70.
26 A rather clear combination of multiple forms of punctuation within the context of a legal document containing textual elements intended for both silent reading as well as vocalization can be found in the royal act establishing the British coronation oath. The majority of the lengthy act is lightly punctuated with the *punctus* until the text turns to the specific words to be spoken by the Archbishop. At that point, the vocalized text is highly punctuated using a variety of orthographic forms indicating intonation, pause, and stop/interrogative. See Mellinkoff, *The Language of the Law*, 161–162.
27 Brown, *A Palaeographer's View*, 79.
28 In late antiquity and the early Middle Ages, the cola indicated a major rhetorical division within a sentence and the comma indicated a minor division. Punctuation *per cola et commata* indicates spatial disambiguation of "sense-units." See Clemens and Graham, *Introduction to Manuscript Studies*, 82.
29 See, generally, Derk Bodde, "Punctuation: Its Use in China and Elsewhere," *Rocznik Orientalistyczny* 47, no. 2 (1991): 15–23.
30 Imre Galambos, "Scribal Notation in Medieval Chinese Manuscripts: The Hewen (Ligature) and the Chongwen (Duplication) Marks," *Manuscript Cultures*, 2009.
31 Hsu Fu-chang conducted an extended examination of the Shuihudi materials and his analysis does contain several pages dedicated to the various forms of punctuation

present in the manuscripts; however, little attempt is made to expand on the interpretive implications of the markers. See Hsu Fu-chang, *Shuihudi Qin jian yanjiu*, 194–210.

32 Bodde, "Punctuation," 22–23.

33 Two exceptions for the study of punctuation in early China would be Matthias Richter's work on the forms and functions of punctuation markers found in the Warring States Period excavated manuscripts, *Xing zi ming chu* 性自命出 and *Xing qing lun* 性情論, and Guan Xihua's analysis of punctuation in ancient and medieval China. See Matthias Richter, *Embodied Text: Establishing Textual Identity in Early Chinese Manuscripts* (Leiden: Brill, 2013), 184–187; Guan Xihua, *Zhongguo gudai biaodian fuhao fazhan shi* (Chengdu: Ba Shu shu she, 2002).

34 See Javier Calle-Martin and Antonio Miranda-Garcia, "The Punctuation System of Elizabethan Legal Documents: The Case of G.U.L. MS Hunter 3 (S.1.3)," *Review of English Studies* 59, no. 240 (2007): 357, 361–369.

35 The *Xiao lü* manuscript also contains a title; however, I will review the significance of this feature in the next chapter.

36 For a discussion of "blank space" punctuation in Shang oracle bones, see Guan Xihua, *Zhongguo gudai biaodian fuhao fazhan shi*, 35–38.

37 Qinghua University published a Warring States Period manuscript entitled, *Xi nian* 繫年. The 138 bamboo slips comprising the manuscript contain 23 individual textual units related to pre-Qin historical episodes. The remaining space on a bamboo slip upon which the last graphs of an individual textual unit are written is left blank and a new slip is used to begin the next textual unit. See Li Xueqin, ed., *Qinghua daxue cang zhanguo zhu jian*, vol. 2 (Shanghai: Zhong xi shuju, 2012).

38 As mentioned, the *Xiao lü* manuscript will be the focus of this chapter; however, I will make reference to other Shuihudi and Qin excavated materials when necessary. The *Xiao lü* employs a simpler method of spatial organization than that of the *Qin lü shiba zhong*, yet an analysis of the latter is still important.

39 The "source title" is the title of the original legal statute from which the present textual unit was excerpted. These titles are usually one to three characters in length (e.g., 金布律 [Statute on Metal and Cloth/(=Currency)], 行書 [(Statute on) Dispatch of Documents], and 效 [(Statute on) Checking]), and provide no additional information concerning the exact location of the excerpted textual unit within the original statute text. I follow Hulsewé in adding the implied word *lü* or statute where needed.

40 In saying this, I am merely pointing out the fact that the composer of this manuscript wanted to convey the fact that these excerpts come from another text. It possibly also signals to the reader that the excerpts do not represent the complete text of the source document, as layout alone is not sufficient and more context would likely be needed.

41 By "often employed" I do not mean to imply that in *all* types of legal documents Qin scribes utilized blank space to disambiguate independent articles of a legal statute. In the *Qin lü zachao* manuscript, for example, individual excerpts of legal statutes (similar to *Qin lü shiba zhong*) do not begin a new bamboo slip, but instead run continuously throughout the manuscript. In that manuscript, the individual textual units are separated by bold, black dots [•].

42 For more on the textual style of ancient Greek laws, see Michael Gagarin, *Writing Greek Law* (Cambridge: Cambridge University Press, 2008), 46–47.

43 The early Chinese *hewen* is, in many ways, analogous to the use of *ligatures* in European print culture. Common European ligatures, some of which are still used today, include: ﬄ for "ffl," Æ for "AE," and Œ for "OE."

44 For *hewen* examples from Western Zhou inscriptions, Houma covenant texts, and Shuihudi manuscripts, see Guan, *Zhongguo gudai biaodian fuhao fazhan shi*, 42–44, 49–50, and 62–63; for *hewen* examples in newly published Chu bamboo manuscripts, see Ma Chengyuan, *Shanghai bowuguan cang zhanguo chu zhushu (si)* (Shanghai: Shanghai guji chuban she, 2004), passim.

45 Galambos, "Scribal Notation in Medieval Chinese Manuscripts," 5–6.
46 Translation (A) based on the reading of Li Xueqin and the Shuihudi editors. See Shuihudi Qin mu zhujian zhengli xiaozu, *Shuihudi Qin Mu Zhujian*, 73.
47 Translation (B) from A.F.P. Hulsewé, *Remnants of Ch'in Law* (Leiden: E.J. Brill, 1985), 96.
48 Li Xueqin, "Qin jian de guwenzixue kaocha," in *Yunmeng Qin jian yanjiu*, ed. Zhonghua shuju bianji bu (Beijing: Zhonghua shuju, 1981), 341.
49 Shuihudi Qin mu zhujian zhengli xiaozu, *Shuihudi Qin mu zhujian*, 73.
50 Hulsewé, *Remnants of Ch'in Law*, 96.
51 One Qin *chi* 尺 was approximately 23.1 cm and there are ten Qin *cun* 寸 per *chi.* Hulsewé states this horse measurement would likely be 1.35 m. Hulsewé, *Remnants of Ch'in Law*, 107.
52 Zang Kehe and Wang Ping, eds., *Shuowen jiezi xinding* (Beijing: Zhonghua shuju, 2002), 641.
53 Hulsewé, *Remnants of Ch'in Law*, 107; Shuihudi Qin mu zhujian zhengli xiaozu, *Shuihudi Qin mu zhujian*, 81.
54 This linguistic feature is not unique to legal texts of the Qin. As mentioned above, there are several examples of *hewen* constructions in a variety of literary genres dating from the Shang through to the Han. My focus for this chapter, however, is on legal manuscripts.
55 See the arguments set out in Galambos, "Scribal Notation in Medieval Chinese Manuscripts."
56 For examples of [=] usage as a *chongwen* indicator in the Shang dynasty, see Qiu Xigui, "Jiaguwen zhong chongwen he hewen chongfu pianpang de shenlüe," in *Guwenzi lunji*, by Qiu Xigui (Beijing: Zhonghua shuju, 1992), 141–146; and Qiu Xigui, "Zai tan jiaguwen zhong chongwen de shenglüe," in *Guwenzi lunji*, by Qiu Xigui (Beijing: Zhonghua shuju, 1992), 147–150; for later examples see Galambos, "Scribal Notation in Medieval Chinese Manuscripts."
57 For other examples drawn from Shuihudi, see Guan, *Zhongguo gudai biaodian fuhao fazhan shi*, 62–63; and Hsu Fu-chang, *Shuihudi Qin jian yanjiu*, 200–205.
58 I have not found an example of the use of a *chongwen* construction for an AABBCCDDEE reading; however, if one came across an $A_{=}B_{=}C_{=}D_{=}E_{=}$ phrase, then one would, however quickly, need to dismiss the possibly of an AABBCCDDEE construction.
59 For examples drawn from bronze inscriptions through Han dynasty manuscripts, see Guan, *Zhongguo gudai biaodian fuhao fazhan shi*, 39, 61, and 67.
60 See Ma Chengyuan, *Shanghai bowuguan cang Zhanguo Chu zhushu (si).*
61 This arrangement follows that found in Ji Xusheng, ed. 《*Shanghai bowuguan cang Zhanguo Chu zhushu* (*si*)》 *duben* (Taipei: Wanjuan chuban she, 2007). See also, Ernest Caldwell, "Promoting Action in Early Chinese Political Philosophy: A First Look at the Warring States Period Bamboo Manuscript Cao Mie's Battle Arrays," *Early China* 37 (2014): 259–289.
62 This manuscript was part of a collection purchased by the Shanghai Museum on the Hong Kong antiquities market. Without archeological context, there was little physical evidence to date the manuscripts other than calligraphic similarity to other Warring States manuscripts with a known provenance. C-14 dating of the Shanghai manuscripts resulted in a 2257±65 BP (306±65 BCE) date for the manuscripts which makes them likely contemporaries of manuscripts discovered at sites such as Baoshan 包山 and Guodian 郭店. See Ma Chengyuan, "Ma Chengyuan xiansheng tan Shangbo jian" in *Shang boguan cang Zhanguo Chu zhushu yanjiu* ed. Liao Mingchun and Zhu Yuanqing (Shanghai: Shanghai shudian, 2002), 3.
63 For examples from other texts in the corpus, see Guan, *Zhongguo gudai biaodian fuhao fazhan shi*, 61–62; and Hsu Fu-chang, *Shuihudi Qin jian yanjiu*, 205–207.

64 For a more comprehensive analysis of these measurement devices, see Table 5.6 in the next chapter. See also, Wu Hung, "Qin quan yanjiu," *Gugong jikan* 4 (1979): 33–47; Qiu Guangming, ed., *Zhongguo lidai duliangheng kao* (Beijing: Kexue chuban she, 1992).

65 Matthias Richter claims that for Warring States Period bamboo manuscripts the [乚] marks frequently occur between graphs that are rather consistently spaced. Richter argues that this could indicate that the marks were added *after* the manuscript was composed. Therefore, they should not be considered "original" elements of the text, but later reader marks added to the manuscript. See Richter, "Punctuation" (unpublished manuscript).

66 Hunan sheng wenwu kaogu yanjiu suo, *Liye fajue baogao* (Changsha: Yuelu shushe, 2006). For an English language overview of the Liye corpus, see Robin D.S. Yates, "The Qin Slips and Boards from Well No. 1, Liye, Hunan: A Brief Introduction to the Qin Qianling County Archives," *Early China* 35–36 (2012–2013): 291–329.

67 Wang Huanlin, *Liye Qinjian jiaoku* (Beijing: Zhongguo wenlian chubanshe, 2007), 5–6.

68 See *Qin lü shiba zhong*, Slips 131–132.

69 See examples found in Michael Loewe, *Records of Han Administration*, 2 vols. (Cambridge: Cambridge University Press, 1967).

70 For more on the use of *shou* 手 in Liye documents, see Wang Guihai, "Cong Xiangxi Liye Qin jian kan Qin guanwenshu zhidu," in *Liye gucheng: Qin jian yu Qin wenhua yanjiu*, ed. Zhongguo shehui kexue yuan kaogu yanjiu suo, Zhongguo shehui kexue yuan lishi yanjiu suo, and Hunan sheng wenwu kaogu yanjiu suo (Beijing: Kexue chuban she, 2009), 142–145; Wang Huanlin, *Liye Qinjian jiaoku* (Beijing: Zhongguo wenlian chubanshe, 2007), 7.

71 For an English language analysis of "scribal signatures" in Qin and Han period excavated manuscripts, see Enno Giele, "Signatures of 'Scribes' in Early Imperial China," *Asiatische Studien/Etudes Asiatiques* 59, no. 1 (2005): 353–387.

72 Parkes, *Pause and Effect*, 1.

73 Ibid., 5.

5 The anatomy of a Qin Legal Statute Part II

Introduction

The previous chapter examined the codicological features utilized by Qin government officials to produce clear and readable legal texts. Such features demonstrate the ways in which the Qin government's anxiety over interpretive inconsistency and the potential judicial discretion influenced the very physical form in which legal statutes were produced. Concomitantly, one can postulate that because these specific manuscripts were found in the tomb of a low-level administrator, who would likely have received censure from higher authorities for improper use or interpretation, the physical features were also specifically intended by the copyist to ensure that the reader (official) did not misinterpret or misapply the statutory provisions. I further noted how the *Xiao lü* manuscript employed fairly standardized graphic forms laid out in orderly columns upon bamboo slips. Individual legal articles were clearly distinguished through the use of blank space and by beginning a new article on a new slip. Within individual statutory articles additional specialized orthographic forms were employed to perform specific punctuation functions in an attempt to produce greater internal clarity when reading the text of the statute. Thus, the physical layout and arrangement of text was consciously crafted to better facilitate consistent and unambiguous readings by those possessing a level of governmental training required for obtaining at least the official rank of *ling shi* 令史 or chief scribe. We do not know the specific nature of training for scribes and government officials during the Qin conquest or during the short-lived Qin dynasty; however, using the information found in the Shuihudi manuscript, *Recorded Annals* 編年記, and the Han dynasty *Statute on Scribes*, *Shi lü* 史律, found in Tomb 247 of Zhangjiashan we can deduce some basic forms of knowledge necessary to carry out the functions of a Qin scribal official. These primarily dealt with the ability to recognize and reproduce words in their written forms.[1]

In the present chapter, I will turn my attention to the linguistic features of Qin legal statutes. Specifically, I will examine the linguistic composition of the statutory articles found in the *Xiao lü* manuscript in order to demonstrate how the Qin government utilized specific linguistic forms in an attempt to curb judicial discretion and ensure consistent textual interpretation. Furthermore, I will highlight certain linguistic features which could potentially hinder the realization of this goal of consistency in statutory interpretation.

My analysis of Qin legal statutes will utilize the theories and methods employed by modern legal linguists. These methods, developed in the burgeoning field of legal linguistics and comparative legal linguistics, are particularly instructive when examining any modern or premodern legal text. Considerations of the value of linguistic analysis for legal studies has a long history in the West, yet few works seriously attempted to meld the two fields of linguistics and legal studies into a coherent methodology. Since the 1990s, numerous works have been published that analyze legal texts and legal language from a variety of perspectives.[2] For the purposes of this chapter, I am primarily interested in those works which examine the linguistic composition of legislative and statutory texts, as well as those works examining the influence of the intended textual function on the practice of textual composition.[3]

The previous chapter argued that producing a clearly written and spatially organized textual document is quite important; however, if the linguistic composition of the actual *text* is not conducive to consistent and clear readings, then regardless of any perfection in physical design, the compositional and organizational features will not jointly facilitate consistent readings. Several linguists argue that the particular function of any text plays a crucial role in determining its linguistic form.[4] Similarly, it has been argued that the intended audience also contributes to how a text is linguistically composed. Chartier comments that "[w]riting deploys strategies that are meant to produce effects, dictate a posture, and oblige the reader."[5] Yet, even so, Chartier notes that the selection of such strategies is dependent upon specific characteristics of the intended audience. Thus the social status, education, political affiliation, or even the gender of the intended audience of a text can potentially condition the linguistic choices of the document's composer.

Scholars within the field of legal linguistics analyze the specific ways in which legislators, particularly legislative drafters, construct legal statutes. For linguists, the act of drafting legal statutes is a predictive exercise requiring a conscious selectivity of terminology embedded with specialized legal meaning, phrasal or sentential formulae specifically employed to elicit desired interpretations consistently, and an informational organization familiar to the target audience, thus facilitating consistent readings. In other words, legal linguists are most interested in performing reader-centric analyses of statutory language which attempt to elucidate the various levels of interpretive ambiguity resulting from the linguistic composition choices of drafters.

Two primary influences are often considered simultaneously by linguists when analyzing the linguistic decisions made by drafters when composing legal statutes. The first decision-conditioning influence is the education and "literacy" of the target audience. A legal text is often written with the intention of being read by a specific audience and subsequently eliciting a desired response. When making linguistic choices, the drafter must consider whether the target audience is the general public, a specialized legal profession, or a combination of the two.

The French tradition of legal codification and the German tradition offer excellent examples of two very different legislative ideologies and their linguistic consequences. The French codification utilizes generalized and fairly non-technical linguistic conventions to produce a legal document that is intended to be accessible to the general populace. Contra to this, the German codification tends to be linguistically very technical and highly stylized as the intended audience of such texts is the legal professional possessing a high level of specialized training in the law. Therefore, the "legal-literacy" background of the target audience affects the potential levels of interpretive ambiguity and, as such, directly influences the ways in which legal information can be conveyed in written form.

The second influence often considered in legal linguistic analysis is the level of interpretive discretion provided by the legal system being studied to those individuals tasked with executing or obeying the laws. In systems allowing a wider range of interpretive discretion, the language of the statutes is often more general (such as France) and the canons of interpretation are typically more liberal.[6] The more restricted the level of discretion, however, the greater emphasis is required to employ compositional features which limit potential ambiguity of meaning and application.[7] Within many European traditions of statutory interpretation, the common canons of interpretation prescribe the limits of expanding or restricting the legal meaning of words found in a statutory provision. As an example, the canon of *ejusdem generis* (of the same kind) is a rule of construction that limits the meaning of a broad meaning word which follows a list of specific words. If a statutory article makes reference to "houses, semi-detached houses, flats, condominiums, or any other buildings," then under the rules of *ejusdem generis* the meaning of the phrase "any other buildings" would be restrictively constructed as residential buildings and not, as it were, commercial properties. A more restrictive canon would be *expression unius est exclusion alterius* (that expressed puts end to that which is silent). Such an interpretive construction restricts the interpretive statutory ambit to *only* those things expressly mentioned in the provision.

For the Qin case, as we have seen in Chapter 3, the government required strict adherence to the language of the law and required strict interpretation of statutory provisions. One of the primary reasons for the introduction and continued use of written law was its perceived ability to curtail the judicial discretion of hereditary aristocratic offices, as well as to ensure the same discretion throughout all levels of the salaried Qin bureaucracy. In theory, the Qin drafters of statutory provisions needed to be conscious of the potential for ambiguity in their use of words and phrasings, and the potential consequences such ambiguity might have on the interpretive consistency between different audience members.

In the remainder of this chapter, I examine the compositional features of the Qin legal manuscripts discovered in Tomb 11 of Shuihudi. As with the previous chapter, I focus primarily on the *Xiao lü* manuscript, yet I make supplementary reference to several companion Shuihudi manuscripts such as, the *Qin lü shiba zhong*, the *Qin lü zachao*, and the *Questions and Answers Concerning Law and Statutes*, *Fa lü dawen* 法律答問.[8] Following the work of the above-mentioned legal linguists, I examine the text of the *Xiao lü* manuscript on several levels looking for specific compositional strategies employed with the intent of providing greater reading clarity, as well as potential compositional features which could potentially impede consistent interpretation or cause a level of reading ambiguity. To do this, I first examine the opening lines of the *Xiao lü* text. I then turn my attention to the compositional framework of the text in order of increasing linguistic complexity. That is, I examine linguistic issues related to embedding individual words with legal meaning. Afterwards, I examine the compositional structures of individual legal articles with specific reference to the problematics of increasing levels of complexity and increasing levels of linguistic ambiguity. Finally, I examine the meta-compositional feature of text-mapping utilized by drafters to produce an internally "coherent" legal statute, as well as integrate a single legal statute into an extant corpus of several statutes in use by the Qin.

Statute title, initial articles, and jurisdictional clarity

Several linguistic and compositional strategies can be employed to ensure that a reader will come to a desired interpretation or reading of a text; however, such strategies are wasted if one is not reading the proper text! To that end, many legal texts around the world (both modern and premodern) use titling strategies designed to convey specific information to the reader regarding the particular manuscript's contents, audience, and jurisdiction.

Example 5.1—*Xiao lü*—Articles 1 and 2, Slips 1–2[9]
{1}
效 【背】

[Statute on] Checking[10] (recto)

為都官及縣效律其有贏不備物值之以其價多者罪之勿纍 [1]

Being the Statute on Checking for general offices as well as counties: If there are surpluses or shortages of things, value them, and use that which has the highest value to hold them responsible. Do not compound. (1)

{2}
官嗇夫冗吏皆共償不備之貨而入贏 [2]

The *sefu* of the office and assigned clerks all jointly make restitution for shortages in goods; however, take in that which is surplus. (2)

Although the first article of the statute consists of only one bamboo slip and 25 graphs, its textual contents provide valuable information about the structural relationship between the written text and the physical manuscript, as well as information concerning the ways in which the potential reader would initially engage the manuscript. Slip 1 is the only bamboo slip of the *Xiao lü* manuscript that contains writing on both the recto and verso sides. This feature allows us to postulate the way in which this particular manuscript of 60 slips was stored and first viewed by the reader. It would likely have been rolled—with the text facing inward—beginning from the last slip and proceeding towards the first slip. In this way, the graph *xiao* 效 written on the recto side of Slip 1 would provide a visible, external title of the rolled manuscript.[11] It is again likely that the external title would facilitate its quick discovery by an official searching through a collection of statutes or legal documents stored together.

Further facilitating the speed at which an official could ascertain the utility of the legal document in hand, as the manuscript is unrolled for reading the first two textual units the eye comes into contact with clearly define the statute's intended audience, the relevant jurisdiction of these legal norms, the legal content of the document, and the basic application of the legal document. The opening phrase of the manuscript provides what it is, the "Statute on Checking," *xiao lü* 效律, and its intended audience and jurisdictional scope, "the general offices and counties," *duguan ji xian* 都官及縣.

The remainder of the text in this article provides an implicit definition of "checking," namely, that checking consists of ascertaining within the general offices and counties "the existence of surpluses and shortages of things," *qi you ying bu bei* 其有贏不備物. The article describes the general method for calculating the severity of the offense based upon the estimated worth of the highest valued good, *yi qi jia duo zhe zui zhi* 以其價多者罪之. The drafter of the statute evinces a level of legal prescience as the text presupposes the potential for the concurrent discovery of multiple surpluses or shortages. Should such a case arise, the official tasked with executing the dictates of the statute is required to calculate the value of all the shortages and surpluses, but to charge only the liable party based on the amount of the highest total. The official is clearly instructed not to combine the values of multiple shortages and surpluses when calculating the severity of the offense, *wu lei* 勿纍.

Article 2 follows quite logically after Article 1. The latter, written in rather broad, generic language, describes an offense associated with two types of discrepancies arising from "checking" and provides a general method for ascertaining the severity of such an offense. Article 2 then provides the next crucial element when applying the law, namely specifying the parties liable for such offenses once discovered. Similar to Article 1, the language of Article 2 is generalized. That is to say, this article provides the reader/user with the general parameters of *who* will be liable for the existence of shortages and surpluses, "the *sefu* of the office and assigned clerks," *guan sefu rong li* 官嗇夫冗吏, while the subsequent articles in the statute contain refined and qualified terms of liability associated with categorically diverse legal situations and specific mitigating circumstances.

When read together, Articles 1 and 2 provide the general statement of law informing the intended function of the *Xiao lü*. The use of such an initial disquisition allows the reader to know the intended purpose of the text and its potential applicability to the present situation without the necessity of reading through the full text. Furthermore, it is composed in the very broad, general language of "surplus" and "shortage," which are qualified and specified in subsequent articles of the *Xiao lü* manuscript. This type of compositional practice is actively used today in many legal jurisdictions as a means of ensuring that a piece of legislation is applied to jurisdictionally correct and categorically accurate situations.

Terminological clarity

Organizational clarity is an extremely important feature of a well-composed legal text. Just as important as the organization, however, is the very language used to compose the legal statute. The Qin government promulgated legal texts with the intention that they would be dispatched throughout the kingdom, and later empire, and that the texts would be consistently interpreted and applied.[12] By ascribing such a function to legal texts, the Qin concomitantly necessitated the use of specific linguistic features which would ensure that the officials tasked with executing the dictates of a particular statute understood the specific legal meaning ascribed to the terms used within the text, and, by extension, come to a consistent interpretation regardless of whether they were serving in the Qin capital of Xianyang 咸陽 or in the peripheral southern county of Qianling 遷陵.

One particularly problematic aspect of legal composition is the use and interpretation of legal terminology. Legal linguists agree that in most cultures and most contexts legal language is not created *ex nihilo*, and, as such, it should not be considered a specifically engineered technolect.[13] Often, a legal term is "created" when a word in ordinary use acquires "a specialized or enlarged meaning in legal contexts as a result of a more or less spontaneous linguistic evolution."[14] Today, the majority of terms found in legal documents are in fact drawn from everyday language, yet over time they acquired specialized meaning when located in a legal context.[15] For example, the term *agreement* can mean two very different things if it is used as an ordinary term versus when it is used in the context of contract law. In the former, an agreement between two friends can seem to bind them socially to a specific set of terms; however, in the latter context *agreement* is one of three necessary conditions that must be met to produce a legally enforceable set of contractual obligations.[16] Simply put, within a specific legal culture, a legal language develops to serve as "a language for a specialized purpose."[17]

The Shuihudi legal texts do not necessarily contain a great deal of law-specific terminology. That is, the texts of the corpus to do not appear to rely exclusively on words specifically created for *legal* purposes (notable exceptions being terminology for specific forms of punishment). Instead, many of the terms used throughout the texts are commonly found in other genres of texts both excavated and received. In the Shuihudi legal materials, however, many common terms have become imbued with specialized legal meaning.[18]

The drafter can deal with the issue of ambiguity from terminological choices in three ways. First, the drafter can rely upon specialized training of the target audience. So an individual reading a particular statute would be familiar through training of the legal meaning attached to the term being employed in this context. Second, the drafter can use additional prose to elaborate, within the text, the specific legal meaning of the term. Third, the specific legal meaning of terms can be disambiguated through supplementary texts, a form of exegetical text of legal terminology. Even today, supplementary texts are used in the legal profession, such as dictionaries or legislative interpretations. Therefore, the level of interpretive ambiguity in the text is often dependent upon either the reader's knowledge of the specialized meaning of terms found within the text, the ability of the drafter to adequately describe the legal meaning of the term in this specific context, or the use of, as well as availability of, supplementary exegetical texts.

In this section, I will examine several ways in which the *Xiao lü* manuscript illustrates conscious effort to encode specific legal meaning into individual terms or phrases. Such efforts were intended to provide a clear reading and interpretation of the legal significance of the term's usage in this particular context as opposed to its everyday use. To do this, I will examine the practice of legal definition, enumeration, subject repetition, and finally consider evidence of retained ambiguity and alternative methods for dealing with such ambiguity.

Definition, enumeration, and definitional enumeration

Lexical enumeration is a commonly employed compositional strategy found in many legislative texts, both modern and premodern. Linguistically, enumeration functions as a specialized form of definitional composition. In many legal texts, a specific situation is outlined and the categories of consequential objects or subjects are provided through an enumerative list. There are, of course, several issues related to the use of enumeration. For example, one must consider whether or not a specific list is exclusive or inclusive. That is to say, are items of a similar type or category that are not explicitly enumerated in the statutory language to be considered subject to the stated provision? For many legal systems, specialized statutory interpretation methods have been specifically devised or have grown out of customary practices. Below, I analyze several examples of enumeration that demonstrate how Qin drafters employed lists to encode specific *legal* meaning to ordinary or commonly used terms.

> Example 5.2—*Xiao lü*—Article 3, Slips 3–4
> {3}
> 衡石不正十六兩以上貲官嗇夫一甲不盈十六兩到八兩貲一盾∟桶不正二 [3] 升以上貲一甲不盈二升到一升貲一盾 [4]
>
> If the *hengdan* is not accurate by 16 *liang* or more, then fine the office's *sefu* one suit of armor. If not fully 16 *liang* to eight *liang*, then fine one shield. ∟ If the *tong* is not accurate by two (3) *sheng* or more, then fine one suit of armor. If not fully two *sheng* to one *sheng*, then fine one shield. (4)

In this example, we can observe an attempt to clearly and unambiguously embed specific legal meaning to three commonly used words *hengdan* 衡石, *tong* 桶, and *zheng* 正. Each of these terms can be found in a variety of pre-Qin and Qin texts, yet once the terms are placed within the context of a Qin legal statute they acquire a definitional specificity replete with legal consequences.

To begin, the two measurement terms, *hengdan* and *tong*, are immediately qualified and defined by the composer of the article as existing in two potential forms; *bu zheng* 不正 meaning "improper" or "inaccurate" and its inferred opposite, *zheng* meaning "proper" or "accurate." Historical sources reveal that measurement devices during the Warring States Period were not standardized vis-à-vis different kingdoms, and one of the great policies of the Qin government was to compel metrological uniformity in weights and measures within newly acquired regions. This uniformity was achieved through legislation, as well as a large-scale visual propaganda campaign as evidenced by the "Twenty-sixth Year Edict" inscribed on several unearthed measurement devices.[19] Thus, the definitional significance of these two terms, *hengdan* and *tong*, shifted away from the common parlance of measurement devices—terms used earlier by various kingdoms for potentially different quantities—and into the Qin legal sphere by assigning a statutory definition of what legally, or officially, constitutes a *hengdan* or *tong* within Qin. Based upon this statute, an "accurate" *hengdan* would measure to within less than eight *liang* of the standard and a *tong* would measure to within less than one *sheng* of the standard. Because the Qin government went to great lengths to ensure metrological uniformity in all measurement devices, such definitional specificity would nullify the validity of any previous measurement forms used within newly annexed lands and signify a uniform government sanctioned (i.e., legal) measurement standard.

Second, the legal significance of the qualifying term *zheng* is further elaborated. The graph *zheng* 正 is a commonly used term in early Chinese received texts and manuscripts. In early Chinese texts, the semantic net of the term frequently envelops a range of meanings including "appropriate," "correct," and "standard." Once it is established that there is a correct path, method, or model, there is a resultant implied concept of "improper" or *bu zheng*. In the current example, the legal article is phrased as a negative—emphasizing the legal significance of incorrectness—yet the wording provides an elaborated conceptualization of the *zheng-bu zheng* that is graded into levels of incorrectness, not simply a correct–incorrect dyad. While this might seem like a rather obvious statement to make, the graded distinctions have quite significant legal consequences. A layperson might simply consider a weight measure as being accurate or inaccurate, yet based on this legal article, we now know that a Qin official tasked with ensuring the reliability of instruments of measure would understand that there was not only an "accurate" or "inaccurate" categorization, but that legally there existed three levels of accuracy for a *tong* measurement vessel. Any *tong* instrument calibrated to within a one *sheng* 升 discrepancy of the standard unit measurement would legally be considered *zheng* or "accurate." Those instruments inaccurately calibrated between one *sheng* to two *sheng* off the standard measurement are considered sufficiently "inaccurate" to the extent that they warrant a sanction of "one shield," *yi dun* 一盾, applied to the person responsible for their accuracy. Furthermore, an additional level of inaccuracy is provided for those instruments deviating from the standard measure by more than two *sheng* and such an occurrence warrants an increased sanction of "one suit of armor," *yi jia* 一甲.

Thus we see that in keeping with the Qin mandate of metrological uniformity, the measurement instruments mentioned within this legal article are specifically defined according to a Qin standard of accuracy, and yet the legal importance of the phrase *bu zheng* differs significantly. A calibration discrepancy of one *sheng* for a *tong* measurement vessel or eight *liang* 兩 for a *hengdan* measurement instrument deviating from the standard measurement would certainly be considered "inaccurate" or *bu zheng*; however, legally, Qin statutes acknowledge and condone metrological inaccuracy to a specified level. Thus, a *tong* calibrated to 0.99 *sheng* higher than the statutory standard measurement would not fall under the legal definition of an "inaccurate *tong* instrument" (*bu zheng zhi tong* 不正之桶 or *tong buzheng* 桶不正). Instead of creating a linguistically simple legal article providing that inaccuracies of measurement devices are to be punished, whoever composed this particular legal article opted to provide a series of coordinated phrases intended to elaborate and clearly qualify the legal distinction between accurate and inaccurate *tong* and *hengdan* devices.

One finds similar definitional phrasing in other articles within the *Xiao lü* manuscript. In such cases, the meaning of a commonly used word is slightly elaborated and imbued with legal significance.

Example 5.3—*Xiao lü*—Article 5, Slips 8–10
{5}
數而贏不備值百一十錢以到二百廿錢誶官嗇夫過二百廿錢以到千一百 [8] 錢貲嗇夫一盾過千一百錢以到二千二百錢貲官嗇夫一甲過二千二百錢 [9] 以上貲官嗇夫二甲 [10]

When counting and there is a surplus or shortage valued at 110 cash to 220 cash, reprimand the *sefu* of the office; if exceeding 220 cash to 1100 (8) cash, fine the *sefu* of the office one shield; if exceeding 1100 cash to 2200 cash, fine the *sefu* of the office one suit of armor; if exceeding 2200 or higher, (9) fine the *sefu* of the office two suits of armor. (10)

Article 5 provides specific administrative sanctions for surpluses and shortages discovered when counting. As in the previous example, the terms surplus, *ying* 贏, and shortage, *bu bei* 不備, are the key concepts requiring specific legal definition in order to facilitate a desired interpretation by the reader. What constitutes a surplus or shortage? How are such phenomena calculated? These questions are only partially answered within the phrasing of this particular article. To begin, the concepts of shortage and surplus are defined in terms of coins or *qian* 錢. The reader of the article is not told whether or not what is being counted is in fact government stored *qian*. Alternatively, one could—though acknowledging the lack of context—interpret the shortages and surpluses found when counting to be physical items for which a *qian* value is calculated. Again, just as with the concept of *bu zheng*, we see the Qin drafters devising a statistical measure of leeway with what is considered to be a shortage or surplus. Not all incidences of excess or lack are legally considered to be shortages or surpluses. That is, certain levels of discrepancy discovered while counting do not warrant penal sanction, and are, therefore, under the statutory definition implicitly provided for in this article, not deemed to be *punishable* shortages or surpluses. Furthermore, we see that these two concepts are also divided into grades of surplus and shortage determined by the calculated *qian* value of each. The significance is that one must determine where to place the liability for such occurrence and each carries a specific sanction. Thus, within the sphere of Qin law, the simple concepts of "shortage" and "surplus" require specialized definitional specificity for accurate interpretation and application.

> Example 5.4—*Qin lü shiba zhong*—Slip 66
> 布袤八尺幅廣二尺五寸布惡其廣袤不如式者不行　　　金布 [66]
>
> Cloth measures eight *chi* in length and two *chi* and five *cun* in width. When cloth is inferior or its width and length do not accord with the standard-model, do not circulate. [Statute on] Currency (66)

Cloth was an important commodity in early China and in many instances was indeed considered to be a form of currency. This article is found in the *Qin lü shiba zhong* manuscript and according to its label was excerpted from a larger statute entitled [*Statute on*] *Currency*, *Jinbu lü* 金布律. Like instruments of measurement, the Qin government exercised control over the quality, quantity, and distribution of cloth. Their anxiety over such control is reflected in the present article which clearly and unambiguously provides the Qin statutory definition of "cloth," *bu* 布, that was permitted to be circulated as currency. Permissible "cloth" is first defined according to its physical dimensions. Only cloth measuring "eight *chi* in length and 2 *chi* and five *cun* in width" conforms to the statutorily defined "standard model," *shi* 式. Any cloth not conforming to these exact dimensions should not be circulated, and, by extension, would not fall into the statutory definition of "cloth." Following this, the article then elaborates and clarifies what legally constitutes permissible cloth by stating that any cloth of which the quality is deemed "inferior," *e* 惡 or which does not conform to the model-standard is not to be circulated.

A similar way in which drafters attempt to achieve terminological clarity is through enumeration. The practice of enumeration allows the drafter to explicitly define those items which fall within the jurisdictional ambit of a particular piece of legislation. Under a rather strict set of interpretive parameters, one would only apply the statutory provisions to those items specified. However, under a less strict system of interpretation, one might take these listed items to represent a class or category of items of which other similar items might be considered analogous and therefore fall under this provision.[20] Considering the Qin emphasis on consistent interpretation and limited judicial discretion, I would argue that when an article explicitly uses a linguistic enumeration device, the intent is to convey a rather closed interpretation.

> Example 5.5—*Xiao lü*—Article 22, Slip 45
> {22}
> 殳戟弩鬃[汧]相易殹勿以為贏不備以識耳不當之律論之 [45]
>
> When black or cinnabar-marked quarterstaffs, halberds, or crossbows are exchanged, one ought not take this to be a surplus or shortage; adjudicate in accordance with the statute concerning markings not corresponding. (45)

Article 22 of the *Xiao lü* provides a procedure for determining any penal liability for surpluses or shortages of military weaponry caused by exchanges. Specificity is clearly evinced in the wording of the article. Instead of utilizing a broad categorical term, such as "weapon," *bingqi* 兵器 or *wuqi* 武器, the individual terms falling into the jurisdiction of this particular provision are explicitly enumerated: quarter-staffs, *shu* 殳, halberds, *ji* 戟, and crossbows, *nu* 弩. It is apparent that only these three specific military weapons are covered by this article. This clarifies any potential applicability of this article to other types of weaponry which may be marked and later exchanged. For example, this statutory article does not provide for potential shortages or surpluses of swords, *jian* 劍, knives, *dao* 刀, or pieces of armor, *jia* 甲. Those officials tasked with auditing the proper numbers of weaponry within a county arsenal would necessarily need to know the types of weapons held, as well as how shortages or surpluses of each type are statutorily governed.

> Example 5.6—*Qin lü shiba zhong*—Slip 34
> 計禾別黃白青秫勿以稟人　　倉 [34]
>
> When calculating grains, isolate the yellow, white, green, and sorghum and do not use to ration the people. [Statute on] Granaries (34)

In this legal article, we see a prescriptive statement providing that when registering the quantities of grains still in the ear, an official is required to distinguish four specific types of grains that are not to be distributed as official rations. Though we are uncertain as to the reason for the distinction of these particular grain types, we can clearly see that the drafter of this document specifically singled them out for scrutiny. By utilizing the linguistic technique of enumeration, the meta-category of grains in the ear is subdivided into two distinct categories: those grains which can be used to ration the people and those that cannot. It is thus clear that grains are not all equal under the law. For the latter category, this article further provides a specific enumerated list that clearly distinguishes the permissible grains from impermissible. A Qin official tasked with rationing the people would be able to read this article and distinguish those grains he would be allowed to dispense to the populace, and those for which he would be statutorily liable for a sanction should they be dispensed.

Each of the examples above demonstrates an attempt to imbue specific legal meaning to commonly used terms. Consistency in legal meaning of these terms was important for Qin governance as was the fact that many of these statutory articles provide sanctions for any deviation from the statutory definitions. As such, the wording of legal statutes within the Qin reflects conscious attempts to produce a written text that clearly defines specific, legally significant terms. Yet, no written form is perfect, nor is any statutory language composed in such a way as to totally preclude ambiguity. Indeed, assessing the legal meaning of specific terms within statutes still causes problems within present day legal systems. For a Qin official, this was even more important as he was required to interpret and apply the law in a manner consistent with the desires of the Qin central government, and simultaneously he would be liable for punishments should he improperly interpret or apply a statutory provision.

Keeping terms clear: exegetical texts and statutory language

Among the many manuscripts interred in Tomb 11 at Shuihudi, archeologists also discovered an interesting legal manuscript entitled, *Falü dawen*. The content of the manuscript is composed in a dialogic question and answer style format, wherein a specific question related either to the language of a statute or the application of statute is posed and a response is recorded. While it is difficult to assess how widespread the use of such texts might have been among Qin officials, the types of questions posed within the *Falü dawen* do evince—at least for the person possessing this particular document—an anxiety over the proper interpretation and application of Qin legal statutes. Continuing with the line of inquiry relating to Qin legal terminology, I examine how the *Falü dawen* functions to disambiguate specific legal connotations for individual words, as well as phrases.

According to the excavators, and subsequent Shuihudi editors, the *Falü dawen* consists of 210 bamboo slips, each roughly 25 cm in length. The calligraphy is small and cramped. The text of the manuscript contains 190 individual articles wherein a question related to the law is posed and a response recorded. Each article is distinct and this distinction is represented by the spatial practice of beginning a new article on a fresh bamboo slip. Thus, slips containing text at the end of the article might have large amounts of blank space.

The textual contents of the manuscript are clearly reflected in its title. All of the articles are intended to clarify the language or application of the statutes. It does so primarily in one of two ways. First, advice is sought on the proper application of a statute by posing a specific "fact" pattern—at times with direct reference to a statutory provision—and then requesting guidance on how to apply the law in a case that does not perfectly match. Such inquiries typically include the phrase "how [is this] to be adjudicated?" *ke* (*he*) *lun* 可(何)論.

The second question and answer formulation is more pertinent to the present section. In this format, the questions do not concern the appropriate form of punishment or application of law; but instead deal specifically with disambiguating language found in legal statutes. This form of questioning is quite prevalent with 63 articles specifically pertaining to questions over linguistic ambiguity. Within these articles, the phrase *ke* (*he*) *wei* X 可(何)謂 X is often employed to seek clarification. This phrase is often translated as "what is the meaning of X?" or "what is meant by X?"

In terms of its use in guiding the individual's interpretation of statutory language, the *Falü dawen* articles disambiguate legal language on four levels: legal definition of specific terms, distinguishing an important semantic difference between two or more similar terms when found in a legal context, exegesis of particular phrases, and exegesis of complete sentences. Within each of these types, the main purpose appears to be to provide a standard or proper interpretation that would ensure consistency in legal application.

In this section, I am primarily interested in the ways in which the *Falü dawen* is employed to disambiguate the legal significance of specific terms or phrases. The question posed seeks clarification of the meaning of a specific term used in a passage of a statute. Frequently, a sentence or phrase from an unidentified statute will be directly cited, after which the question will refer specifically to a term within the phrase for which there is interpretative ambiguity over the precise *legal* meaning.

Example 5.7—*Falü dawen*—Slip 91
以梃賊傷人●何謂梃木可以伐者為梃 [91]

"The use of a cudgel to wantonly injure a person" ● What is meant by "cudgel?" Wood that can be used to attack is considered a cudgel. (91)

This represents a classic example of the "*he wei* X" interrogative sentence pattern which seeks elaboration upon the meaning of specific legal terms. The present example provides a five graph quote from the text of an undesignated legal statute. The quote from this statute is clearly demarcated from the remainder of the dialogue through the use of a [●] marker. The quote concerns the use of an object called a *ting* 梃 for the purpose of wantonly injuring another person. Because the legal quote explicitly cites the use of a specific item in the performance of the crime, the question posed seeks clarification on what legally constitutes a *ting*. As we only have a small quote—not the full statutory provision—we can only postulate that correctly determining what items may be categorized as a *ting* or not is of great importance for the proper application of this statutory provision. The response clarifies the categorical characteristics of items that can potentially be considered *ting*-like objects. Although the answer is rather broad, being any wooden piece capable of being used to attack a person, it is clear that the proper application of this article depended upon the official correctly determining if the weapon used by an assailant was a *ting* or not.

Example 5.8—*Falü dawen*—Slip 190
何謂甸人甸人守孝公獻公冢者殹 [190]

What is meant by "field personnel?" "Field personnel" are those who stand guard over the graves of Duke Xiao and Duke Xian.[21] (190)

This article also represents one of the most basic forms of the *he wei* 何謂 interrogative sentence structure. There are numerous examples of this simple construction found in the *Falü dawen* manuscript. The present slip begins with the simple sentence of "What is meant by field personnel?" The term *dian ren* 甸人 is apparently an official title; however, that title seems to hold some form of legal significance. Because of this significance, a question was posed seeking elaboration over what specific official functions may be categorized as *dian ren*.

The answer to the question specifies that only those individuals guarding the graves of two former dukes, Xiao and Xian. From this, we may assume that those individuals tasked with guarding the final resting places of other Qin nobility would *not* be categorized under the administrative or legal title of *dian ren*.

Example 5.9—*Falü dawen*—Slip 142
何如為犯令灋（廢）令律所謂者令曰勿為而為之是謂犯令₌(令)曰為之弗為是謂灋（廢）令殹 [142]

What is it to "contravene an ordinance" and to "disregard an ordinance?" Now what the statute refers to is when an ordinance provides that one ought not do [something], yet one does it, this is called "contravening an ordinance." When an ordinance provides that one is to do something, but one does not, this is what is called "disregarding an ordinance." (142)

In the present example, we see a request for clarification of two terms with seemingly similar semantic values, but which clearly possess demarcated legal meanings. To *fan* 犯 an ordinance and to *fei* (灋=廢) an ordinance both indicate an act going against the dictates of an officially promulgated ordinance; however, for the individual posing the question the circumstances of each act appears to be ambiguous. The question posed seeks to clarify what is specifically meant by each phrase. Although both words imply going against the ordinances, each possesses a very specific meaning which includes very different actions. In the first instance, the crime would be an active offense. In the latter, to *fei* an ordinance indicates a passive crime of inaction. Though we are not told, it seems as though the difference between the active and passive breaking of an ordinance implies a separate punishment or distinctive considerations of punishments. A proper understanding of the distinction between these two terms would, therefore, be very important.

The existence of a text like the *Falü dawen* clearly demonstrates not only the importance of legal language in Qin administrative culture, but, more specifically, the importance attached to obtaining uniformity and consistency when interpreting terms embedded with specialized legal meaning. Having examined the legal linguistic features of individual words, I will now turn my attention to the construction of individual statutory articles. Beginning with the simplest form, the single sentence conditional, and progressing to highly complex multi-conditional articles, I again look for evidence of the purposive use of linguistic features to ensure consistent readability as well as evidence of compositional practices which might actually impede interpretive continuity.

Compositional features of legal articles in the *Xiao lü*

As previously mentioned in various parts of this book, the *Xiao lü* manuscript represents a single Qin legal statute comprising 30 individual legal articles. This meta-architectonic feature directly influenced the way in which Qin drafters and scribes visually produced and reproduced the statute. Chapter 4 demonstrated that the copyist of the Shuihudi *Xiao lü* manuscript distinguished individual articles of the text by employing the punctuation-functioning visual features of blank space and beginning each new article on a separate bamboo slip. Likewise, in the other legal texts from Shuihudi, the *Qin lü shiba zhong* and *Qin lü zachao*, individual legal articles were distinguished using various punctuation methods, such as blank space, statute title, or the orthographic punctuation marker [•].

These latter two texts comprise multiple extracts from a variety of legal statutes. The fact that these articles could be excerpted from their original source further emphasizes the quasi-independent nature of individual legal articles. From a compositional perspective, this level of contextual independence also indicates that legal articles, the very building blocks of a statute, were composed in such a way as to be comprehensible on their own, with little or no reference to the larger text of which they were an integral textual component.

This section explores the compositional nature of statutory articles found in the *Xiao lü* manuscript. In particular, it considers what types of legal information were meant to be conveyed via individual articles and how such articles—intentionally conceptualized to have some level of interpretive-cognitive independence—were in fact composed.

In previous chapters, I have argued that remnant historical materials related to the Qin provide clear evidence of the government's concern over consistency in legal interpretation and application. It was shown that this anxiety over legal consistency, so palpable in philosophical and historical texts, as well as excavated materials, directly influenced the visual or codicological features of legal manuscripts during their production. One would, therefore, expect this anxiety over producing texts capable of consistent interpretation to affect the selection of specific, or perhaps formulaic, modes of textual composition which also maintain a level of linguistic consistency.[22] Instead, a cursory examination of the *Xiao lü* legal articles reveals a wide range of stylistic variability.

The high level of structural linguistic variability is evidenced from differing compositional features such as, article length, article content, and the form in which said content is presented. Indeed the shortest article is a mere 12 graphs in length. It is composed as a single casuistic sentence with one protasis outlining an individual situational topic and one apodosis assigning liability and prescribing a punishment.[23] Yet another short article—only 14 graphs—simply consists of two statements of legal "fact" regarding standard measurements for grain and hay piles in two different geographic locations. Alternatively, some of the longest articles consist of dozens of graphs, run the length of several bamboo slips, and demonstrate a high level of compositional complexity interweaving statements of fact, legal principles, situational topics, and numerous multi-layered protasis–apodosis sentences. Below I will analyze several examples of legal articles drawn from the *Xiao lü* manuscript. Each chosen article represents different compositional strategies and their analysis serves to illustrate the textual variations of length, content, and presentation.

Short statements of law

The *Xiao lü* manuscript contains several articles containing less than 20 graphs. This brevity, however, should not be construed as representing a simple, easily understood legal article. While some such articles are fairly precise in their language, others demonstrate a rather marked level of interpretive ambiguity. The following examples represent legal articles not composed in the more common legal "if–then" format, but which provide what might be called informational statements of law.

> Example 5.10—*Xiao lü*—Article 15, Slip 38
> 櫟陽二萬石一積咸陽十萬石一積 [38]
>
> In Yueyang 20,000 *dan* constitutes one pile; in Xianyang 100,000 *dan* constitutes one pile. (38)

At first blush, this particular article of only 14 graphs appears fairly simple and straightforward. It could be translated as two distinct sentences or as a compound sentence comprising two joint clauses each describing the quantitative equivalencies of *dan* unit measurements to a single pile, *ji* 積. The initial clause contains a specific geographic qualifier—Yueyang—and the connected, qualified subject–verb–object segment provides that at the specified location a specified quantity of *dan* is equivalent to a single pile. This is followed by an additional geographic qualifier—Xianyang—and a different specified quantity of *dan* which is also equivalent to a single pile.

Table 5.1 Compositional breakdown of *Xiao lü* Article 15, Slip 38

Geographic qualifier (1) In Yueyang…	**Distinct amount (1)** …20,000 *dan*…	**Standard unit** …constitutes one pile.
Geographic qualifier (2) In Xianyang…	**Distinct amount (2)** …100,000 *dan*…	

The *Xiao lü* manuscript provides numerous articles dictating the duties of an official charged with "checking" or "auditing" government offices thereby necessitating direct access to the appropriate (standard) units and measures against which the locality's figures would be assessed. In this article, it is clear that the primary topic is a "pile" and the information being conveyed is: (a) that the two places mentioned have different equivalencies for *dan* to pile conversions and (b) that those differences are 20,000 *dan* to a pile in Yueyang and 100,000 *dan* to a pile in Xianyang.

What is interesting about this particular article is that it simultaneously evinces both a level of specificity and ambiguity. The article clearly indicates to the reader that different locations maintain different conversions for *dan* and piles. But this brings up further questions not explicitly answered by this specific article. First, is there a *standard* ratio of *dan* units to a pile? The reader is only told of the ratio of *dan* units to a pile for two specific geographic locations, but no mention is made of other areas. How would an official in Dongting Commandery, Qianling County calculate a *dan* to pile conversion? A previous article in the *Xiao lü* manuscript indicates the potential for a standard ratio conversion by providing that when "entering *he* 禾, 10,000 *dan* constitutes one pile."[24] Thus, this article could be read as modifying legal information specified in separate articles, or perhaps even in separate legal statutes.

Alternatively, one must also consider the possibility that the statutory article is clarifying "historical" legal information. That is to say, Yueyang was the capital of Qin from roughly 383–350 BCE, while Xianyang became the capital around 350 BCE. Therefore, the article could be read as clarifying two different ratio conversions used at two different geographic locations during two different time periods. Unfortunately, the composition of this particular article does not convey adequate information to the reader. This ambiguity of phrasing necessitates broader knowledge located external to what is written in the text for proper comprehension.

Second, what is the actual material being measured and converted? That is, a *dan* is a unit of measurement for weight, and can therefore be applied to items or materials that can be weighed. The present article, however, does not specify the actual contents being measured. Other articles contained in the *Xiao lü*, as well as those excerpts from the *Qin lü shiba zhong* and *Qin lü zachao*, reference numerous types of produce capable of being measured by the *dan* or pile. To which does the present article refer? We may only tentatively postulate at this point; however, because adjacent articles reference issues concerning the collection, storage, and distribution of *he* 禾, then one might assume that it is the case for this article. Yet, standing alone, this article would not convey the requisite information for proper interpretation and application. That is to say, if this article were to be excerpted from the current statute without any other context—such as the case with several statutory excerpts in the *Qin lü shiba zhong* and the *Qin lü zachao*—it would be difficult for a reader to determine the specificity required.

A more detailed analysis makes clear that a simple article comprising a single sentence may appear non-ambiguous, yet when read within the context of a Qin legal culture requiring rigid precision in application and interpretation, the very wording of the article leaves a great deal of interpretive leeway. Furthermore, the ambiguity arising from its composition evinces a lessened sense of independence for this particular article. Proper interpretation and application requires a contextualized reading of this article vis-à-vis the whole legal statute. Other articles evince similar levels of compositional ambiguity that deemphasizes the standalone quality of individual articles by necessitating a contextualized interpretation.

Example 5.11—*Xiao lü*—Article 2, Slip 2
官嗇夫冗吏皆共償不備之貨而入贏 [2]

The *sefu* of the office and assigned clerks all jointly make restitution for shortages in goods; however, take in that which is surplus. (2)

This article comprises only 15 graphs and consists of a single sentence with limited linguistic complexity. It contains a compound subject, a verbal phrase indicating collective action, and a coordinated verbal phrase prescribing action back to the original two subjects.

Like the article previously analyzed, this article seems to be fairly straightforward, yet it too contains compositional elements leading to interpretive ambiguity. This ambiguity further limits the "independence" of the individual article from the collective whole.

This statutory article clearly provides for joint liability among members of the same office whenever shortages and surpluses are discovered. While this seems clear enough, one must remember that joint liability does not equate to equal liability. The greater Qin politico-legal philosophy of *xing ming* 形(刑)名 dictates that upon appointment an official is responsible for the success or failure of those duties ascribed to a particular office.[25] Indeed, several articles of the *Xiao lü* manuscript explicitly provide differing levels of liability for offenses and differing levels of severity in punishment among members of the same office.[26] Thus, on the one hand, the reader may comprehend that liability is jointly held by members of the same office, yet, on the other hand, the reader is not informed

Table 5.2 Compositional breakdown of *Xiao lü* Article 2, Slip 2

Compound subject The *sefu* of the office and assigned clerks…	**Adverbial qualifier** …all jointly…	**Command** …make restitution…	**Object**[1] …for shortages in goods…
		Secondary command …however take in…	**Secondary object** …that which is surplus.

Note
1 By "object," I am not implying that this phrase "for shortages in goods" is a direct or indirect object. It merely provides a description of what is being restituted.

how the levels of liability are assigned to the *sefu* versus the other lower ranking officials assigned to that office. To ascertain such information, the reader must engage the greater legal statute (or a separate statute) to locate additional articles dealing with situational issues similar to those confronting him. Again, while the present statutory article provides a clearly worded basic principle of law, its proper interpretation and application to a particular legal case is highly dependent upon supplementary information retained in other statutory articles.

Conditional articles of increasing complexity

Articles providing statements of legal "fact" or principles can be found in many collections of excavated materials from early China. The most common compositional structure for a statutory article, however, is the conditional or casuistic case/situation-based construction.[27] At its most basic, this structure consists of a protasis containing a set of situational facts. Often this set of facts provides fairly specific situational elements which give rise to a legal problem or offense. The protasis format usually begins (in English translation) with "If X situation occurs…" or "When X situation arises…" In its simplest form, the protasis is followed by an apodosis providing the legal liabilities and potential penal sanctions incurred from the situational facts.[28] In English translations, this is often initiated with a "then…" clause. Together the protasis–apodosis phrasing constitutes the formal and commonly used legal compositional form of a causal "if–then" or "when–then" sentence. Alternatively, casuistic sentences in ancient legal sources can be translated in a quasi-nominalized sentence format such as, "For X offense, Y punishment." In the Chinese context, the latter approach is preferred due to the lack of explicit conditional in most Qin legal statutes. That is, the conditional article, *ze* 則, is rarely, if ever, present. As a result, most scholars of early Chinese legal texts tend to eschew the use of "if … then" constructions in their translations.[29]

> Example 5.12—*Xiao lü*—Article 17, Slip 40
> 公器不久刻者官嗇夫貲一盾 [40]
>
> When government implements are not branded or inscribed,[30] the *sefu* of the office is fined one shield. (40)

At only 12 graphs, this article is the shortest found in the *Xiao lü* manuscript. It is composed in a basic single protasis–single apodosis sentence. In this example, I translate the text as a casuistic statement (i.e., When X occurs, Y is to occur in response). I do this to clearly demonstrate that the initial phrase is setting up a specific situation which is required *before* the dictates of the second phrase can be executed. The particle *zhe* 者 is acting to nominalize the phrase *gongqi bu jiu ke* 公器不久刻, thus making it an *event* (hence the "when") that occurs. A structural breakdown of the article illustrates how individual pieces of information are construed within the sentence to formulate a clearly defined legal situation and its consequences.

Table 5.3 Compositional breakdown of *Xiao lü* Article 17, Slip 40

Legal situation	Object of legal action	Legal action	Legal sanction
When government implements are not branded or inscribed…	…the *sefu* of the office…	…is fined…	…one shield.

In the present article, the legal situation is deemed central and thus placed at the head of the sentence. The reader quickly and clearly ascertains that the overall content of this article is the general "case" or situation wherein government tools lacking proper identifying inscriptions are discovered. The legal manuscripts from the Shuihudi corpus contain numerous references to regulating the production, maintenance, loaning out, and recovery of government implements. One statutory excerpt from the *Statute on Artisans*, *Gong ren cheng* 工人程 found in in the *Qin lü shiba zhong* manuscript stipulates that all government implements are to be branded or inscribed with the name of the office overseeing its distribution and collection.[31] Additional excerpts stipulate actions to be taken if implements are returned broken,[32] if they are lost by convict laborers,[33] if they are to be discarded due to loss of utility,[34] and how to request the production of additional or replacement government implements.[35] Furthermore, Anthony Barbieri-Low has argued that craftsmen markings on tools and other government implements also functioned to ensure that proper liability could be placed on artisans or their overseers for problems related to quality or defectiveness.[36] Thus, the presence of these markings was necessary for government officials tasked with ensuring consistency in production and maintaining quality control.

It comes as no surprise then that the *Xiao lü*, a statute concerning checking the status of government offices, contains several articles related to auditing records and verifying official stocks of government implements.[37] The present legal statute falls into this broader legal topic, yet refers more specifically to cases wherein government implements are discovered which are not inscribed at all. Such a discovery would complicate the auditor's ability to properly assess the stock of government implements. The official charged with conducting the check/audit is also required to assign liability and determine the proper penal consequences arising from the situation.

The present article accomplishes all these legal tasks with 12 simple graphs. First, it outlines the general situation. In order for the present article to be applicable, the auditing/checking official must ensure that the factual circumstances of his own audit correspond to the situational outline provided in the article topic phrase. He must, therefore, determine that the objects in question are indeed "government implements," *gongqi* 公器. This is distinct from non-governmental implements (lacking a 公 designation), as well as other, distinctive categories of government owned implements, such as military equipage which is regulated under separate legal articles and statutes. Having done this, the article then proceeds to prescribe the target of legal liability (the *sefu* of the office) and the appropriate level of severity for the corresponding sanction.

The drafter of this article conveyed all this legal information in a simple, yet clear legal-linguistic formula of:

> SITUATION → LIABILITY → LEGAL ACTION → SPECIFIC SANCTION

While this particular compositional protasis/apodosis structure of SITUATION → LEGAL RESULT can be employed as one of the clearest and most concise methods of legal writing, it can also be heavily elaborated in order to convey increasingly complex levels and greater amounts of legal information.[38] The following two examples illustrate these increased levels of compositional complexity by elaborating on the basic protasis/apodosis structure.

> Example 5.13—*Xiao lü*—Article 19, Slip 42
> 官府藏皮革數穆風之有蠹突者貲官嗇夫一甲 [42]
>
> When government storerooms hold hides and leathers, frequently dry[39] and air them. When there are worm boreholes, fine the *sefu* of the office one suit of armor. (42)

In this example, the article utilizes two compositionally similar forms of conditional sentences to convey distinct types of legal information. Though only 19 graphs in length, it provides two distinct sets of conceptually related situational facts and two distinct consequences of such fact sets.

In this statutory article, two distinct sets of situational facts are linked through a shared, single legal subject, *hides* and *leathers*. The drafter of this article embedded this single legal subject within a field of qualifiers providing locational specificity, legal commands (responsibilities), secondary qualifying situations, secondary commands, and targets of liability and sanction.

Table 5.4 Compositional breakdown of *Xiao lü* Article 19, Slip 42

Primary situation					
Subject qualifier When government storehouses hold …	**Legal subject** … hides and leathers …	**(1) Command modifier** … frequently …	**(1a) Command** … air …	**(1b) Command** … and dry …	**(1c) Command direct object** … them.
		(2) Secondary situation When there are worm boreholes …	**(2a) Secondary command** … fine …	**(2b) Secondary command object** … the *sefu* of the office …	**(2c) Secondary command indirect object** … one suit of armor.

The initial segment of the article provides the legal subject and qualifies this legal subject as being specifically to those hides and leathers which are held in government storage. Compositionally, the important use of this sentence-initial qualifier expediently signals to the reader the strict subject limitations of this article's applicability. Then, the first apodosis contains a command related to the care of these specific hides and leathers held by government offices. Though it is not explicitly stated, the targeted audience responsible for executing this particular command would presumably be the *sefu* of the office mentioned later in the article. This first sentence, therefore, provides the scope of the article and a directed command, but it leaves the target of legal liability for its proper execution unspecified.

A subsequent sentence further elaborates the potential scope of situational facts affecting the legal subject. A secondary protasis provides that *when* the previously mentioned legal subject—which is not repeated—is found to be damaged due to insect infestation, then penal action is required. The apodosis segment clearly assigns liability to the *sefu* of the office and prescribes a specific penal sanction of one shield. The initial sentence specifies legal obligations or duties for the *sefu* of the office and these obligations are composed in the form of a command, "frequently air and dry them (hides and leathers)." The intended audience of this initial command is the *sefu* of the office, yet in the second sentence, the composition shifts in perspective and the intended audience of the text is now the official reading this statutory article and charged with executing its provisions. That is, now the text is specifically composed for the person charged with assessing the existence of these situational facts and consequently applying the penal sanction prescribed.

Through this complex protasis–apodosis article construction, the drafter of this statutory article was able to convey two distinct layers of legal information affecting two different audiences. Furthermore, each sentence is necessary for understanding the whole of the article. The legal subject is mentioned in the first sentence, but not repeated in the second. The *sefu* of the office—the very target of responsibility and liability—is not mentioned in the initial sentence, but only in the second sentence. Thus, each element of each sentence performs an integral representative function for interpreting the statutory article in its entirety.

> Example 5.14—*Xiao lü*—Article 29, Slips 56–57
> 計校相謬殹自二百廿錢以下誶官嗇夫過二百廿錢以到二千二百錢貲一盾 [56] 過二千二百錢以上貲一甲人戶馬牛一貲一盾自二以上貲一甲 [57]
>
> When audited figures indicate mistakes, if 220 cash or below, reprimand the *sefu* of the office; if 220 to 2200 cash, fine one shield; (56) if it surpasses 2200 cash and above, fine one suit of armor. If one household, horse, or bull, fine one shield; if two or more, fine one suit of armor. (57)

The present article demonstrates further compositional complexity by linking a single legal situation to a series of dependent protasis–apodosis statements.

Table 5.5 Compositional breakdown of *Xiao lü* Article 29, Slips 56–57

Legal situation	**Value protasis (1)**	**Apodosis action (1)**	**Apodosis object**	**Apodosis sanction**
When audited figures indicate mistakes…	if 220 cash or below…	…reprimand…	…*sefu* of the office…	n.a.
	Value protasis (2) if 220 to 2200 cash…	**Apodosis action (2)** …fine…	[assumed same *sefu*]	…one shield…
	Value protasis (3) if it surpasses 2200 cash or above…	**Apodosis action (3)** …fine…	[assumed same *sefu*]	…one suit of armor.
	Specific protasis (A) If one household, horse, or bull…	**Apodosis action (A)** …fine…	[assumed same *sefu*]	…one shield…
	Specific protasis (B) …if two or more…	**Apodosis action (B)** …fine…	[assumed same *sefu*]	…one suit of armor.

These latter statements provide protasis qualifiers to the initial legal situation and are each paired with a corresponding apodosis segment containing a coordinated sanction.

The present article consists of 57 graphs and covers five potential variables for the primary legal situation that is outlined in the initial five graphs. It deals with a particularly worrisome issue of all administrative systems, the problem of bureaucratic mistakes made with registers or accounting. The Qin government relied heavily upon consistent and accurate reports and registers. As such, many articles in the *Xiao lü* deal specifically with the issue of falsified information, mistaken information, or careless information which somehow manages to be included into officials reports.

From the perspective of legal theory, this article is important because it illustrates the fact that the Qin legal system made a categorical distinction between acts committed purposefully and those committed by mistake or due to carelessness. Thus, we can question the rather unforgiving and "draconian" nature of Qin penal theory portrayed in later dynastic histories. That said, this mere distinction, while certainly important, is not well defined within the present statutory article. While the article provides that mistakes are recognized, the reader, however, is not told what actually *constitutes* a mistake. Most of this article focuses on the type and severity of the mistake, but not what conceptually constitutes a mistake. An official confronted with such a problem would need additional textual sources to distinguish a mistaken action from a purposive action.

Linguistically, the construction is quite similar to those articles found near the beginning of the *Xiao lü* manuscript which provide a series of measurement discrepancies and corresponding punishments, all scaled hierarchically according to increasing levels of discrepancy/severity. The present article consists of an initial statement about the discovery of mistakes and then proceeds to modify this initial statement with five qualifiers composed of protasis–apodosis phrases. Several features of the present article aid us in further understanding the ways in which more complex legal articles were purposively composed in order to facilitate consistent interpretation and application by those charged with their execution.

First, the primary legal issue of the article is the discovery of mistakes in the accounting registers of local government offices. The Qin bureaucracy functioned effectively through a well-developed communications system. The philosophical tenets of Shang Yang found in the *Shangjun shu* argue that the best rulers are aware of all that goes on in their kingdoms, and the documents excavated at Liye attest to the volume of administrative documentation required for the everyday functioning of a single county. Much of the Qin government system—such as taxes and corvée labor—relied heavily upon accurate record-keeping. The graph written for clerical mistake is *jiu* 繆 (OCM *kiu), "to twist," which the Shuihudi editors understand to be a phonetic loan representing the word *miu* 謬 (OCM *miuh), "to lie" or "to make an error."[40] The use of this term, and indeed this entire article, is very important for understanding Qin legal thought. Historically reviled for the harshness of its draconian laws for which there was no room for mitigating circumstances, the Qin legal system evidenced by the excavated legal texts such as the *Xiao lü*, however, depicts a very complex legal culture in which the intent of parties was quite important. In the present article, we see evidence of this in the categorical distinction between mistaken and purposive action.

Second, for all its potential for explaining issues related to legal concepts of intent in Qin legal thought, it does, however, leave a deal of ambiguity. We do not, for example, know what specifically constitutes a "mistake" in accounting. What is the definition of a mistake? How does one "prove" a mistake? How would one distinguish a mistake due to carelessness from a purposive misrepresentation?

Third, the remainder of the article consists of multiple protasis–apodosis qualifiers providing differing levels of "mistake" as well as corresponding sanctions of differing severity. Yet, these "mistakes" are also subdivided into two categories. The first is concerned with assessing the severity of a mistake according to the monetary value of the mistake. Here the reader is provided with three monetary value ranges which correspond to three specific sanctions. The second category is based upon single units of three different items: households, oxen, and horses. For this category, the calculus of punishment is determined by the numerical quantity of the mistake (i.e., a mistaken count of one or more items).

From this example, we can see a heightened level of compositional clarity since the drafter attempted to reduce interpretive ambiguity by distinguishing the conceptual categories of mistake and dealing with them in turn. However, this article still evinces a level of ambiguity. The reader is not told, for example, specifically which "objects" with a monetary value falling in the range provided in this article should be considered to fall within the authority of this statute. The article is clear about households, oxen, and horses, but what items of "value," if mistakenly recorded, should be dealt with under this article? Military weaponry has a monetary value, but is a mistakenly registered number of crossbows punishable under this statutory article? The reader is not told, and so the potential for ambiguity remains.

One finds a slightly different organizational principle informing the compositional structure of Articles 3 and 4. The specific contents of these articles have been discussed in previous sections; however, I have not discussed their overarching organizational principles.

Example 5.15—*Xiao lü*—Articles 3–4, Slips 3–7
{3}
If the *heng-dan* is not accurate by 16 *liang* or more, then fine the office's *sefu* one suit of armor. If not fully 16 *liang* to eight *liang*, then fine one shield. ∟ If the *tong* is not accurate by two (3) *sheng* or more, then fine one suit of armor. If not fully two *sheng* to one *sheng*, then fine one shield. (4)

{4}
斗不正半升以上貲一甲不盈半升到少半升貲一盾∟半石不正八兩以 [5] 上鈞不正四兩以上∟斤不正三銖以上∟半斗不正少半升以上∟參不正六 [6] 分升一以上∟升不正廿分升一以上∟黃金衡纍不正半銖以上貲各一盾 [7]

If the *dou* is not accurate by one-half *sheng* or more, then fine one suit of armor. If not fully one-half *sheng* to one-third *sheng*, then fine one shield. ∟ If the half-*dan* is not accurate by eight *liang* or (5) more, the *jün* is not accurate by four *liang* or more, ∟ the *jin* is not accurate by three *zhu* or more, ∟ the half-*dou* is not accurate by one-third *sheng* or more, ∟ the *can* is not accurate by (6) one-sixth *sheng* or more, ∟ the *sheng* is not accurate by one-twentieth *sheng* or more, ∟ weights of a gold balance are not accurate by a half-*zhu* or more, then for each fine one shield. (7)

As evident from the above example and the illustrative Table 5.6, this pairing of statutory articles provides a series of measurement discrepancies and their correlating penal sanction. What is interesting to note, however, is the compositional strategy employed by the composer of the articles. The information contained within the articles is not arranged categorically. That is, enumeration of discrepancies is not ordered according to the specific form of measurement (weight or volume). Nor is information organized according to specific measurement devices. Instead, the composition transitions to different objects based on the *amount* of discrepancy and the punishment. Thus we see

Table 5.6 Sequence of device/discrepancy/sanction in Articles 3 and 4

Measuring device	*Expected weight/ volume*	*Discrepancy (original)*	*Discrepancy (modern)*	*Sanction*
石	29.5 kg	16 兩 or higher	#≥245.76 g	1 甲
石	29.5 kg	8 兩 to 16 兩	122.88 g<#<245.76 g	1 盾
桶	11.976 L	2 升or higher	#≥398 mL	1 甲
桶	11.976 L	1 升to 2 升	199 mL<#<398 mL	1 盾
斗	1.996 L	半升 or higher	#≥99.5 mL	1 甲
斗	1.996 L	少半升 to 半升	66.33 mL<#<99.5 mL	1 盾
半石	14.75 kg	8 兩 or higher	#≥122.88 g	1 盾
鈞	7.37 kg	4 兩 or higher	#≥61.44 g	1 盾
斤	245 g	3 銖 or higher	#≥1.92 g	1 盾
半斗	0.998 L	少半升 or higher	#≥99.5 mL	1 盾
參	—	1/6 升 or higher	#≥31.16 mL	1 盾
黃金衡纍	n.a.	½ 銖 or higher	#≥0.32 g	1 盾

the *heng dan* and *tong*—measurement devices for weight and volume respectively—linked together in the initial article due to their larger size (i.e., greater potential for higher levels of discrepancy) and the fact that they have two distinct punishments. The subsequent article also organizes the measurement objects based first on the total amount of the discrepancy, yet towards the end it seems that the level of punishment is the primary factor. Single levels of discrepancy are provided in dependent protasis clauses which all share a common apodosis of *one shield* as the penal sanction. Thus, an official reading this article would need to read it entirely in order to fully assess whether or not the discrepancy of a particular measurement device was covered under this statute. Furthermore, the official would need *both* articles if confronted with multiple forms of measurement device.

Complex articles conveying legal principles and situational information

Example 5.16—*Xiao lü*—Article 7, Slips 17–18
同官而各有主殹各坐其所主官嗇夫免縣令₌ (令)人效其官₌ (官)嗇夫坐效以 [17] 貲大嗇夫及丞除縣令免新嗇夫自效殹故嗇夫及丞皆不得除 [18]

Within the same office, each has that which he superintends. Each is liable for that which he superintends. When the *sefu* of an office is dismissed, the County Prefect orders another to audit[41] his office. The *sefu* of the office is liable for (17) fines determined by the audit. The *grand sefu* and assistants are excused. When the County Prefect is dismissed, the new *sefu* personally audits. The former *sefu* and assistants are unable to be excused. (18)

Table 5.7 Componential breakdown of *Xiao lü* Article 7, Slips 17–18

Legal principle (A) →	**Legal situation (1)**	**Liability (1a)**	**Liability (1b)**
Within the same office, each has that which he superintends.	When the *sefu* of an office is dismissed, the Prefect orders another to audit his office.	The *sefu* of the office is liable for fines determined by the audit.	The *grand sefu* and assistants are excused.
Legal principle (B) →	**Legal situation (2)**	**Liability (2a)**	
Each is liable for that which he superintends.	When the prefect is dismissed, the new *sefu* personally audits.	The former *sefu* and assistants are unable to be excused.	

In the present example, we find a legal article providing two interrelated legal norms or principles, and supplements both norms with particular situations in which these norms are applicable and relevant or distinguishable.

One of the most important aspects of prosecuting a legal case is the proper determination of appropriate levels of liability for each of the parties involved. The present article is solely concerned with establishing specific liability relations between bureaucratic superiors and inferiors within the same office. To do this, the drafter composed the article in three distinct layers.

The initial layer outlines the theoretical underpinning of liability for administrative offenses. A bureaucracy is divided and subdivided many times over, and within each division and subdivision numerous personnel deal with a variety of separate, but interrelated tasks. This occupational interconnectedness within individual offices can create a legal problem when attempting to assign liability for an individual administrative offense. The opening of the article clearly articulates that within a bureaucratic system each office contains individual officials assigned a particular area of responsibility, and that official is liable for sanction should something go wrong. Indeed, the second sentence explicitly provides for this, "each is liable for that which he superintends" *ge zuo qi suo zhu* 各坐其所主. Thus, the initial section of this article provides a highly generalized legal principle of administrative liability, yet does not necessarily provide liability risks for subordinate officials when a superior in charge of the overall office is accused of an offense.

In the second and third layer of the composition, we see a conscious effort to further modify the general principles outlined in the initial section in order to clarify their applicability in specific cases. This particular article seems concerned with the liability of subordinates when administrative malpractice by a superior is discovered. Two potential "legal situations" are provided for, and the appropriate method with which to assign liability is detailed.

Thus, in the present article we see the compositional features steering the reader from the general to the specific. Each segment of the article provides the reader (presumed to be the one tasked with applying this statute) with an additional layer of information allowing a clearer comprehension of the article's specific applicability.

Other compositional features of statutory articles

Noun repetition

Another important compositional strategy that facilitates consistent interpretation and decreased ambiguity is the repetition of full subject or object nouns within a sentence and throughout a textual unit. As Tiersma states, "[o]ne of the most salient ways in which lawyers try to enhance precision is by avoiding pronouns."[42] Likewise, Mattila argues that accuracy within legal texts often "presupposes that a noun in a sentence is not replaced by a pronoun if that can cause ambiguity as to the subject or the object of the sentence."[43] Such ambiguity is easily demonstrated through a simple sentence.

> *Sally told Lucy* ***she*** *kissed* ***her*** *boyfriend.*

Without additional context, the meaning of this sentence can potentially be interpreted in four different ways.

> Sally informed Lucy that Sally had kissed Sally's boyfriend.
> Sally informed Lucy that Sally had kissed Lucy's boyfriend.
> Sally informed Lucy that Lucy had kissed Sally's boyfriend.
> Sally informed Lucy that Lucy had kissed Lucy's boyfriend.

The efficacy of legal language is dependent upon a compositional consciousness striving for interpretive clarity. In the above example, if legal liability arose depending upon who kissed whom, then the use of pronouns in such decontextualized statements could create a problematic level of ambiguity for legal application. As such, drafters of legal documents are quite hesitant to employ pronouns for fear of increasing the ambiguity of the text through linguistic impersonalization. When composing a complex sentence, the key substantives are often times repeated with the addition of precision words such as the *aforementioned* X or *the said* X.[44] Such practice might mean that the words "the Tenant" can be found four to five times within the same sentence of an apartment rental contract; however, those working with documents embedded with potential legal consequences prefer prolixity over the succinct, if such repetition ensures increased clarity.

In the *Xiao lü* manuscript, we see varying levels of specificity with noun–pronoun usage. In certain articles, the object of a penal sanction, the liable official, is often repeated in each apodosis phrase; however, in very similarly constructed articles, the official liable for an offense is mentioned in the initial apodosis, yet never again mentioned, only implied. This would not be a problem in cases where one individual was solely liable for an offense; however, if an administrative offense could implicate colleagues or subordinate officials, then specificity in liabilities would be required.

Additionally, we find a few compositional features within the *Xiao lü* manuscript indicating that the practice of noun or substantive repetition was certainly utilized, yet that it was not consistently employed. Compare the use of the official title *sefu* 嗇夫 in Articles 3, 4, and 5.

> Example 5.17—*Xiao lü*—Articles 3 and 4—Slips 3–7
> {3}
> If the *heng-dan* is not accurate by 16 *liang* or more, then fine the office's *sefu* one suit of armor. If not fully 16 *liang* to eight *liang*, then fine one shield. ∟ If the *tong* is not accurate by two (3) *sheng* or more, then fine one suit of armor. If not fully two *sheng* to one *sheng*, then fine one shield. (4)
>
> {4}
> If the *dou* is not accurate by one-half *sheng* or more, then fine one suit of armor. If not fully one-half *sheng* to one-third *sheng*, then fine one shield. ∟ If the half-*dan* is not accurate by eight *liang* or (5) more, the *jün* is not accurate by four *liang* or more, ∟ the *jin* is not accurate by three *zhu* or more, ∟ the half-*dou* is not accurate by one-third *sheng* or more, ∟ the *can* is not accurate by (6) one-sixth *sheng* or more, ∟ the *sheng* is not accurate by one-twentieth *sheng* or more, ∟ weights of a gold balance are not accurate by a half-*zhu* or more, then for each fine one shield. (7)
>
> {5}
> When counting and there is a surplus or shortage valued at 110 cash to 220 cash, reprimand the *sefu* of the office; if exceeding 220 cash to 1100 (8) cash, fine the *sefu* of the office one shield; if exceeding 1100 cash to 2200 cash, fine the *sefu* of the office one suit of armor; if exceeding 2200 or higher, (9) fine the *sefu* of the office two suits of armor. (10)

The contents of the previous articles are similar; however, the explicit reference to the object of penal sanction, the *sefu*, is repeated in each apodosis of Article 5, while is only written once in the space of *two* different articles (3 and 4).

In Article 3, the *sefu* is mentioned in the initial apodosis, yet all subsequent apodosis statements merely assume the same subject. The retention of blank space beginning a new article is a clear indication that Article 4 is distinct from Article 3; however, there is no subject in the initial apodosis of Article 4. It appears that the reader must infer the transference of the previous article's subject to the present article.

Introducing the subject of a sentence and then adding several subordinated clauses or separate sentences describing or modifying the initial, non-repeated subject is a common linguistic form in classical Chinese. For legal texts, however, this succinct grammar pattern can prove quite problematic as correctly ascertaining the culpability of individuals and their level of liability within the statutory language is of the utmost importance for officials serving in judicial capacities. The opening lines of the Statute on Checking provide that for all shortages and surpluses the *sefu* and clerks are jointly liable. Yet, this liability is not strictly equal, so clearly articulating the individual to which a specific statutory provision applies would be very important. The complexity of properly assigning levels of liability is demonstrated in Article 8 (Slips 17–18) and Article 9 (Slips 19–21). Each of these articles provides specific circumstances in which the initial statement of Article 2 (that in cases of shortages or surpluses, the *sefu* of the office and subordinate officials are jointly liable)[45] is significantly qualified. Article 8, for example, provides that when a *sefu* is dismissed due to a crime, then there is the possibility for mitigation of penalties for subordinates; however, if a prefect is dismissed, then those under his command are unable to escape punishment. Similarly, Article 9 provides a timeline of liability for surpluses or shortages wherein a dismissed official can be exempt from punishment if his replacement fails to conduct the appropriate audit within one year. These examples demonstrate the importance of clearly demarcating the subject–object of any legal liability through the repetitive use of nouns and the limited or non-use of pronouns.

Based on the above examples, we can postulate that the composers of Qin statutes at times made use of noun repetition for the purposes of clarity; however, the practice was not universal or consistent, even within a single text. The examples drawn from the *Xiao lü* clearly indicate the inconsistency in this matter. Such inconsistency could potentially give rise to varying levels of interpretative ambiguity, especially when an official would need to properly ascertain specific levels of liability for different individuals based upon a written text.

Broadened audience through impersonal sentence constructions

Most legal statutes in premodern societies are constructed of casuistic or conditional sentences like those outlined above. To increase the applicability of the statutory language, drafters often composed such statutory sentences so as to make them generalized, and, therefore, not to restrict them to a limited category of individual. Even today, many modern legal drafters continue to compose legislation in ways that indicate the general applicability of the encoded legal norms.[46] This is often done using impersonal constructions. That is, present day drafters commonly construct sentences that are phrased in the third person, while first and second person phrasings are avoided. The argument against first and second person constructions stems from the way in which personalized phrasing limits the target audience of the law. This is particularly problematic if a legal provision is being composed with the intention of having a broad or universal jurisdiction. By phrasing the sentence in the second person, the primary audience of the legal provision could become narrower than what the legislator originally intended. In the ancient world, however, one commonly finds laws written as prescriptive or proscriptive statements personally directed towards the specific category of person, for example, "you shall" or "you shall not," or the biblical "thou shall not."[47] Sentences framed in the first person, "I order" or "I declare" can also be found in the ancient world, though one typically sees such language employed in legislative prologues like that found on the stele of Hammurabi.[48] Most legislation language, however, uses the impersonal, third person phrasing to maximize the potential audience of the written text.

As mentioned above, the *Xiao lü* manuscript explicitly states its intended audience and jurisdiction. Slip 1 provides that this particular statute is intended for the "general offices and counties." After this, the language of the statutory provisions is completely impersonal. One does not find directed first or second person phrasal constructions. The more common classical Chinese personal pronouns, *wo* 我, *wu* 吾, *ru* 汝, *er* 爾, *zi* 子, are not found in Qin legal statutes. In terms of audience, we can then argue that the phrasing of the statutory provisions found in the Shuihudi corpus could be more generally directed at either the official tasked with carrying out the prescriptions of the provision or the official tasked with properly censuring an individual who has transgressed the provisions. The use of such impersonalized language within the *Xiao lü* manuscript provides us with a hint at the universality of legislation in Qin legal culture.

Inter/intra-textuality, textual-mapping and legal referencing

The presence of referential qualifications within legal statutes constitutes another set of important compositional features that can greatly aid our understanding of statutory drafting in Qin legal culture. In particular, an analysis of the forms and functions of referential qualifications within extant Qin statutes provides a window through which to view how drafters of a single legal statute—consisting of several individual textual units—organized the multiple layers of legal information into an internally coherent textual whole. Furthermore, referential qualifications allow us to consider how an individual statute was contextualized into an existing, systematized body of written law. In this section, I will introduce the various forms and functions of referential qualifications within the context of statutory composition, and then proceed to analyze the evidence of its uses in the Shuihudi legal materials.

Referencing is an important feature of modern legislation; however, its use is well attested in earlier forms of legal writing ranging from laws of ancient Greece to medieval European legal compilations. At its most basic, referencing involves the embedding of compositional devices within a single textual unit which then serve to indicate a specific relationship of that textual unit to another preceding or preceded textual unit.[49] These textual units can be part of a larger, complex text or they may be a distinct part of a larger textual corpus. Linguists often term this compositional feature textual-mapping, referencing, referential qualification, or cross-referencing, and within the context of law it is referred to as legal referencing, legislative mapping, or statutory linkage.

Referencing functions on multiple textual and cognitive levels and can take a variety of forms. However, according to most linguistic research on legal statutes, referencing primarily serves one of two functions, or both simultaneously: a text-cohesive function and a text-claritive function. Referential devices serving a text-cohesive function often "indicate textual relations between various (sub) sections of the same or related provisions."[50] Such references often point to specific preceded or preceding textual units. By adding this form of referential qualification distant, yet interrelated, textual units of a lengthy and complex text can be cognitively connected at various points throughout the text, thereby increasing reader comprehension and interpretive consistency.[51] In modern legislation, these references frequently take the form of directional phrases such as; "*see section* 113 *below*," "*as specified in article* 4 *of this Act*," or "*as found in paragraph* 8 *of the above section* 12."

Alternatively, the text-claritive function indicates a specific legal relationship between textual units, such as the jurisdictional ambit of a statute or a reference to definitional statements required to understand the language of the statute in question. In the first instance, the text-claritive function is typically used to distinguish a particular legislative hierarchy between pieces of legislation (or within a single piece of legislation). Thus, for example, one could find a statement such as, "the provisions of statute A are applicable in all cases except those situations found in statute B." In the second instance, a preceding piece of legislation can hold a particular legal definition of a word or phrase, and instead of writing the definition again into the new piece of legislation, the drafters merely reference the location of the legal meaning of the term: *as defined in X*.[52]

There are four modes of referencing that are common in legal statutes. The first two are "directional" in that they convey the location of the specific reference to the reader. Directional indicators are either internal (i.e., a reference to a different part of the same text) or external (i.e., a reference to a different text). The other two features are related to the level of linguistic precision of the reference and are articulated as either a direct reference (i.e., a direct citation to a specific text or section of a text) or an indirect reference (i.e., a reference to a legal norm but where no specific textual source for this norm is cited). The former two features and the latter two features are conceptually linked, so one will have a direct external reference to another legal statute or an indirect internal reference to a legal norm found in an unspecified section of the same statute.

In the remainder of this section, I will analyze the forms and functions of referential qualifications found in the *Xiao lü* manuscript, as well as the *Qin lü shiba zhong* and *Qin lü zachao*, and conclude with a consideration of what referencing can tell us about the composition of early Chinese legal manuscripts, specifically statutes within Qin legal culture.

Evidence of legal referencing from the **Xiao lü** *manuscript*

The *Xiao lü* manuscript contains several examples of legal referencing with varying levels of specificity. Examples of direct external, indirect external, direct internal, and indirect internal are all attested in the *Xiao lü* and these examples allow us to make a limited reconstruction of specific compositional norms informing the textual production of statutes in Qin legal culture.

Direct internal referencing

Example 5.18—*Xiao lü*—Article 5, Slips 8–16
{5}

When counting and there is a surplus or shortage valued at 110 cash to 220 cash, reprimand the *sefu* of the office; if exceeding 220 cash to 1100 (8) cash, fine the *sefu* of the office one shield; if exceeding 1100 cash to 2200 cash, fine the *sefu* of the office one suit of armor; if exceeding 2200 or higher, (9) fine the *sefu* of the office two suits of armor. (10)

{6}
縣料而不備者欽書其縣料殹之數 [11]

When weighing and there is a shortage, carefully record the numbers of the weighing. (11)

{7}
縣料而不備其現數五分一以上值其價其貲誶如數者然十分一以到不盈 [12] 五分一值過二百廿錢以到千一百錢誶官嗇夫過千一百錢以到二千二百錢 [13] 貲官嗇夫一盾過二千二百錢以上貲官嗇夫一甲百分一以到不盈十分一 [14] 值過千一百錢以到二千二百錢誶官嗇夫過二千二百錢以上貲官嗇夫 [15] 一 盾 [16]

When weighing and there is a shortage of one-fifth or higher of its present/expected number, value its worth, and its fines and reprimands are like those of counting. [If it] is one-tenth to not fully one-fifth (12) and the value exceeds 220 cash to 1100 cash, reprimand the *sefu* of the office; if exceeding 1100 cash to 2200 cash, (13) fine the *sefu* of the office one shield; [if] exceeding 2200 cash or higher, fine the *sefu* of the office one suit of armor. If it is one-hundredth to not fully one-tenth (14) and the value exceeds 1100 cash to 2200 cash, reprimand the *sefu* of the office; if exceeding 2200 cash or higher, fine the *sefu* of the office (15) one shield. (16)

Article 6 of this grouping requires the careful recording of any shortages found when a county conducts an audit. Articles 5 and 7 also pertain to discrepancies found during administrative auditing (assessing proper quantities and weights of things) and the appropriate penal sanctions for such discrepancies. In terms of their linguistic composition, Articles 6 and 8 follow a syntactic pattern similar to that of other related legal articles in the *Xiao lü* manuscript. The formula begins with the presentation of a legal topic, "when counting there is a surplus or shortage" (Article 5) or "when weighing there is a shortage" (Article 7). After this, one finds a series of complex casuistic phrases in the protasis–apodosis format intended to clearly differentiate specific levels of measurement discrepancy and the appropriate level of severity of the sanction.

There is, however, one distinct difference between the two articles (5 and 7). Article 7 related to "weighing things" should contain eight protasis–apodosis sentences defining eight separate levels of measurement discrepancy and eight corresponding sanctions. Instead, the article clearly defines four levels of discrepancy with their corresponding sanction, but the initial level of weight discrepancy (one-fifth or above) and its sanctions are defined via a direct internal reference to the preceding Article 5: "its fines and reprimands are like those of counting" *qi zi sui ru shu zhe ran* 其貲誶如數者然. Table 5.8 illustrates the totality of discrepancies and sanctions covered by Article 7, as well as the sources required for determining each.

Table 5.8 demonstrates that while the content of Article 7 is distinct and insular, in order to properly interpret and apply the penal provisions, however, one must have access to Article 5. Indeed, any official lacking access to both of these statutory articles would be unable to determine the appropriate punishment prescribed for all eight potential levels of discrepancy. Clearly there is a consciousness of the interconnectedness between individual articles to form a cohesive statutory whole.

Indirect internal referencing

> Example 5.19—*Xiao lü*, Article 24, Slip 50
> 計用律不審而贏不備以效贏不備之律貲之而勿令償 [50]
>
> When auditing, and the use of statutes is careless and results in a surplus or shortage, fine [the guilty person] in accordance with the Statute pertaining to checking for surpluses and shortages; however, one ought not order repayment. (50)

Similar to the previous example, this article utilizes internal referencing to outline the scope of the legal topic, define its levels of discrepancy, and delineate the severity of its sanctions. Here the primary topic is the presence of a surplus or shortage; however, the numerical discrepancy of concern is the direct result of a careless administrative error and is not an actual surplus or shortage of materials. This is of course different from discovering an actual surplus or shortage, hence the added provision that the guilty party is not liable to repay any shortage carelessly recorded.[53]

Table 5.8 Location of proper sanction for counting discrepancies in Article 7

Source	*% discrepancy*	*Value (in 錢)*	*Sanction*
Cross-ref to Article 5	1/5 or higher	110 to 220	誶
Cross-ref to Article 5	1/5 or higher	220 to 1100	1 盾
Cross-ref to Article 5	1/5 or higher	1100 to 2200	1 甲
Cross-ref to Article 5	1/5 or higher	2200 or higher	2 甲
Article 7	1/10 to 1/5	220 to 1100	誶
Article 7	1/10 to 1/5	1100 to 2200	1 盾
Article 7	1/100 to 1/10	1100 to 2200	誶
Article 7	1/100 to 1/10	2200 or higher	1 盾

The proper application of this particular article requires multiple steps due to the use of internal referencing. One would need to first assess whether or not the accounting discrepancy is actual or a clerical error based on the careless application of statutory provisions. Once a clerical error is determined as the cause of the discrepancy, the reader would then need to locate within the *Xiao lü* text the pertinent legal article covering the type of discrepancy and calculate the appropriate sanction. As a final step, the person charged with executing some sanction upon the guilty party would need to once again reference the original article to adjust the severity of the sanction because the party guilty of a shortage caused by a clerical error is not liable for repayment of the shortage, whereas the party guilty of an actual shortage is liable.

This article makes use of a broader, more indirect scope of referencing than in the previous example. In the previous example, the article pertaining to weight discrepancies references a particular section of the *Xiao lü* dealing with counting and only a portion of this referenced article on counting is applicable for weighing. The present article, however, defines the legal topic of a clerical error-based discrepancy with a very broad referential qualification, and its proper application would require access not just to a particular article, but to the totality of statutory provisions related to surpluses and shortages. This clearly evinces a strong interconnectedness between individual legal articles of a larger textual whole and a conscious use of referential qualifications as text-claritive and text-cohesive compositional features.

External direct referencing

> Example 5.20—*Xiao lü*—Article 16, Slip 39
> 效公器贏不備以齎律論及償毋齎者乃值之 [39]
>
> When checking public implements, surpluses and shortages are to be adjudicated according to the Statute on Equipment and [shortages] must be repaid. If something is not considered "equipment," then value it.[54] (39)

This example is a rather clear use of a direct external reference. The article is part of a larger statute on checking, yet its topic relates not only to checking within the ambit of this present statute, but is also connected to administrative requirements covered under separate statutes. Once the article demonstrates that under the system of "checking" a surplus or shortage is a legal issue, it then utilizes a referential qualification to perform three functions. First, the reference indicates to the reader that there is a link between the legal topic in this statute and additional legislation/statutes found elsewhere. Second, although it is clearly listed as a punishable offense in the present statute, the referenced statute must be sought to determine the level of the offense and the severity of its corresponding punishment. As such, a surplus or shortage of public implements would be considered legal offenses under the *Xiao lü*, but must be adjudicated in accordance with the stipulations found within the *Ji lü*.

As in the examples of internal referencing, the use of direct external referencing can serve both a text-cohesive and a text-claritive function. The referencing of required information found in a separate and topically distinct statute demonstrates the interconnectedness of different statutes in Qin legal culture, and is indicative of the text-cohesive function of referencing. Furthermore, the text-claritive function of this referential qualification signals how this particular provision in this particular statute relates, in terms of a hierarchy of authority, to contemporaneous statutes of the Qin legal corpus.

External indirect referencing

> Example 5.21—*Xiao lü*—Article 22, Slip 45
> 殳戟弩髹[汧]相易毆勿以為贏不備以識耳不當之律論之 [45]
>
> When staffs, halberds, or crossbows bearing lacquer or cinnabar [markings] are exchanged, this ought not be considered as surplus or shortage; adjudicate according to the Statute pertaining to markings not matching. (45)

The legal texts of the Shuihudi corpus contain numerous references to government marks/seals which were applied to military weapons or public tools. The Qin took great care in regulating the dispersal and collection of these types of items, and, as such, it is little surprise that a statute related to administrative checking contains sanctions for their loss or surplus. Yet, while the exchange of military weapons—to the extent that the number of weapons registered and the number of weapons accounted for differ—is a concern for administrative checking, the article explicitly states that this particular legal issue should not be adjudicated under the *Xiao lü*, but instead in accordance with the provisions of another legal statute.

I classify this particular reference as an *indirect* external qualification because I understand the *zhi* 之 graph in the phrase *shi er bu dang zhi lü* 識耳不當之律 to serve a linguistic function indicating a statute containing provisions related to marks not corresponding, but not indicative of a particular statute entitled, *Statute on Markings Not Matching*. The present format is similar to that of Example 5.19 above in which the phrase "Statute pertaining to checking for surpluses and shortages" *xiao ying bu bei zhi lü* 效贏不備之律 indicates a broad category of potential statutory provisions that would need to be consulted. To qualify as a *direct* external reference, I argue that the specific statute should be named as in the use of *Ji lü* in Example 5.20 above.

> Example 5.22—*Xiao lü*—Article 11, Slips 25–26
> 度禾芻稾而不備十分一以下令復其故數過十分以上先索以稾人而 [25]
> 以律論其不備 [26]
>
> When measuring grain in the ear,[55] hay or straw and there is a shortage of one-tenth or less, then order its former quantity to be restored. When

> exceeding one-tenth or more, first empty it to ration the people, and then (25) in accordance with the statute(s) adjudicate its shortage. (26)

This article covers the sanctions corresponding to discrepancies discovered when measuring specific types of grains, grasses, and hay. The lesser offense, a shortage of one-tenth or less, merely requires restitution for the missing amount. The more severe offense found in the second conditional statement, however, is more complex. Instead of providing a list of amounts and their corresponding sanctions, the text states that shortages of one-tenth or more are to be adjudicated in accordance with the statute, *yi lü lun qi bu bei* 以律論其不備. The question is, of course, which statute is to be consulted and applied? The *Xiao lü* manuscript contains several references to shortages; however, the *Qin lü shiba zhong* also contains excerpts from the *Cang lü* 倉律 or *Statute on Granaries*. The *Statute on Granaries* excerpts outline similar legal topics and provide penal sanctions for shortages. If these two statutes (and possibly other statutes) contain overlapping or duplicate legal provisions, an official faced with applying this particular article would require knowledge of all the relevant statutes for this legal topic, as well as the jurisdictional hierarchy of the statutes. Such reference types do serve a text-cohesive function; however, the level of referential ambiguity potentially limits its efficacy in directing the reader to the correct provision and instead relies heavily upon the reader's familiarity and access to other statutes.

> Example 5.23—*Xiao lü*—Article 30, Slips 58–60
> 計脫實及出實多於律程及不當出而出之值其價不盈廿二 [58] 錢除廿 二錢以到六百六十錢貲官嗇夫一盾過六百六十錢以上貲官嗇夫一甲而復 [59] 責其出殹 [60]
>
> When calculating and grain stores have been omitted, and if grain stores are dispensed in greater quantities than the statutory limit, as well as if what does not warrant to be dispensed is dispensed, then estimate its value. If not 22 (58) cash, it is absolved; if 22 cash to 660 cash, fine the office's *sefu* one shield; if exceeding 660 cash or more, fine the office's *sefu* one suit of armor and [he] is responsible for restoring (59) that which was dispensed. (60)

Many of the provisions in the *Xiao lü* are concerned with public stores of grains, as well as public property such as weapons and utensils. Whereas the previous examples of referential qualifications primarily reference texts (either directly or indirectly), the present article contains the rather oblique reference to a "statutory limit" 律程 for the dispersal of grain stores. The source of this statutory standard, however, is not clearly articulated. The ambiguous nature of this particular reference demonstrates that an official charged with carrying out the provisions of this article would require the knowledge of where to find the definition of this limit and, after ascertaining that information, then refer back to the present article in order to assess the severity of sanction for the offense.

Indirect external/internal referencing

> Example 5.24—*Xiao lü*—Article 9—Slips 20–21
> 實官佐史柀免徙 … [19] … 故吏弗效新吏居之未盈歲去者與居吏坐之新吏弗坐∟其 [20] 盈歲雖弗效新吏與居吏坐之去者弗坐它如律 [21]
>
> When assistants or scribes of an office related to stores are dismissed, removed, or relocated … (19) … If the former official does not check and the new official has not been in office for a full year, then the departed [official] and those remaining officials are jointly liable for it [shortages/surplus]. The new official is not liable. ∟If (20) a full year, then although not checked, the new official and those remaining officials are liable for it. The departed [official] is not liable. All else is to be done in accordance with the statutes. (21)

The above example contains perhaps the broadest and most indirect form of referencing, but it is also one of the most common. The article describes a series of complex legal situations in which the key issue is determining individual liability for surpluses and shortages. Interestingly, after differentiating the two levels of liability, the phrase "all else is to be done in accordance with the statutes" *ta ru lü* 它如律 is appended to the end of the article. So what is this indirect referencing doing?

To understand what is being referenced, one must consider the purpose of this particular article. First, its primary focus is ascertaining the appropriate levels of liability for officials under a specified set of circumstances. The issue of liability is linked to the issue of shortages and surpluses, but the article takes the existence of the shortage/surplus as a matter of fact. Therefore, once the reader has determined those individuals liable, as well as their respective levels of liability, the legal issue of the shortage or surplus must then be dealt with. Here the referential phrase, *ta ru lü* 它如律 indicates the next step in the process. It signals to the reader that the individuals described in the present article are liable for any offenses or sanctions related to surpluses or shortages found in this or any other statute. This necessitates both knowledge of and access to those statutory provisions related to surpluses and shortages that are found in the *Xiao lü*, and also to those statutes referenced within the *Xiao lü*. It is for this reason that I consider this phrase to have the dual function of both an indirect external statute and an indirect internal statute.

In summary, the *Xiao lü* manuscript contains several referential qualifications of varying levels of ambiguity and precision. These examples demonstrate that during the composition of this particular statute there was a conscious emphasis to include textual devices that would cognitively unite distant segments of the same statute to create a greater sense of textual coherence, as well as to link legal provisions found in different statutes.

Referential qualifications in the* Qin lü zachao *and* Qin lü shiba zhong *manuscripts

The *Xiao lü* manuscript is an individual legal statute containing a vast range of legal topics instructing a newly appointed official on the proper methods of auditing the records of his predecessor and providing clear allotment of liability and sanctions for any discrepancies discovered during such auditing. The *Xiao lü* utilizes several referential qualifications allowing the modern researcher to postulate a variety of compositional norms employed to produce internal textual cohesion, as well as textual methods applied during the Qin to link individual statutes, thus creating a systematic body of statutory texts. Yet, the *Xiao lü* is only one example of a legal statute. Do the referential qualification practices evidenced in this particular manuscript appear in other legal manuscripts? If so, do these manuscripts employ similar forms of referential qualifications and with the intent of serving similar functions?

Luckily, the *Xiao lü* was not the only legal text within the Shuihudi corpus, and, as has been previously noted, the tomb of Xi also yielded two additional manuscripts that contain statutory provisions, the *Qin lü zachao* and *Qin lü shiba zhong*. Interestingly, these two manuscripts are in and of themselves representative of a form of legal referencing. Each consists of multiple excerpts drawn from a variety of legal statutes and compiled into a single document. These excerpts are individually distinguished and are referentially labeled with the statute title from which they were taken. Embedded within the actual text of these individual excerpts, however, one finds several referential qualifications—both internal and external—which evince compositional features strikingly similar to those found in the *Xiao lü* manuscript.

Below, I translate a small selection of referential qualifications drawn from these two manuscripts. In doing so, the compositional and conceptual similarities between the form and function of referential qualifications in all three manuscripts become clear.

Direct referencing

Example 5.25—*Qin lü shiba zhong*—Slip 57
日食城旦盡月而以其餘益為後九月稟所城旦為安事而益其食以犯令律論吏主者 [57]

For daily rations of *cheng dan*, when the month is completed take their remainders/excess to serve as the latter ninth month's rations. When a *cheng dan* performs simple services,[56] yet his rations are increased, then adjudicate the official in charge in accordance with the Statute on Disobeying Ordinances. (57)

Table 5.9 Direct and indirect referencing

	Qin lü shiba zhong	*Qin lü zachao*
Direct	4	0
Indirect	16	3
Total	**20**	**3**

Example 5.26—*Qin lü shiba zhong*—Slips 102–103
公甲兵各以其官名刻久之其不可刻久者以丹若鬃書之其叚百姓甲兵必書其久受之以久入叚而₌(而) [102] 毋久及非其官之久也皆沒入公以齎律責之 工 [103]

Government armor and weaponry must each be inscribed/branded with the name of its office. Those which cannot be inscribed or branded, mark them with cinnabar. When armor and weaponry is loaned to the hundred-names, one must record its brand. When returned, take it in according to its brand. When borrowed, and (102) it is not branded, as well as if it is not the brand of its office, all are to be seized and taken in by the office. Fine them in accordance with the Statute on Equipment. (103)

Example 5.27—*Qin lü shiba zhong*, Slip 190
除佐必當壯以上毋除士伍新傅苑嗇夫不存縣為置守如廄律 [190]

When appointing assistants, they must be *zhuang* or older. One ought not appoint from the rank and file or the newly registered. When the *sefu* of parks is not present, the county assigns an interim [assistant] in accordance with the Statute on Stables. (190)

The *Qin lü zachao* manuscript does not contain direct referential qualifications; however, the *Qin lü shiba zhong* contains a total of four examples. In the three examples translated above, one sees a pattern of direct referencing similar to that found in the *Xiao lü*. Typically a legal topic is outlined, yet in order to fully prosecute an infraction of the article, the reader must reference a separate statute. The language employed frequently utilizes an *yi* 以 serving a verbal function indicating "to use" the following noun phrase, *Jiu lü*, to complete the task of the final verb "adjudicate," or "fine," *lun/zi* 論/貲, the person liable, indicated with either a direct object pronoun *zhi* 之 or the actual office title, *guan sefu*.

The second example (5.26) drawn from the *Qin lü shiba zhong* is of great interest because of the title of the statute mentioned through direct external referencing. This excerpted article comes from the *Statute on Artisans*, *Gong lü* 工律, and consists of multiple segments related to military equipage. The first part is hortatory prescribing that all public armor and weaponry must be inscribed with the markings of their office, or, if inscription is not possible, then marked with lacquer or cinnabar. The second part states that the relevant marks on military equipage should be properly recorded when such equipment is dispensed to the populace. In the final segment, a protasis–apodosis sentence describes a legal problem in which military equipment is lent out; however, when returned, the equipment lacks the appropriate office's markings or lacks markings altogether. Such an occurrence is a legal problem from the standpoint of the statute from which this article is excerpted; however, the present statute (or article) does not provide the authorized procedure or penal sanctions required for adjudicating such an issue. Instead, the article refers the reader to the *Ji lü* which should contain the information needed to correctly assign liability and determine the appropriate penalty for the offense.

The importance of this particular reference to the *Ji lü* becomes clear once it is considered in conjunction with a similar reference found in the *Xiao lü*. As noted above, the *Xiao lü* manuscript also contains articles related to military equipage and contains a direct external reference to provisions found in the *Ji lü*. Therefore, we have evidence of three legal statutes that are in varying degrees interconnected, and an official would possibly need access to all three in order to adjudicate certain legal situations.

Indirect referencing

Example 5.28—*Qin lü shiba zhong*, Slip 56
城旦舂舂司寇白粲操土功參食之不操土功以律食之 [56]

Cheng dan, grain-pounders, grain-pounder robber guards, and white rice sifters when engaged in construction labors use one-third (a *dou*) to feed them; when not engaged in construction labors feed them in accordance to the Statutes. (56)

Example 5.29—*Qin lü zachao*, Slip 39
●戍律曰同居毋并行縣嗇夫尉及士吏行戍不以律貲二甲 [39]

●The Statute on Conscription provides: "Members of the same household ought not be concurrently mustered. If a County *sefu*, the Commander, or sergeant musters conscripts not in accordance with the Statute(s), then fine two suits of armor." (39)

In these two examples, we again see a level of ambiguity arising from the use of indirect referencing of statutory provisions. Example 5.28 drawn from the *Qin lü shiba zhong* provides directions for feeding personnel assigned to specific construction duties. Yet, when the same individuals are not actively engaged in construction, their rations are altered. This excerpted provision explicitly provides for differential rationing; however, it does not explicitly contain the altered measurement for *cheng-dan*, grain-pounders, grain-pounder robber guards, and white rice sifters who are not actively engaged in construction. Instead, the excerpted article provides that such personnel are to be "fed in accordance with the Statute(s)" *yi lü shi zhi* 以律食之. Is this referring to the same statute from which this article was excerpted, or perhaps from a different statute? The reader is not clearly told; however, the inclusion of the phrase does inform the reader that *somewhere* within the corpus of Qin legal statutes, there is an article dealing with this specific issue.

The other example, drawn from the *Qin lü zachao* contains an explicit quote from the *Statute on Conscription* providing limitations on government imposed conscription for individual family units. If an official musters conscripts in a manner “not in accordance with the Statute(s)” *bu yi lü* 不以律, then he is to be fined two suits of armor. The potential ambiguity here comes from the generic use of *lü* 律 which does not expressly provide the direct location of relevant text detailing *how* one can ascertain if a conscription selection has been properly carried out. Does “in accordance with the Statute(s)” refer to the *Statute on Conscription*? If so, where in the statute can one find this? Does it refer specifically to conscriptions which do not conform to the principle provided in this excerpt? Or does it perhaps refer to a series of articles, or even series of statutes, dealing with the proper way to muster conscripts? This particular reference is likely directed at this specific excerpted article; however, there is some room for questioning given that there is a *Statute on Conscription* which, like the *Xiao lü*, potentially contains several interrelated articles.

The above examples, drawn from the *Qin lü shiba zhong* and *Qin lü zachao* manuscripts, clearly demonstrate the use of referential qualifications within statutes in ways similar to those found in the *Xiao lü* manuscript. This indicates compositional practices whereby those drafting Qin statutes make consistent use of specific types of referential qualification to conceptually unite disparate textual units within one legal text or between multiple legal texts.

Yet, interestingly, while the *Qin lü shiba zhong* contains a few examples of direct referencing the vast majority of referential qualifications in both manuscripts are indirect and rather ambiguous. This level of referential ambiguity could in some way be potentially linked to the very referential nature of these composite texts, or it could merely be the result of the particular excerpted selections chosen for each text.

Regardless of the true reason for such ambiguity, the majority of the references contained within these two manuscripts appears to rely heavily on the reader’s familiarity with the legal topics excerpted, the overall content of the excerpt source, and also the reader’s access to the complete statutory texts referenced. Without such familiarity and access, it would be difficult to obtain any measure of interpretative consistency of the statutory provisions by different individuals. These three texts, the *Xiao lü*, *Qin lü shiba zhong*, and *Qin lü zachao*, each demonstrate a variety of interactions between the form and functions of referential qualifications within different genres of legal text.

Interpretative issues related to textual-mapping in Qin legal manuscripts

A detailed analysis of the forms and functions of referential qualifications found in the Shuihudi legal manuscripts sheds some new light on the “compositional mindset” of Qin legislators. First, by embedding internal referential devices into the very text of the statute—producing implicit or explicit links between individual articles—the drafters were able to visibly indicate a conceptual interconnectedness between the individual textual units, and thereby increasing the cohesiveness and readability of the overall statute. Many linguists have argued that the use of referential qualifications within legislation evinces an increased consciousness of a systematized order amongst a body of written texts. Just as an internal reference indicates a sense of textual unity, so too can an external reference demonstrate a broader connectedness between differing texts.[57]

This is an important point to consider for the Qin as some scholars have attempted to dismiss the cohesiveness of Qin legislation. Liu Yongping, for example, has argued that the Shuihudi materials actually represent a random collection of legal rules which could never constitute a "codified" body of systematically legislated law.[58] Liu argues that the Qin ruler legislated at will and as such we find random and often trivial statutory provisions. I would argue two points. First, Liu seems to misunderstand the function, form, and development of the different legal texts found within the Shuihudi corpus. The statutory excerpts in the *Qin lü shiba zhong* and *Qin lü zachao* do not represent complete statutes. Nor should they be considered representative of the way in which laws were transmitted from the central government to the periphery. Second, an analysis of the use of referential qualifications within the Shuihudi materials shows that the Qin legal drafters were conscious of extant legislation and made conscious efforts through the use of compositional-linguistic measures to demonstrate a "corpus" approach to legislating and to the very use of legal statutes.

The lack of a direct form of citation/reference, however, does create a level of interpretive ambiguity. The examples above demonstrate that while the Qin did take care to title their legal statutes, they did not have a precise or standardized method of referencing individual sub-sections or articles of a statute. Nor did drafters necessarily always supply clear references to the statute title when making external references. For the official, such practices could make proper interpretation and application quite problematic. From the perspective of Qin legal theory, particularly the Qin concern with interpretive consistency, the lack of a slightly more refined cross-referencing system is surprising.

Thus we see in Qin legal culture that central authorities conceptualized legal statutes as potentially semi-independent pieces of legislation, yet these legislative statutes provided the textual pieces to the jigsaw puzzle of a legal system predicated upon codified law. Further, presence of references demonstrates that officials tasked with interpreting and applying statutory provisions would have required a broad knowledge of a wide range of interconnected legal documents as well as direct access to such documents. In short, the Qin developed a fairly sophisticated understanding of legal codification wherein multiple statutes are produced, promulgated, and internally linked via cross-referencing; yet this system was not necessarily optimally calibrated to ensure maximum consistency in interpretation and application of statutory provisions.

Conclusion

This analysis of the linguistic features of extant legal statutes from Qin provides valuable information related to Qin views on writing and law. Within Qin political and legal thought there was an overt emphasis on producing clearly worded laws that could be promulgated throughout the kingdom, and later empire, and could also be consistently interpreted by officials at the local level. Such a requirement of law necessitated the use of specific compositional strategies that would limit any potential areas of interpretive ambiguity. The fragments of Qin legal statutes recovered from Xi's tomb at Shuihudi allow us to consider how Qin legal theory was translated into legal practice.

What the analysis found was a clear attempt to provide specific legal definitions for terms which held significant penal consequences. The statute composers utilized a variety of definitional techniques to provide the clearest possible contextualization of specific words. That said, the existence of the *Falü dawen* manuscript and the types of questions posed within it, demonstrates that the Qin—just like modern legislators—were unable to completely stamp out all definitional ambiguity. There was apparently a genre of text like the *Falü dawen* that functioned to supplement statutory language and provide further guidance to ensure interpretive consistency. We simply do not know, however, whether such texts were the product of individuals fearful of administrative punishment for misreading and misapplying the law or if such texts were centrally produced and circulated.

The linguistic analysis also demonstrated that the composers of Qin statutes utilized a variety of sentential and organizational patterns to produce individual statutory articles. Given the Qin emphasis on standardization and consistency of interpretation, it is slightly surprising that more formalized language and sentence patterns were not utilized.[59] Indeed, the language of legal statutes in China gradually became more formulaic and by the time of the Tang dynasty (唐朝, CE 618–907), the individual articles of statutes found in the *Tang lü shuyi* 唐律疏議 all utilized a consistent formulaic sentence pattern. Every article begins with a situational protasis of varying degrees of complexity that is headed by the particle *zhu* 諸 and often translated as "In all cases of…"[60] Often, though not always, the protasis is further nominalized with a *zhe* 者 particle ending the clause. This is then followed by an apodosis dictating the prescribed consequences (punishments) for those who cause the event depicted in the protasis to occur.

Example 5.30—*Tang lü shuyi*
諸有妻更娶妻者徒一年

In all cases of one who has a wife and further marries an [additional] wife, [sentence] to penal servitude for one year.[61]

This is an example of a fairly standard Tang construction of a legal sentence. It is written in a casuistic style that provides a protasis containing the punishable situation/act and an apodosis providing the corresponding punishment.

The sentence begins with the particle *zhu* 諸 indicating the beginning of the protasis. The use of this particle further increases the general application of this article by stating "In all cases of…" Next, the clause of the protasis provides the situational "facts" covered by this article. In this instance the offense is "having

Table 5.10 Structure of *Tang lü shuyi* sentence

Protasis			*Apodosis*
Particle	*Situation*	*Nominalizing particle*	*Sanction*
諸	有妻更娶妻	者	徒一年
In all cases of	having a wife and further marries another wife	one who	[sentence] to penal servitude for one year.

a wife and further marrying a wife" *you qi geng qu qi* 有妻更娶妻. Under medieval and later imperial Chinese law, a male was only allowed one official wife, yet could retain additional women in his household as concubines or *qie* 妾.[62] This phrase is followed by a nominalizing particle *zhe* 者 that I translate as "one who." Thus, the protasis has general applicability to *any* person (here, male) who marries a second wife while already married. Finally, we have the apodosis providing the corresponding type of punishment "penal servitude," *tu* 徒, and the severity of the punishment "one year." Although other articles might contain compound or complex protasis clauses, the vast majority of legal articles within the *Tang lü shuyi* employ this basic, casuistic sentence structure.

Though not as consistently formulaic as later codes, the Qin patterns of statutory construction do contain a logic, and they evidence a consciousness of creating a text that would be consistently interpreted by different people in different locations. And, finally, we see that the Qin composer utilized various forms of legal referencing to produce an internally coherent text and to situate a specific legal statute within an existing larger body of written law. Though thousands of years removed from present day forms of legislation, the remnants of Qin law found in Shuihudi and other archaeological sites demonstrate an advanced legal system predicated upon well thought out written legal texts.

Notes

1 See Robin D.S. Yates, "Soldiers, Scribes, and Women: Literacy among the Lower Orders in Early China," in *Writing and Literacy in Early China: Studies from the Columbia Early China Seminar*, ed. Li Feng and David Prager Branner (Seattle: University of Washington Press, 2011), 339–369; Robin D.S. Yates, "Introduction: The Empire of the Scribes," in *Birth of an Empire: The State of Qin Revisited*, ed. Yuri Pines, Lothar von Falkenhausen, Gideon Shelach, and Robin D.S. Yates (Berkeley: Global, Area, and International Archive, University of California Press, 2013), 141–154.

2 For one of the earliest works to seriously consider the potential for linguistic analysis in law, primarily from a Common Law perspective, see David Mellinkoff, *The Language of the Law* (Boston, MA: Little, Brown, & Company, 1963). More recent monographs on the subject of legal linguistics are: Peter M. Tiersma, *Legal Language* (Chicago, IL: University of Chicago Press, 1999); Heikki Mattila, *Comparative Legal Linguistics* (Farnham, UK: Ashgate, 2006); Marcus Galdia, *Legal Linguistics* (Frankfurt am Main: Peter Lang, 2009); Peter Tiersma and Lawrence Solan, eds., *The Oxford Handbook of Language and Law* (Oxford: Oxford University Press, 2012).

3 The best examples of this work can be found in Risto Hiltunen, "The Grammar and Structure of Legal Texts," in *The Oxford Handbook of Language and Law*, ed. Peter M. Tiersma and Lawrence M. Solan (Oxford: Oxford University Press, 2012), 39–51; Vijay Bhatia, "Textual-Mapping in British Legislative Writing," *World Englishes: Journal of English as an International and Intranational Language* 6, no. 1 (1987): 1–10; Lawrence Solan, *The Language of Statutes: Laws and Their Interpretation* (Chicago, IL: University of Chicago Press, 2010). For a more recent application of historical and legal linguistic methodologies to analyze the development of a "legal language" in fifteenth and sixteenth century Scotland, see Joanna Kopaczyk, *The Legal Language of Scottish Burghs: Standardization and Lexical Bundles 1380–1560* (Oxford: Oxford University Press, 2013).

4 For an analysis of non-legal textual forms, see Roger Chartier, *Forms and Meanings: Texts, Performances, and Audiences from Codex to Computer* (Philadelphia: University of Pennsylvania Press, 1995). For examples related to statutory texts, see Solan, *The Language of Statutes*, chap. 2; Hiltunen, "The Grammar and Structure of Legal Texts"; Maurizio Gotti, "Text and Genre," in *The Oxford Handbook of Language and Law*, ed. Peter M. Tiersma and Lawrence M. Solan (Oxford: Oxford University Press, 2012), 52–66.

5 See, Chartier, *Forms and Meanings*, 1.

6 Solan, *The Language of Statutes*, 50–66.

7 Ralf Poscher, "Ambiguity and Vagueness in Legal Interpretation," in *The Oxford Handbook of Language and Law*, ed. Peter M. Tiersma and Lawrence M. Solan (Oxford: Oxford University Press, 2012), 129–134.

8 As with previous chapters, I will not translate the titles of individual manuscripts, but will instead refer to them by the *pinyin* transcription.

9 As with previous chapters, I provide my own translations of the Shuihudi materials; however, in the production of my own translations I have frequently referenced the translations of A.F.P. Hulsewé and the annotations of the editors of the *Shuihudi Qin mu zhujian*. See A.F.P. Hulsewé, *Remnants of Ch'in Law* (Leiden: E.J. Brill, 1985); Shuihudi Qin mu zhujian zhengli xiaozu, ed., *Shuihudi Qin mu zhujian* (Beijing: Wenwu chuban she, 1990).

10 Only one graph is visible on the recto side of the bamboo slip, *xiao* 效, "to check," or "to audit" (OCM *grâuh); however, I translate the title as "Statute on Checking" due to the self-reference of *xiao lü* 效律 on the verso side of the same slip.

11 Several recently published Warring States Period manuscripts from the kingdom of Chu 楚 are self-titled on the recto side of a manuscript. For example, the four graph title, 曹蔑之陳 *Cao Mie's Battle Array*, is found on the recto side of Slip 2 of the Shanghai corpus manuscript bearing that text. Several other manuscripts (though not all) follow similar titling practices which further demonstrates the convention of rolling the bamboo manuscripts inward and allowing an external and visible indicator of the manuscript's textual contents. See Ma Chengyuan, *Shanghai bowuguan cang Zhanguo Chu zhushu (si)* (Shanghai: Shanghai guji chuban she, 2004).

12 The institutionalized feature of strict interpretation is clearly evidenced in Governor Teng's letter found in Tomb 11 at Shuihudi. As mentioned in Chapter 3, Governor Teng's letter admonished local officials for not following the laws of Qin and for allowing heretical interpretations to flourish. Such lapses in legal procedure were deemed detrimental to the overall sustainability of the Qin kingdom and later empire.

13 Mattila, *Comparative Legal Linguistics*, 3–4.

14 Heikki Mattila, "Legal Vocabulary," in *The Oxford Handbook of Language and Law*, ed. Peter M. Tiersma and Lawrence M. Solan (Oxford: Oxford University Press, 2012), 33.

15 Tiersma, *Legal Language*, 106–110.

16 Edwin Peel, ed., *Treitel: The Law of Contract*, 13th ed. (London: Sweet & Maxwell, 2011), chap. 2.

17 Mattila, *Comparative Legal Linguistics*, 3.
18 For more analysis on legal language of Han statutes, see Anthony J. Barbieri-Low and Robin D.S. Yates, *Law, State, and Society in Early Imperial China: A Study with Critical Edition and Translation of the Legal Texts from Zhangjiashan Tomb No. 247* (Leiden: Brill, 2015), 32–37.
19 See discussion in Chapter 3.
20 The use of enumerative lists always brings up the question of whether or not a list is exhaustive or simply explanatory (i.e., a general category of things which could be expanded if relevant). See Mattila, *Comparative Legal Linguistics*, 71–72.
21 Duke Xian 獻公 reigned from 384–362 BCE. His son, Duke Xiao 孝公, reigned from 361–338 BCE.
22 The development of formulaic language patterns and textual forms is a fairly common phenomenon within legal systems as they shift to a greater emphasis on the use of writing within legal contexts. For an examination of formulaic language predating Hammurabi's Stele in the Near East, see Reuven Yaron, "Forms in the Laws of Eshnunna," *Revue Internationale Des Droits de L'antiquité* 3, no. 9 (1962): 137–138. Joanna Kopaczyk has similarly studied the increased use of formulaic language within the context of Scottish legal culture in the fourteenth to sixteenth centuries, see Kopaczyk, *The Legal Language of Scottish Burghs*, chap. 4.
23 For more on the concept of *casuistic* constructions in legal texts, see discussion below pp. 149–156.
24 禾入萬石一積, see *Xiao lü*, Slip 27.
25 See Geoffrey MacCormack, "The Legalist School and Its Influence upon Traditional Chinese Law," *Archiv Für Rechts-Und Sozialphilosophie* 92 (2006): 59–81. See, also, John Makeham, "The Legalist Concept of Hsing-Ming: An Example of the Contribution of Archaeological Evidence to the Re-Interpretation of Transmitted Texts," *Monumenta Serica* 39 (1991 1990): 87–114.
26 See *Xiao lü*, Articles 8 and 9.
27 The frequent composition of casuistic or conditional sentence patterns for legal statutes is common in most ancient legal systems that use writing. See Russ VerSteeg, *Early Mesopotamian Law* (Durham, NC: Carolina Academic Press, 2000), 10–11; Martha T. Roth, *Law Collections from Mesopotamia and Asia Minor* (Atlanta, GA: Society of Biblical Literature and Scholars Press, 1997), 2–4; Elizabeth A. Meyer, *Legitimacy and Law in the Roman World: Tabulae in Roman Belief and Practice* (Cambridge: Cambridge University Press, 2004), 44–52.
28 B.L. Eichler, "Literary Structure in the Laws of Eshnunna," in *Language, Literature, and History: Philological and Historical Studies Presented to Erica Reiner*, ed. Francesca Rochberg-Halton (New Haven, CT: American Oriental Society, 1987), 71.
29 Barbieri-Low and Yates, *Law, State, and Society in Early Imperial China*, 34.
30 The phrase *jiu ke* 久刻 is interpreted by Hulsewé to mean two distinct actions. The first, *jiu*, he understands to mean "branded" while the second, *ke*, means to be inscribed. Hulsewé argues that different types of materials would require different methods of marking. See Hulsewé, *Remnants of Ch'in Law*, 54.
31 *Qin lü shiba zhong*, Slips 104–107.
32 Ibid., Slip 15.
33 Ibid., Slips 77–79.
34 Ibid., Slips 86–88.
35 Ibid., Slip 199.
36 Anthony J. Barbieri-Low, "Craftsman's Literacy: Uses of Writing by Male and Female Artisans in Qin and Han China," in *Writing and Literacy in Early China: Studies from the Columbia Early China Seminar*, ed. Li Feng and David Prager Branner (Seattle: University of Washington Press, 2011), 370–372.

37 Article 16, for example, requires the county equipment stocks to be checked and those in charge of the equipment are, via the Statute on Equipage and the present statute, liable for any shortages. See *Xiao lü*, Slip 39.

38 Vijay Bhatia, "Cognitive Structuring in Legislative Provisions," in *Language and the Law*, ed. John Gibbons (Harlow: Longman Group UK, 1994), 140–149.

39 The Shuihudi editors read the graph *yang* 楊 as a loan word for *yang* 煬, "to dry out." See Shuihudi Qin mu zhujian zhengli xiaozu, *Shuihudi Qin mu zhujian*, 73.

40 The loan is highly probable as both graphs are in the same *xiesheng* 諧聲 series (*you bu* 幽部). See Axel Schuessler, *Minimal Old Chinese and Later Han Chinese: A Companion to Grammata Serica Recensa* (Honolulu: University of Hawai'i Press, 2009), 178–179.

41 I translate the title of this manuscript *Xiao lü* as Statute on Checking; however, it could also be translated as Statute on Auditing. In the present example, I translate the term *xiao* 效 as "to audit." I do this because in this particular situation, the "checking" likely entails a full audit of the county finances, grain stocks, military equipment, etc. The translation "audit" reads as more formal and inclusive.

42 Tiersma, *Legal Language*, 71.

43 Mattila, *Comparative Legal Linguistics*, 66.

44 Ibid., 66.

45 See above, Example 4.1.

46 Tiersma, *Legal Language*, 67.

47 Ibid., 67–68.

48 For example, the prologue found on the Hammurabi Stele extolls the greatness of King Hammurabi and legitimizes his promulgation of the laws recorded on the stele. The prologue uses a great deal of personalized language; yet once the text shifts to the actual legal provisions, the personalized language disappears. See Roth, *Law Collections from Mesopotamia and Asia Minor*, 76–81.

49 Mattila, *Comparative Legal Linguistics*, 77–79.

50 Bhatia, "Textual-Mapping in British Legislative Writing," 2.

51 Mattila, *Comparative Legal Linguistics*, 79.

52 Bhatia, "Textual-Mapping in British Legislative Writing," 3.

53 Article 2 (Slip 2) of the *Xiao lü* manuscript provides that when a shortage is discovered the office *sefu* and other relevant officials are to jointly liable to repay any losses.

54 In the *Xiao lü* manuscript, the graph *ji* 賫 is not present. This leaves the ungrammatical and awkward ending of *zhe nai zhi zhi* 者乃值之. The same sentence found in the *Qin lü shiba zhong* does contain the missing phrase. I follow the Shuihudi editors in inserting the missing phrase.

55 Hulsewé, *Remnants of Ch'in Law*, 79.

56 The Shuihudi editors interpret *an shi* 安事 to mean simple tasks, or non-heavy labor tasks. See Shuihudi Qin mu zhujian zhengli xiaozu, *Shuihudi Qin mu zhujian*, 34.

57 Mattila, *Comparative Legal Linguistics*, 79.

58 Liu Yongping, *Origins of Chinese Law: Penal and Administrative Law in Its Early Development* (Oxford: Oxford University Press, 1998), 203–207. This line of argument is also evident in Michael Loewe's more recent analysis of Qin and Han excavated legal materials. See Michael Loewe, "The Laws of 186 BCE," in *China's Early Empires: A Re-Appraisal*, ed. Michael Nylan and Michael Loewe (Cambridge: Cambridge University Press, 2010), 257–258.

59 In other societies evincing a tendency towards linguistic standardization, one tends to find a quicker development in standardized and formulaic legal language. For example, in her study of Scottish legal language, Joanna Kopaczyk demonstrates how during the period of CE 1380–1560, Scottish vernacular became increasingly standardized in an effort to distinguish it as a formal language distinct from English. She

concludes that this standardization quite quickly influenced the legal language of Scotland as evidenced by a marked rise and standardization of formulaic phrases. See, Kopaczyk, *The Legal Language of Scottish Burghs*.

60 Wallace Stephen Johnson, *The T'ang Code*, vol. 1 (Princeton, NJ: Princeton University Press, 1979), 43.

61 Chang-sun Wuji, *Tang lü shuyi* (Taipei: Taiwan shangwu, 1965), 178.

62 The reasoning has to do with the status of women within the household and the legal rights of these women and their children in areas of succession and inheritance.

6 Conclusion

The introduction to this book began with several questions related to the development of Chinese law in general, and of Chinese written law in particular. Of overarching concern was the question of how a civilization that for several millennia openly condemned its legal past and the use of legal forms and legal punishments continually maintained a series of legal institutions predicated upon written criminal law. That is, if law and punishment were considered to be of such little value in the overall government and social structure, then why did all Chinese governments rely so heavily upon them for maintaining social order and control over the government officials? Furthermore, law and punishment, particularly as manifested in written or codified law, were commonly associated with the Qin dynasty. This dynasty, along with the First Emperor (Qin Shi Huang Di 秦始皇帝), were vilified for their use of brutal law and punishments to strictly control government officials and the populace. Yet, the successor to the Qin, the Han dynasty, inherited much of the Qin legal practices, and although these institutions were reformed and refined by subsequent dynasties, the essence of Qin theories and conceptualizations of written law as a tool capable of maintaining strict centralized control over the bureaucracy as well as the general populace continued to be influential for over two millennia.

This book has tried to argue that Qin views on the nature of socio-legal change influenced the development of a government system and society that was regulated by written legal statutes. Although an extensive analysis of the influences of Qin legal thought and practices on subsequent dynasties is outside the purview of this book, advances in archeological discoveries of legal manuscripts excavated from Qin tombs make possible an examination of Qin theories of written law and how those theories translated to the production of legal statutes.

Law, language, and writing in Qin

This book has not aimed to uncover the "origins" of written law in China per se, but rather has focused on one period for which we have both received and excavated legal texts to provide some indication of how the Qin envisioned a place for written law within the overall structure of government and society. I hoped to trace the developing relationship between early Chinese theories of writing and theories of law, and to examine how these theories influenced the production of the earliest extant forms of legal statutes in the kingdom of Qin. To do this, I have adopted a *form and function* approach commonly employed in literary studies and discourse analysis. However, I have reversed the order and first examined how the Chinese conceptualized the intended function of law. I have then considered how this predetermined function potentially influenced the actual physical and linguistic forms of written law, specifically the forms of legal statutes.

My examination of the *function* of written law began in Chapter 2 by looking at some of the earliest debates over the implementation of written law as recorded in the *Zuo zhuan* 左傳. These debates represent an early Chinese historical understanding that the transition to promulgating written law often arose as a response to social and political turmoil that threatened the continuation of the kingdom. Drawing further on modern socio-legal analytic frameworks, we can interpret this increased emphasis on written law as arising from social and political pressures which decreased (or perhaps completely nullified) the efficacy of previous legal institutions. Laws that were previously sufficient to maintain control over the government and the populace no longer resonated with the changing social and political reality. Yet, legal reform was conceptualized to be more than just a reaction to social and political change. It was also understood to be a catalyst for new social and political changes. By reforming laws or institutions deemed no longer efficacious, one could potentially produce targeted changes within those institutions deemed detrimental to the kingdom. That is, by reforming the legal institutions one could address the social or political issues causing problems and thereby re-align law and society. We thus see a continuation of the law and society cycle wherein social changes effect legal changes and responsive legal changes effect social changes.

The available sources for the kingdom and later empire of Qin allow us to see this interplay between social and legal change, and further allow us to reconstruct the role of writing and especially written law within these various changes. The received and traditional historical sources are fraught with issues of authenticity as well as historiographical bias; however, they do demonstrate a historical consciousness that the Qin government suffered from the internal turmoil wrought by the machinations of its own hereditary ministerial elite. Usurpations and political assassinations severely disempowered the Qin ruling family for decades. Under the rule of Duke Xian 秦獻公 and Duke Xiao 秦孝公, however, the Qin began a systematic reform of its social and political institutions. Evidence that such reforms were predicated upon changing social and political conditions is clearly evident in the writings of the influential "Legalist" scholars, such as Shang Yang 商鞅, Han Feizi 韓非子, and Li Si 李斯. For the reforms carried out by Qin rulers and advocated by these ministers, writing and law were key resources and were heavily utilized to maintain the stability of newly formed or newly reformed institutions. The received texts and Han histories reveal that the Qin clearly understood the dynamics of socio-legal change. They were able to articulate their own views of how social and political changes necessitate legal change, as well as how responsive legal changes could be used to address and alter problematic social or political institutions. The primary problem addressed by the Qin through law was the re-centralization of control over the government through strictly defined official posts and hefty sanctions for failing to conform to the requirements of one's post.

Although the received materials and traditional histories are greatly useful, archeological discoveries since the 1970s have provided new materials to confirm, refute, or expand the characterizations of Qin legal thought found in traditional sources. Excavated sources such as the tiger tallies and the edict inscriptions on measuring devices all demonstrate the various platforms and textual forms the Qin government employed to visually demonstrate their centralized control over the military and ensure that key functions of government such as tax collection via grain (hence, the need for standardized measuring devices) were carried out solely according to the dictates of the central government. To further extend and maintain their control over lower level officials, the Qin required all officials to perform their duties exactly as prescribed by law; formulaic administrative phrases developed as a constant reminder of this obligation. The phrase "carry out this matter in accordance with the statutes and ordinances" *yi lü ling cong shi* 以律令從事 is found in numerous excavated legal and administrative texts from the Qin.

Furthermore, the use of writing and law as a form of centralized control extended not just to the lower reaches of the Qin bureaucracy, but was also employed to centrally regulate the general populace. The Qin exacted various taxes from its population including a monetary/grain tax, as well as a military and corvée labor service tax. To ensure compliance with its tax regime the Qin legally required all males to register as "adults" and thus officially establish their tax liability. The Qin established an extensive registration system to regulate taxes and labor, and this system relied upon the maintenance of detailed household registration ledgers recording all members of the household (male and female), as well as their ages and rank. Just as officials in the bureaucracy were required to serve "in accordance with the statutes" and could be punished for failing to do so, those individuals serving their statutory labor service or working in government sponsored workshops, such as artisans, also had the quality of their work regulated by legal statutes. Failure to perform or produce items in accordance with the statutory standards could result in sanctions. All evidence indicates that writing and law were combined by the Qin and employed to maintain strict centralized control over the government, as well as the entire population.

Reconstructing the intended function of law and the role of writing for the Qin is quite important for understanding the "legislative mind" of Qin rulers; however, equally important from a text-history perspective is the actual composition of legal statutes. That is, one should also consider the textual forms arising when one transitions from a concept of law to the actual production of written laws. Edward Finegan argues the language of law should not merely be studied as a phenomenon of lexical usage, but should also be understood in terms of the grammar of language employed in legal contexts.[1] Joanna Kopaczyk takes this further in her study of Scottish legal language and states the "language of specific legal text types is linked to the functions they perform, while the written mode helps to achieve the stability of record or legal act."[2] Working with methodologies employed by modern legal linguists, I have considered the transition from theory to praxis in Chapters 4 and 5. These chapters have examined the physical and linguistic attributes of extant legal materials recovered from Tomb 11 at Shuihudi, and also compared them to other legal and administrative materials dated to the late Warring States kingdom of Qin and the later Qin dynasty.

As mentioned, prior to the 1970s, scholars working on Qin law were necessarily restricted to using post-Qin historical materials or the received philosophical texts. Such sources contain scattered information regarding legal philosophy, legal history, and critiques of Qin legal institutions and practice. While these sources are certainly useful, they tell us surprisingly little about how Qin laws were actually composed. The discovery of the Shuihudi legal corpus provided modern scholars with the first chance to examine and interpret contemporary legal materials from the Qin. With actual Qin statutes and other legal texts, one could begin to answer questions related to the physical form and linguistic composition of such texts. As shown in Chapter 4, an analysis of these legal manuscripts illustrates the fact that the Qin did employ several codicological features designed to facilitate transmission and, at least in theory, ensure textual fidelity and interpretative consistency over a large and geographically dispersed audience. For example, most legal and administrative texts from the Qin employ a common proto-clerical script. Those trained to work as scribes or officials in the Qin bureaucracy would have been familiar with this script form and thus any text written in an official capacity could, in theory, have been read by any official in the Qin government. Furthermore, the texts from Shuihudi illustrate a fairly consistent use of punctuation markers to facilitate the reading of the text. Although we do not know whether or not an original Qin legal statute promulgated from the capital would have included such markers, by comparing the use of punctuation markers in the Shuihudi materials to those found in the Liye administrative tablets, we do see a consistency in the form and ascribed function of the markers which could be indicative of a greater scribal practice designed to ensure consistent interpretation of texts by different audiences.

The platform of the Shuihudi legal statutes, bamboo slips, also influenced the production of written law. As demonstrated by the *Xiao lü* manuscript, Qin legal statutes were composed of multiple individual articles. An official required to maintain a collection of those statutory provisions relevant to his post could excerpt individual articles and produce a statute compilation text such as the *Qin lü shiba zhong* or the *Qin lü zachao*. In all of these texts, however, punctuation, blank space, and titles were clearly employed to ensure the individual articles would not be confused and read together. Furthermore, by using bamboo slips, which could be easily unthreaded and rethreaded, local Qin officials could, in theory, keep their collections of statutes pertaining to their office up-to-date and edit any necessary changes which might occur within the year.

The form of statutes from Shuihudi tells us a great deal about how lower ranked officials, like the tomb occupant Xi, might have engaged the physical form of a legal manuscript. The physical features of the manuscript form can further tell us what practices were employed to ensure that a particular text would be read in a specified manner—that is, how the physical features evince the consciousness of a need for consistent readings. This formatting is of course extremely important and is still debated today among legislative drafters throughout the world; however, equally if not more important is the *textual content* of the manuscripts. The Qin desire for consistent readings and interpretations of laws combined with the level of administrative and criminal liability associated with the improper application of written law necessitated the production of clearly written sentence forms. "Legalist" philosophers such as Shang Yang argued that for laws to be effective, they must be clear (*ming* 明) and known to all. Extant legal texts demonstrate that the Qin did not appear to compose general laws for fear that ambiguity would lead to increased instances of varying interpretations. The push to utilize written law was predicated on the perceived ability of the central government to control the interpretation of written laws by lower ranking officials.

The Shuihudi manuscripts provide evidence of compositional strategies designed to facilitate consistent readings. One key issue with all legal texts is ascertaining the precise meaning of specific words. Qin legal language, like most legal languages of the world, did not develop as a *sui generis* technolect, but instead developed through the ascription of legal meaning to ordinary words. Through the linguistic practice of definitional encoding, the Qin drafters relied on a variety of techniques to clearly define the legal meaning of a term within the context of a legal text. The Shuihudi materials contain various examples of such techniques including direct definition, subject repetition, and enumeration. Yet even the best defined words can, if drawn from ordinary language, still contain inherent definitional ambiguities within legal contexts, and the Qin, or at least Mr. Xi, maintained a question and answer style digest that clarified the language of statutes. This text, the *Falü dawen* 法律答問, disambiguated seemingly synonymous words, as well as provided more detailed explanations of the "legal" meaning of specific words in specific legal contexts. Awareness of the importance of interpreting legal language "correctly" thus perhaps led to the production of a genre of specialized exegetical legal texts.

A structural examination of individual articles within the *Xiao lü* manuscript further demonstrates the ways in which the Qin attempted to produce legal texts that would, at least in theory, preclude the need for individualized interpretation by those officials tasked with applying them. Most of the articles within the manuscript utilize a casuistic pattern. This pattern, commonly employed in texts from numerous legal traditions of the ancient world, typically begins with a protasis segment prescribing or proscribing a specific legal situation. For the Qin, the protasis segments were quite specific and they eschewed overly general statements which might be considered ambiguous and open to interpretation. The protasis was followed by the "consequence" or apodosis segment that often specified the individual or individuals liable for sanction in the situation described in the protasis, and also prescribed the specific sanction. The *Xiao lü* manuscript contains articles of varying degrees of complexity and length. Yet, surprisingly, given the Qin government's concern with *consistency*, the casuistic sentence constructions within the Shuihudi corpus do not evince an overly *formulaic* pattern. That is, the casuistic patterns of Qin statutes are formulated in a variety of ways at times utilizing linguistic particles indicating a conditional statement (e.g., *qi* 其, *ru* 如, *er* 而), and at other times using a simple nominalized statement that does not contain any linguistic particles: "The armor has bore-holes; fine *sefu* two shields." One would perhaps expect greater use of formulaic sentence patterns to facilitate consistent readings, yet the use of such formulas did not stabilize until later dynasties.

Lastly, the use of textual-mapping within legal statutes demonstrates a consciousness of inter- and intra-coherence of statutory materials. Despite several scholarly arguments to the contrary, the Shuihudi materials utilize complex forms of referencing within individual statutes. These references demonstrate the cohesion between the different articles comprising an individual legal statute. Furthermore, cross-references to other statutes demonstrate two things. First, the drafters were conscious of the existence of other legislation and the potential connections and overlap between different legislations. Second, references requiring officials to engage statutes not included in the Shuihudi corpus demonstrate that lower officials had some level of access to statutes they did not personally own a copy of, perhaps statutes held at the county office.[3]

Taking all these features together, the legal manuscripts from the Shuihudi corpus demonstrate awareness of the need to produce legal statutes that would require minimal interpretation by those officials tasked with reading and applying them. This concern over the *function* of the text influenced choices related to the physical features of the manuscripts containing the texts, as well as the texts' linguistic composition.

The next step: expanded synchronic comparison of Shuihudi legal materials with other Qin sources

The core chapters of this book (Chapters 2–5) have brought together the study of the forms and functions of written law in Qin as seen in received texts, historical records, and selected excavated manuscripts. When analyzing the influence of early Chinese theories of the function of written law on the physical forms of legal statutes, I have restricted my analysis primarily to a collection of statutory materials discovered in a single tomb at Shuihudi, in particular the *Xiao lü* manuscript. As the most complete statute currently known for the Qin, such a close examination of the *Xiao lü* has allowed me to consider, on a micro-level, the effects of an intended *function* on the physical *form* of a document. The representative nature of the findings from such an analysis for the Qin in particular and early imperial China in general is of course limited; however, the methods and findings of this book provide a foundation for the expansion of the project to include an extended mono-dynastic examination of Qin legal development.

To expand the project synchronically and overcome the limitation of a single-corpus-based approach, one could take into consideration other sources of Qin statutory language—some well known, and others newly discovered. The Shuihudi legal materials are no longer the sole excavated sources we have for examining the role of writing and law within the Qin legal system. Limited reference has been made throughout this book to excavated materials from other Qin period sites. The statute fragments from Longgang, for example, provide imperfect information on laws related to the maintenance of Qin Forbidden Gardens. Due to the level of physical deterioration of the bamboo slips, which precludes detailed analysis of complete articles or even full sentences, I have not fully integrated their contents into the book. That said, an expanded account of Qin statutory language (such as specific terminology and phrasing) could more fully incorporate the fragmented Longgang materials.

Likewise, the legal materials recently purchased on the Hong Kong antiquities market by Changsha's Yuelu Academy will eventually greatly contribute to our understanding of Qin statutory composition and construction. At the time of writing, the legal materials have just become available from Yuelu. Now that the Yuelu legal materials are published, a comparative linguistic analysis of the Yuelu and Shuihudi statutes will likely provide three great benefits to the study of written law in Qin. First, a comparative analysis of the Shuihudi and the Yuelu statutory materials could shed light on any potential questions related to the Yuelu materials' authenticity. Because we have no archeological provenance for the Yuelu materials, by contextualizing them vis-à-vis other extant Qin statutes, we could better understand the likely source of these documents. For example, a comparison between the physical forms and linguistic attributes of the two sets of statutes could provide insight into the identity of their composer, their social and governmental rank, and perhaps the general location from which these documents were looted.

Second, the Yuelu materials will represent another large corpus of Qin statutory materials with which we can compare the Shuihudi materials and test the scope of the findings of this book. That is, a comparison between the Shuihudi and Yuelu materials will allow us to test whether or not the statutory composition styles found in Shuihudi legal documents are truly representative of a greater Qin legal written culture, or if they are merely particular to the tomb occupant, Xi. The lengthy statutory documents contained in the corpus will serve as better comparands than the Longgang materials. That said, a comprehensive comparison between the three corpuses will provide a detailed account of Qin statutory composition practices.

Third, the Yuelu corpus contains portions of *ling* 令 "ordinances." The existence of ordinances is well documented in received and historical sources, and the common phrase *lüling* 律令 "statutes and ordinances" occurs frequently in excavated materials from the Qin and Han dynasties. That said, scholars have not been able to precisely determine the relationship between *lü* and *ling* in early China.[4] Determining this relationship is important if one wishes to fully understand the forms and functions of written laws in early China. To what extent does the content of a *lü* take precedence over the contents of a *ling*? Understanding this is very important, especially for later imperial periods. For the Tang and later dynasties, it was exceedingly important that a local prefect adjudicating legal cases to correctly understand the hierarchical relationship between a *lü* "statute" and a *li* 例 "sub-statute." The sub-statute typically arose in response to a legal question or issue found in applying a specified statute and the answer to that question, once codified as a *li* would then take precedence over the original statute. With the discovery of *ling* from the Qin dynasty, we will be able to start reconstructing the various forms of written law, understand their ascribed function, and also compare linguistically how these two distinct legal forms (*lü* and *ling*) differed in construction.

Lastly, one will be able to enhance a mono-dynastic analysis of the statute-based Qin legal system via a thorough examination of the Liye administrative documents. Unfortunately, only a small amount of the corpus has been published to date; however, the incorporation of Liye materials will enable us to see how law actually functioned and what role writing and written statutes played within the legal process and everyday administrative life. Chapters 2 and 3 have already made limited use of the Liye materials. Yet, even that limited use has demonstrated the importance of these manuscripts. In Chapter 2, for example, we saw how legal language permeated the communications of everyday bureaucratic practice and influenced official decision making. Governor Li's command to the counties under his authority to fully employ all government workers before conscripting service from the general populace very closely mirrored the language of the Qin ordinance that he directly cites. As mentioned above, we know very little about the form and function of ordinances in the Qin. An examination of direct and indirect references to *ling* 令 texts in the Liye materials will provide more clues to the similarities and differences in the compositional structures of statutes and ordinances. Furthermore, such references will also enhance our understanding of the hierarchical relationship between statutes and ordinances within the context of greater Qin legal culture. Similarly, the ubiquitous presence of the phrase "carry out this matter in accordance with the statutes" in the Liye documents cited throughout this book clearly demonstrates that local officials were conscious of their statutory obligations and that this consciousness was translated into the language of everyday administration. As more Liye materials are published, we will be able to begin to examine the various ways in which citations to written laws were composed in the Qin, and just how ubiquitous such direct or indirect citations were in Qin official communication. Qin laws were designed to regulate and monitor behavior, and the administrative scope of the Liye materials will allow us to at least begin to piece together how these written laws actually functioned.

By incorporating and comparing these additional Qin sources, one will be able to expand the sample size. This increased sample size will allow one to test, refine, and/or expand the conclusions of this book. Thus, we will be able to produce a more comprehensive illustration of the function, form, and influence of written laws within the Qin government.

The Qin desired the creation of a legal system in which written laws were universally promulgated and consistently interpreted and applied throughout the kingdom and later empire. This book has demonstrated the importance of approaching early Chinese legal materials from a *form and function* perspective, as well as a legal linguistic perspective. By understanding the desired function ascribed to written law by the early Chinese, we are better able to interpret the ways in which the extant physical remains of written law demonstrate codicological and compositional strategies designed to facilitate that function. As more excavated legal and administrative manuscripts become available, our knowledge of the role of law in the development of Qin society and government will become clearer and clearer.

Notes

1 Edward Finegan, "Form and Function in Testament Language," in *Linguistics and the Professions: Proceedings of the Second Annual Delaware Symposium on Language Studies*, ed. Robert Di Pietro (Norwood, NJ: Ablex, 1982), 113–120.

2 Joanna Kopaczyk, *The Legal Language of Scottish Burghs: Standardization and Lexical Bundles 1380–1560* (Oxford: Oxford University Press, 2013), 25.

3 There is, of course, the possibility that the documents found buried in Xi's tomb do not represent the entirety of his collection and the number of statutes personally "owned" by Xi could have been much greater.

4 For a more recent analysis of the various forms of "legislation" in early China, see Anthony J. Barbieri-Low and Robin D.S. Yates, *Law, State, and Society in Early Imperial China: A Study with Critical Edition and Translation of the Legal Texts from Zhangjiashan Tomb No. 247* (Leiden: Brill, 2015), 64–66.

Bibliography

Barbieri-Low, Anthony J. *Artisans in Early Imperial China*. Seattle: University of Washington Press, 2007.

Barbieri-Low, Anthony J. "Craftsman's Literacy: Uses of Writing by Male and Female Artisans in Qin and Han China." In *Writing and Literacy in Early China: Studies from the Columbia Early China Seminar*, edited by Feng Li and David Prager Branner, 370–400. Seattle: University of Washington Press, 2011.

Barbieri-Low, Anthony J. and Robin D.S. Yates. *Law, State, and Society in Early Imperial China: A Study with Critical Edition and Translation of the Legal Texts from Zhangjiashan Tomb no. 247*. 2 vols. Leiden: Brill, 2015.

Beck, Mansvelt. "The First Emperor's Taboo Character and the Three Day Reign of King Xiaowen: Two Moot Points Raised by the Qin Chronicle Unearthed in Shuihudi in 1975." *T'oung Pao* 73 (1987): 68–85.

Bhatia, Vijay. "Textual-Mapping in British Legislative Writing." *World Englishes: Journal of English as an International and Intranational Language* 6, no. 1 (1987): 1–10.

Bhatia, Vijay. "Cognitive Structuring in Legislative Provisions." In *Language and the Law*, edited by John Gibbons, 136–155. Harlow: Longman Group UK, 1994.

Bielenstein, Hans. *The Bureaucracy of Han Times*. Cambridge and New York: Cambridge University Press, 1980.

Bodde, Derk. *China's First Unifier: A Study of Th Ch'in Dynasty as Seen in the Life of Li Ssu*. Leiden: E.J. Brill, 1938.

Bodde, Derk. "Punctuation: Its Use in China and Elsewhere." *Rocznik Orientalistyczny* 47, no. 2 (1991): 15–23.

Boltz, William. "The Composite Nature of Early Chinese Texts." In *Text and Ritual in Early China*, edited by Martin Kern, 50–78. Seattle: University of Washington Press, 2005.

Brown, T. Julian. *A Palaeographer's View : The Selected Writings of Julian Brown*. London: Harvey Miller, 1993.

Calle-Martin, Javier, and Antonio Miranda-Garcia. "The Punctuation System of Elizabethan Legal Documents: The Case of G.U.L. MS Hunter 3 (S.1.3)." *Review of English Studies* 59, no. 240 (2007): 356–378.

Cao Lüning 曹旅寧. *Qin lü xin tan* 秦律新探. Beijing: Zhongguo she hui ke xue chu ban she, 2002.

Chang, Leo S. and Wang Hsiao-po. *The Philosophical Foundations of Han Fei's Political Theory*. Honolulu: University of Hawai'i Press, 1986.

Chang-sun Wuji 長孫無忌. *Tang lü shuyi* 唐律疏義. Taipei: Taiwan shangwu, 1965.

Chartier, Roger. *Forms and Meanings: Texts, Performances, and Audiences from Codex to Computer*. Philadelphia: University of Pennsylvania Press, 1995.

Chen Jie 陳絜. "Liye 'huji jian' yu Zhanguo moqi de jiceng shehui" 里耶'戶籍簡'與戰國 末期的基層社會. *Lishi yanjiu* 歷史研究 5 (2009): 23–40.

Chen Songchang 陳松長. "Yuelu shuyuan suo cang Qin jian zongshu" 嶽麓書院所藏秦簡綜述. *Wenwu* 文物, no. 3 (2009): 75–88.

Chen Songchang 陳松長. *Yuelu shuyuan cang Qin jian de zhengli yu yanjiu* 岳麓書院藏秦簡的整理與研 究. Shanghai: Zhong xi shu ju, 2014.

Chen Wei 陳偉. "Qin yu Han chu de wenshu zhuandi xitong" 秦與漢初的文書傳遞系統. In *Liye gucheng: Qin jian yu Qin wenhua yanjiu* 里耶古城—秦簡與秦文化研究, edited by Zhongguo shehui kexue yuan kaogu yanjiu suo 中國社會科學院考古研究所, Zhongguo shehui kexue yuan lishi yanjiu suo 中國社會科學院歷史研究所, and Hunan sheng wenwu kaogu yanjiu suo 湖南省文物考古研究所, 150–157. Beijing: Kexue chuban she, 2009.

Chen Wei 陳偉, ed. *Liye Qin jiandu jiaoshi* 里耶秦簡牘校釋. Vol. 1. Wuhan: Wuhan daxue chuban she, 2012.

Chen Zhaorong 陳昭容. *Qin xi wenzi yanjiu* 秦系文字研究. Taipei: Zhongyang yanjiu yuan lishi yuyan yanjiu suo, 2003.

Chen Zunxiang 陳尊祥. "Du hufu zhenwei kaobian" 杜虎符真僞考辯. *Wenbo* 文博 9 (1985): 29.

Chü, T'ung-tsu. *Law and Society in Traditional China*. Paris: Mouton, 1961.

Clemens, Raymond and Timothy Graham. *Introduction to Manuscript Studies*. Ithaca, NY: Cornell University Press, 2007.

Cook, Scott. "The Use and Abuse of History in Early China from Xunzi to Lüshi Chunqiu." *Asia Major* 18, no. 1 (2006): 48–78.

Cotterrell, Roger. *The Sociology of Law*. 2nd ed. Oxford: Oxford University Press, 1992.

Creel, Herrlee Glessner. *What Is Taoism? And Other Studies in Chinese Cultural History*. Chicago, IL: University of Chicago Press, 1970.

Creel, Herrlee Glessner. *Shen Pu-Hai: A Chinese Political Philosopher of the Fourth Century B.C.* Chicago, IL: University of Chicago Press, 1974.

Creel, Herrlee Glessner. "Legal Institutions and Procedures during the Chou Dynasty." In *Essays on China's Legal Tradition*, edited by Jerome Alan Cohen, R. Randle Edwards, and Chen Chang Fu-mei, 26–55. Princeton, NJ: Princeton University Press, 1980.

Davies, John K. "Deconstructing Gortyn: When Is a Code a Code?" In *Greek Law in Its Political Setting: Justification Not Justice*, edited by Lin Foxhall and Andrew Lewis, 33–56. Oxford: Oxford University Press, 1996.

De Hamel, Christopher. *A History of Illuminated Manuscripts*. 2nd ed. London: Phaidon Press, 1994.

Duyvendak, J.J.L. *The Book of Lord Shang: A Classic of the Chinese School of Law*. London: Probsthain & Co., 1928.

Eichler, B.L. "Literary Structure in the Laws of Eshnunna." In *Language, Literature, and History: Philological and Historical Studies Presented to Erica Reiner*, edited by Francesca Rochberg-Halton, 71–84. New Haven, CT: American Oriental Society, 1987.

Endicott, Timothy A.O. "Legal Indeterminacy." *Oxford Journal of Legal Studies* 16, no. 4 (1996): 667–697.

Falkenhausen, Lothar von. "The E Jun Qi Metal Tallies: Inscribed Texts and Ritual Contexts." In *Text and Ritual in Early China*, edited by Martin Kern, 79–123. Seattle: University of Washington Press, 2005.

Falkenhausen, Lothar von. *Chinese Society in the Age of Confucius (1000–250 BC): The Archaeological Evidence*. Los Angeles: Cotsen Institute of Archaeology, University of California, Los Angeles, 2006.

Finegan, Edward. "Form and Function in Testament Language." In *Linguistics and the Professions: Proceedings of the Second Annual Delaware Symposium on Language Studies*, edited by Robert Di Pietro, 113–120. Norwood, NJ: Ablex, 1982.

Friedman, Lawrence M. "Legal Culture and Social Development." *Law and Society Review* 4, no. 1 (1969): 29–44.

Friedman, Lawrence M. *Law and Society: An Introduction*. Englewood Cliffs, NJ: Prentice-Hall, 1977.

Fu Rongke 傅榮珂. *Shuihudi Qin jian xinglü yanjiu* 睡虎地秦簡刑律研究. Taipei: Shang ding wenhua chuban, 1992.

Fu Zhengyuan. *China's Legalists: The Earliest Totalitarians and Their Art of Ruling*. New Studies in Asian Culture. Armonk, NY: M.E. Sharpe, 1996.

Gagarin, Michael. *Writing Greek Law*. Cambridge: Cambridge University Press, 2008.

Galambos, Imre. *Orthography of Early Chinese Writing: Evidence from Newly Excavated Manuscripts*. Budapest: Department of East Asian Studies, Eötvös Lorand University, 2006.

Galambos, Imre. "Scribal Notation in Medieval Chinese Manuscripts: The Hewen (Ligature) and the Chongwen (Duplication) Marks." *Manuscript Cultures*, 2009.

Galdia, Marcus. *Legal Linguistics*. Frankfurt am Main: Peter Lang, 2009.

Gao Min 高敏. *Shuihudi Qin jian chutan* 睡虎地秦簡初探. Taipei: Wanjuan chuban she, 2000.

Gao Rong 高榮. "Jiandu suojian Qin Han youshu zhuandi fangshi kaobian" 簡牘所見秦漢郵書傳遞方式考辯. *Zhongguo lishi wenwu* 中國歷史文物 6 (2007): 63–70.

Giele, Enno. "Signatures of 'Scribes' in Early Imperial China." *Asiatische Studien/Etudes Asiatiques* 59, no. 1 (2005): 353–387.

Goody, Jack. *The Logic of Writing and the Organization of Society*. Cambridge: Cambridge University Press, 1986.

Goody, Jack. *The Power of the Written Tradition*. Washington, DC: Smithsonian Institution, 2000.

Gotti, Maurizio. "Text and Genre." In *The Oxford Handbook of Language and Law*, edited by Peter M. Tiersma and Lawrence M. Solan, 52–66. Oxford: Oxford University Press, 2012.

Guan Xihua 管錫華. *Zhongguo gudai biaodian fuhao fazhan shi* 中國古代標點符號發展史. Chengdu: Ba Shu shu she, 2002.

Hanfeizi jishi 韓非子集釋. critical reprint with annotations by Chen Qiyou 陳奇猷. 2 vols. Beijing: Zhonghua shuju, 1959.

Havelock, Erik. *The Muse Learns to Write: Reflections on Orality and Literacy from Antiquity to the Present*. New Haven, CT: Yale University Press, 1986.

Head, John W. and Yanping Wang. *Law Codes in Dynastic China: A Synopsis of Chinese Legal History in the Thirty Centuries from Zhou to Qing*. Durham, NC: Carolina Academic Press, 2005.

Hei Guang 黑光. "Xi'an shijiao faxian Qin guo Du hufu" 西安市郊發現秦國杜虎符. *Wenwu* 文物 9 (1979): 93–94.

Hiltunen, Risto. "The Grammar and Structure of Legal Texts." In *The Oxford Handbook of Language and Law*, edited by Peter M. Tiersma and Lawrence M. Solan, 39–51. Oxford: Oxford University Press, 2012.

Hou Xiaorong 后曉榮. *Qindai zhengqu dili* 秦代政區地理. Beijing: Shehui kexue wenxian chuban she, 2009.

Hsing I-tien. "Qin-Han Census and Tax and Corvee Administration: Notes on Newly Discovered Materials." In *Birth of an Empire: The State of Qin Revisited*, edited by Yuri Pines, Lothar von Falkenhausen, Gideon Shelach, and Robin D.S. Yates, 155–186. Berkeley: Global, Area, and International Archive, University of California Press, 2014.

Hsu Fu-chang 徐福昌. *Shuihudi Qin jian yanjiu* 睡虎地秦簡研究. Taipei: Wen shi zhe, 1993.

Huang Zhanyue 黃展岳. "Liye Qin Jian 'Zhuan Song Wei Shu' Zhe de Shenfen." In *Liye gucheng: Qin jian yu Qin wenhua yanjiu* 里耶古城—秦簡與秦文化研究, edited by Zhongguo shehui kexue yuan kaogu yanjiu suo 中國社會科學院考古研究所, Zhongguo shehui kexue yuan lishi yanjiu suo 中國社會科學院歷史研究所, and Hunan sheng wenwu kaogu yanjiu suo 湖南省文物考古研究所, 114–121. Beijing: Kexue chuban she, 2009.

Hulsewé, A.F.P. "The Ch'in Documents Discovered in Hupei in 1975." *T'oung Pao* 64, no. 4–5 (1978): 175–217.

Hulsewé, A.F.P. "Some Remarks on Statute Labour during the Ch'in and Han Period." *Orientalia Venetiana* 1 (1984): 195–204.

Hulsewé, A.F.P. *Remnants of Ch'in Law*. Leiden: E.J. Brill, 1985.

Hulsewé, A.F.P. "Shih Chi." In *Early Chinese Texts: A Bibliographical Guide*, edited by Michael Loewe, 405–414. Berkeley: SSEC and IEAS, University of California, Berkeley, 1993.

Hunan sheng wenwu kaogu yanjiu suo 湖南省文物考古研究所, ed. *Liye fajue baogao* 里耶發掘報告. Changsha: Yuelu shushe, 2006.

Hunan sheng wenwu kaogu yanjiu suo 湖南省文物考古研究所, ed. *Liye Qin Jian* 里耶秦簡. Vol. 1. Beijing: Wenwu chuban, 2012.

Ji Xun 季勛. "Yunmeng Shuihudi Qin jian gaishu" 雲夢睡虎地秦簡概述. *Wenwu* 文物 5 (1976): 1–6.

Jiang Lihong 蔣禮鴻. *Shangjun shu zhuizhi* 商君書錐指. Beijing: Zhonghua shuju, 986.

Johnson, Wallace Stephen. *The T'ang Code*. Vol. 1. Princeton, NJ: Princeton University Press, 1979.

Kern, Martin. *The Stele Inscriptions of Ch'in Shih-Huang: Text and Ritual in Early Chinese Imperial Representation*. New Haven, CT: American Oriental Society, 2000.

Kopaczyk, Joanna. *The Legal Language of Scottish Burghs: Standardization and Lexical Bundles 1380–1560*. Oxford: Oxford University Press, 2013.

Lau, Ulrich and Thies Staack. *Legal Practice in the Formative Stages of the Chinese Empire: An Annotated Translation of the Exemplary Qin Criminal Cases from the Yuelu Academy Collection*. Leiden: Brill, 2016.

Levi, Jean. "Shang Jün Shu." In *Early Chinese Texts: A Bibliographical Guide*, edited by Michael Loewe, 368–375. Berkeley: SSEC and IEAS University of California, Berkeley, 1993.

Lévi-Strauss, Claude. *Tristes Tropiques*. Translated by John Russell. New York: Criterion, 1961.

Lewis, Mark Edward. *Writing and Authority in Early China*. New York: SUNY, 1999.

Li Xueqin 李學勤. "Qin jian de gu wenzi xue kaocha." In *Yunmeng Qin jian yanjiu* 雲夢秦簡研究, edited by Zhonghua shuju bianji bu 中華書局編輯部, 336–345. Beijing: Zhonghua shuju, 1981.

Li Xueqin 李學勤. ed. *Qinghua daxue cang Zhanguo zhujian* 清華大學藏戰國竹簡. Vol. 2. Shanghai: Zhong xi shuju, 2012.

Liang Zhu 粮柱 and Liu Xinfang 劉信芳, eds. *Yunmeng Longgang Qin jian* 雲夢龍崗秦 簡. Beijing: Kexue chuban she, 1997.

Liu Hainian 劉海年. “Qin lü xingfa kaoxi” 秦律刑法考習. In *Yunmeng Qin jian yanjiu* 雲 夢秦簡研究, edited by Zhonghua shuju bianji bu 中華書局編輯部, 171–206. Beijing: Zhonghua shuju, 1981.

Liu Hainian 劉海年. *Zhanguo Qindai fazhi guankui* 戰國秦代法制管窺. Beijing: Falu chuban she, 2006.

Liu Xinfang 劉信芳. “Guanyu Yunmeng Qin jian biannian ji de bushu, xubian, he xiaogai deng wenti” 關於雲夢秦簡編年記的補書、續編、和消改等問題. *Jiang-Han kaogu* 江漢考古 3 (1991): 79–84.

Liu Yongping. *Origins of Chinese Law: Penal and Administrative Law in Its Early Development*. Oxford: Oxford University Press, 1998.

Loewe, Michael. *Records of Han Administration*. 2 vols. London: Cambridge University Press, 1967.

Loewe, Michael. “China’s Sense of Unity as Seen in the Early Empires.” *T’oung Pao* 80 (1994): 6–26.

Loewe, Michael. *The Men Who Governed Han China: Companion to a Biographical Dictionary of the Qin, Former Han and Xin Periods*. Leiden: Brill, 2004.

Loewe, Michael. “On the Terms Bao Zi, Yin Gong, Yin Guan, Huan, and Shou Was Zhao Gao a Eunuch?” *T’oung Pao* 91 (2005): 301–319.

Loewe, Michael. *The Government of the Qin and Han Empires: 221 BCE–220 CE*. Indianapolis, IN: Hackett Pub. Co., 2006.

Loewe, Michael. “The Laws of 186 BCE.” In *China’s Early Empires: A Re-Appraisal*, edited by Michael Nylan and Michael Loewe, 253–265. Cambridge: Cambridge University Press, 2010.

Loewe, Michael. “The Orders of Aristocratic Rank of Han China.” *T’oung Pao* 48 (1960): 97–174.

Loewe, Michael and Michael Nylan, eds. *China’s Early Empires: A Re-Appraisal*. Cambridge: Cambridge University Press, 2010.

Lunyu zhushu 論語注疏, commentary by He Yan 何晏 (d. 249), subcommentary by Xing Bing 邢昺 (932–1010); reprint from Wenyuange Sikuquanshu 文淵閣四庫全書, 1782; edition Taibei: Taiwan shangwu yinshuguan, 1983–1986.

Ma Chengyuan 馬承源, ed. *Shanghai Bowuguan cang Zhanguo Chu zhushu (si)* 上海博物館藏戰國楚竹書(四). Shanghai: Shanghai guji chuban she, 2004.

Ma Feibai 馬非百. “Yunmeng Qin jian dashi ji ji zhuan” 雲夢秦簡大事記集傳. *Zhongguo lishi wenxian yanjiu jikan* 中國歷史文獻研究季刊 2 (1981): 66–92.

MacCormack, Geoffrey. “The Transmission of Penal Law (lü) from the Han to the T’ang: A Contribution to the Study of the Early History of Codification in China.” *Revue Internationale Des Droits de L’antiquité* 51 (2004): 47–83.

MacCormack, Geoffrey. “The Legalist School and Its Influence upon Traditional Chinese Law.” *Archiv Für Rechts-Und Sozialphilosophie* 92 (2006): 59–81.

Makeham, John. “The Legalist Concept of Hsing-Ming: An Example of the Contribution of Archaeological Evidence to the Re-Interpretation of Transmitted Texts.” *Monumenta Serica* 39 (1991 1990): 87–114.

Mattila, Heikki. *Comparative Legal Linguistics*. Farnham, UK: Ashgate, 2006.

Mattila, Heikki. “Legal Vocabulary.” In *The Oxford Handbook of Language and Law*, edited by Peter M. Tiersma and Lawrence M. Solan, 27–38. Oxford: Oxford University Press, 2012.

Mellinkoff, David. *The Language of the Law*. Boston, MA: Little, Brown, & Company, 1963.

Meyer, Elizabeth A. *Legitimacy and Law in the Roman World: Tabulae in Roman Belief and Practice*. Cambridge: Cambridge University Press, 2004.

Mittag, Achim. "The Qin Bamboo Annals of Shuihudi: A Random Note from the Perspective of Chinese Historiography." *Monumenta Serica* 51 (2003): 543–570.

Nylan, Michael. "The Rhetoric of 'Empire' in the Classical Era in China." In *Conceiving the Empire: China and Rome Compared*, edited by Achim Mittag and Fritz-Heiner Mutschler, 39–66. Oxford: Oxford University Press, 2008.

Ōba Osamu, David Spafford, Robin D.S. Yates, Enno Giele, and Michael Nylan. "The Ordinances on Fords and Passes Excavated from Han Tomb Number 247, Zhangjiashan." *Asia Major* 14, no. 2 (2001): 119–141.

Ong, Walter. *Orality and Literacy*. 2nd ed. London and New York: Routledge, 2002.

Parkes, M.B. *Scribes, Scripts, and Readers: Studies in the Communication, Presentation and Dissemination of Medieval Texts*. London: Hambledon Press, 1991.

Parkes, M.B. *Pause and Effect: An Introduction to the History of Punctuation in the West*. Berkeley: University of California Press, 1993.

Peel, Edwin, ed. *Treitel: The Law of Contract*. 13th ed. London: Sweet & Maxwell, 2011.

Pines, Yuri. "Biases and Their Sources: Qin History in the Shiji." *Oriens Extremus* 46 (June 2005): 10–34.

Pines, Yuri. "The Messianic Emperor: A New Look at Qin's Place in China's History." In *Birth of an Empire: The State of Qin Revisited*, edited by Yuri Pines, Gideon Shelach, Lothar von Falkenhausen, and Robin D.S. Yates, 258–279. Berkeley: Global, Area, and International Archive, University of California Press, 2014.

Pines, Yuri, Lothar von Falkenhausen, Gideon Shelach, and Robin D.S. Yates, eds. *Birth of an Empire: The State of Qin Revisited*. Berkeley: Global, Area, and International Archive, University of California Press, 2014.

Poscher, Ralf. "Ambiguity and Vagueness in Legal Interpretation." In *The Oxford Handbook of Language and Law*, edited by Peter M. Tiersma and Lawrence M. Solan, 128–144. Oxford: Oxford University Press, 2012.

Qiu Guangming 邱光明, ed. *Zhongguo lidai duliangheng kao* 中國歷代度量衡考. Beijing: Kexue chuban she, 1992.

Qiu, Xigui 裘錫桂. "Jiaguwen zhong chongwen he hewen chongfu pianpang de shenglüe" 甲骨文中重文和合文重複偏旁的省略. In *Guwenzi Lunji* 古文字論集, by Qiu Xigui, 141–146. Beijing: Zhonghua shuju, 1992.

Qiu, Xigui 裘錫桂. "Zai tan jiaguwen zhong chongwen de shenglüe" 再談甲骨文中重文的省略. In *Guwenzi Lunji* 古文字論集, by Qiu Xigui, 147–150. Beijing: Zhonghua shuju, 1992.

Qiu Xigui. *Chinese Writing*. Translated by Jerry Norman and Gilbert L. Mattos. Berkeley: The Society for the Study of Early China and the Institute of East Asian Studies, University of California, 2000.

Richter, Matthias. *Embodied Text: Establishing Textual Identity in Early Chinese Manuscripts*. Leiden: Brill, 2013.

Robertson, Grant. "Comma Quirk Irks Rogers." *Globe and Mail*, 2006. www.theglobeandmail.com/report-on-business/article838561.ece.

Rong Geng 容庚. "Qin Shi Huang ke shi kao" 秦始皇刻石考. *Yanjing xuebao* 燕京學報 17 (1935): 125–171.

Rosen, Mark D. "What Has Happened to the Common Law? Recent American Codifications, and Their Impact on Judicial Practice and the Law's Subsequent Development." *Wisconsin Law Review* no. 5 (1994): 1119–1286.

Roth, Martha T. *Law Collections from Mesopotamia and Asia Minor*. Atlanta, GA: Society of Biblical Literature and Scholars Press, 1997.

Roth, Martha T. "The Law Collection of King Hammurabi: Toward an Understanding of Codification and Text." In *Codification Des Lois Dans L'Antiquite*, edited by E. Lévy, 9–31. Paris: De Boccard, 2000.

Sanft, Charles. *Communication and Cooperation in Early Imperial China: Publicizing the Qin Dynasty*. New York: SUNY, 2014.

Schaberg, David. *A Patterned Past: Form and Thought in Early Chinese Historiography*. Cambridge, MA: Harvard University Press, 2001.

Schuessler, Axel. *Minimal Old Chinese and Later Han Chinese: A Companion to Grammata Serica Recensa*. Honolulu: University of Hawai'i Press, 2009.

Shaughnessy, Edward. *Sources of Western Zhou History: Inscribed Bronze Vessels*. Berkeley: University of California Press, 1991.

Shuihudi Qin mu zhujian zhengli xiaozu 睡虎地秦墓竹簡整理小組, ed. *Shuihudi Qin mu zhujian* 睡虎地秦墓竹簡. Beijing: Wenwu chuban she, 1990.

Sima Qian 司馬遷. *Shiji* 史記. 10 vols. Beijing: Zhonghua shuju, 1959.

Smith, Kidder. "Sima Tan and the Invention of Daoism, 'Legalism,' 'et Cetera.'" *Journal of Asian Studies* 62, no. 1 (2003): 129–156.

Solan, Lawrence. *The Language of Statutes: Laws and Their Interpretation*. Chicago, IL: University of Chicago Press, 2010.

Sun Hong 孫鴻. *Qin jian du shu yanjiu* 秦簡牘書研究. Beijing: Beijing daxue chuban she, 2009.

Sun Jiazhou 孙家洲. *Qin Han falü wenhua yanjiu* 秦漢法律文化研究. Beijing: Zhongguo renmin daxue chuban she, 2007.

Sun Weizu 孫慰祖 and Xu Gefu 徐谷富, eds. *Qin Han jinwen huibian* 秦漢金文匯編. Shanghai: Shanghai shudian, 1997.

Takezoe Kōkō 竹添光鴻. *Saden kaisen* 左傳會箋. 2 vols. Taipei: Tiangong shuju, 1998.

Teng Mingyu. "From Vassal State to Empire: An Archaeological Examination of Qin Culture." In *Birth of an Empire: The State of Qin Revisited*, edited by Yuri Pines, Lothar von Falkenhausen, Gideon Shelach, and Robin D.S. Yates, 71–112. Berkeley: Global, Area, and International Archive, University of California Press, 2014.

Tiersma, Peter M. *Legal Language*. Chicago, IL: University of Chicago Press, 1999.

Tiersma, Peter M. and Lawrence M. Solan, eds. *The Oxford Handbook of Language and Law*. Oxford: Oxford University Press, 2012.

Tomiya Itaru 冨谷至. *Qin Han xingfa zhidu yanjiu* 秦漢刑法制度研究. Translated by Chai Shengfang 柴生芳 and Zhu Hengye 朱恒曄. Guilin: Guanxi shifan daxue chuban, 2006.

Tsien, Tsuen-hsuin. *Written on Bamboo and Silk: The Beginnings of Chinese Books and Inscriptions*. 2nd vol. Chicago, IL: University of Chicago Press, 2004.

Venture, Olivier. "Caractères Interdits et Vocabulaire Officiel Sous Les Qin: L'apport Des Documents Administratifes de Liye." *Études Chinoises* 30 (2011): 73–98.

VerSteeg, Russ. *Early Mesopotamian Law*. Durham, NC: Carolina Academic Press, 2000.

Wang Guihai 汪桂海. "Cong Xiangxi Liye Qin jian kan Qin guan wenshu zhidu" 從湘西里耶秦簡看秦官文書制度. In *Liye gucheng: Qin jian yu Qin wenhua yanjiu* 里耶古城—秦簡與秦文化研究, edited by Zhongguo shehui kexue yuan kaogu yanjiu suo

中國社會科學院考古研究所, Zhongguo shehui kexue yuan lishi yanjiu suo 中國社會科學院歷史研究所, and Hunan sheng wenwu kaogu yanjiu suo 湖南省文物考古研究所, 141–149. Beijing: Kexue chuban she, 2009.

Wang Huanlin 王煥林. *Liye Qin jian jiaogu* 里耶秦簡校詁. Beijing: Zhongguo wenlian chubanshe, 2007.

Watson, Alan. "Legal Change: Sources of Law and Legal Culture." *University of Pennsylvania Law Review* 131 (1983): 1121–1157.

Watson, Alan. *The Evolution of Law*. Baltimore, MD and London: Johns Hopkins University Press, 1985.

Westbrook, Raymond. "Codification and Canonization." In *Codification Des Lois Dans L'Antiquite*, edited by E. Lévy, 33–47. Paris: De Boccard, 2000.

Wu Fuzhu 吳福助. *Qin Shi Huang ke shi kao* 秦始皇刻石考. Taipei: Wen shi zhe, 1994.

Wu Hung 巫鴻. "Qin quan yanjiu" 秦權研究. *Gugong jikan* 故宮季刊 4 (1979): 33–47.

Yaron, Reuven. "Forms in the Laws of Eshnunna." *Revue Internationale Des Droits de L'antiquité* 3, no. 9 (1962): 137–153.

Yates, Robin D.S. "Social Status in the Ch'in: Evidence from the Yun-Meng Legal Documents. Part One: Commoners." *Harvard Journal of Asiatic Studies* 47, no. 1 (1987): 197–237.

Yates, Robin D.S. "State Control of Bureaucrats under the Qin: Techniques and Procedures." *Early China* 20 (1995): 331–365.

Yates, Robin D.S. "Soldiers, Scribes, and Women: Literacy among the Lower Orders in Early China." In *Writing and Literacy in Early China: Studies from the Columbia Early China Seminar*, edited by Feng Li and David Prager Branner, 339–369. Seattle: University of Washington Press, 2011.

Yates, Robin D.S. "Introduction: The Empire of the Scribes." In *Birth of an Empire: The State of Qin Revisited*, 141–154. Berkeley: Global, Area, and International Archive, University of California Press, 2013.

Yates, Robin D.S. "The Qin Slips and Boards from Well No. 1, Liye, Hunan: A Brief Introduction to the Qin Qianling County Archives." *Early China* 35–36 (2012–2013): 291–329.

Yates, Robin D.S. and Katrina C.D. McLeod. "Forms of Ch'in Law: An Annotated Translation of the Feng-Chen Shih." *Harvard Journal of Asiatic Studies* 41, no. 1 (June 1981): 111–163.

Yunmeng Shuihudi Qin mu bianxie zu 雲夢睡虎地秦墓編寫組, ed. *Yunmeng Shuihudi Qin mu* 雲夢睡虎地秦墓. Beijing: Wenwu chuban she, 1981.

Zang Kehe 臧克和 and Wang Ping 王平, eds. *Shuowen jiezi xinding* 説文解字新訂. Beijing: Zhonghua shuju, 2002.

Zhang Chunlong 張春龍. "Liye Qin jian suojian de huji he renkou guanli" 里耶秦簡所見 的戶籍和人口管理. In *Liye gucheng: Qin jian yu Qin wenhua yanjiu* 里耶古城—秦簡與秦文化研究, edited by Zhongguo shehui kexue yuan kaogu yanjiu suo 中國社會科學院考古研究所, Zhongguo shehui kexue yuan lishi yanjiu suo 中國社會科學院歷史研究所, and Hunan sheng wenwu kaogu yanjiu suo 湖南省文物考古研究所, 188–195. Beijing: Kexue chuban she, 2009.

Zhangjiashan ersiqihao Han mu zhujian zhengli xiaozu 張家山二四七號漢墓竹簡真理小組. *Zhangjiashan Han mu zhujian* 張家山漢墓竹簡. Beijing: Wenwu chubanshe, 2001.

Zhao Huacheng. "New Explorations of Early Qin Culture." In *Birth of an Empire: The State of Qin Revisited*, edited by Yuri Pines, Lothar von Falkenhausen, Gideon Shelach, and Robin D.S. Yates, 53–70. Berkeley: Global, Area, and International Archive, University of California Press, 2014.

Zhongguo wenwu yanjiu suo 中國文物研究所 and Hubei sheng wenwu kaogu yanjiu suo 湖北省文物考古研究所, eds. *Longgang Qin jian* 龍崗秦簡. Beijing: Zhonghua shuju, 2001.

Zhu Shiche 朱師徹. *Shangjun shu jiegu dingben* 商君書解詁定本. Taipei: He Luo tushu chuban she, 1975.

Index

Page numbers in **bold** denote tables.

FSC
www.fsc.org
MIX
Papier | Fördert
gute Waldnutzung
FSC® C083411

Kolibri 360 GmbH
Ferdinand-Jühlke-Straße 7
99095 Erfurt, Deutschland
produktsicherheit@kolibri360.de